Chow MAINE

Chow MAINE

THE BEST Restaurants, Cafés, Lobster Shacks & Markets on the Coast

SECOND EDITION

Nancy English

The Countryman Press
Woodstock, Vermont

We welcome your comments and suggestions. Please contact Editor, The Countryman Press, P.O. Box 748, Woodstock, Vermont 05091, or e-mail countrymanpress@wwnorton.com.

ISBN 978-0-88150-774-4

Book design by Melanie Jolicoeur
Page composition by Chelsea Cloeter
Cover photograph by Jason Drew
Clip art from Nova Development Corporation
Interior photographs by the author unless otherwise indicated

Published by The Countryman Press, P.O. Box 748, Woodstock, VT 05091

Distributed by W. W. Norton & Company, Inc.,
500 Fifth Avenue, New York, NY 10110

Printed in the United States of America

10 9 8 7 6 5 4 3 2 1

To EJDWE,
and her nose for fine distinctions

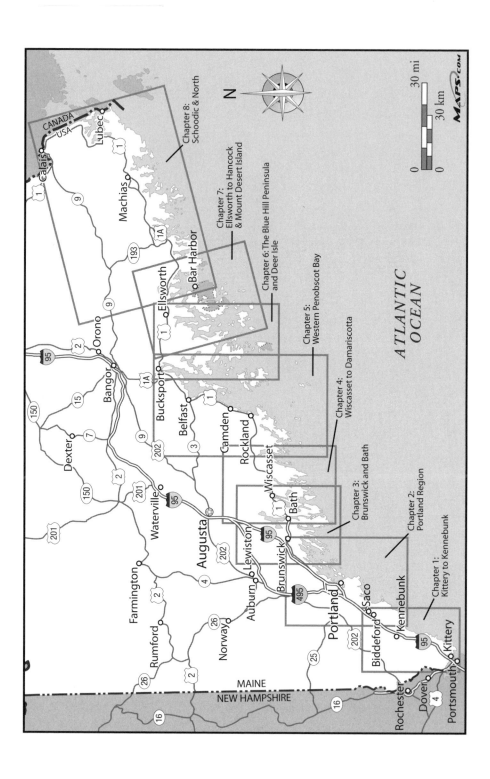

Willhoite, copy editor, my work gets a polish before it gets out to the public eye, and I am grateful.

The words in this book go through several reads, and I want to thank free-lance project editor and copy editor Pamela Benner for helping to improve my sentences and grammar, and proofreader Tim Zink, for checking up on my spelling and punctuation.

For the first edition particular thanks go to Ed and Nancy Ludwig of Thomaston, Roy Kasindorf and Helene Harton of Bar Harbor, Jonathan Chase of Blue Hill, Jane Hurd of Boothbay Harbor, Ellen Barnes of Camden, Bob Bartlett of Gouldsboro, Michael and Sarah Coughlin of Cumberland, and Nancy Swenson at Beach Farm Inn in Wells. All guided me to great places along the coast, and they have my gratitude. Many others gave tips along the way, like Miles, who drove the golf cart at Spruce Point Inn in summer 2004 and loves the doughnuts at Boothbay Harbor's 88 Baker's Way. Thanks also to Daphne Sprague, who knows where to go with her wheelchair.

Friends, of course, made many of the meals described in here better with their company and conversation. Thanks to Lori Eschholz, Nicholas Vasilatos, Elyse Tipton, Bill Curtsinger, Eva Goetz, John and Simone Reynolds, Elizabeth Edwardsen, Robert Solomon, and Nancy Barba and Cynthia Wheelock for heading out to dinner, sometimes many times. I know it was hard work, but someone had to do it.

The person who spent the most nights out was my daughter, who was 11 years old when this book was first written and 13 during the second round of research. Thanks to Emma, whose companionship on the road, aside from the rare moments when we were driving each other crazy, improves my own discernment as she develops better and better taste.

Thanks to Kermit Hummel, editorial director of The Countryman Press, who continues to support this project. Jennifer Thompson, managing editor at Countryman, always responds to questions quickly, making difficulties fade away.

Thanks also to David Corey, from The Countryman Press, who was inspired by his love of lobster to write the Lobster Primer on page 208.

This book's range would not have been possible without the assistance of Chris Tree, travel writer and my coauthor on *Maine: An Explorer's Guide,* among many other books. Chris's experience and long familiarity with the state gave me a fighting chance of finding the coast's great places. Many thanks go to Chris for all her help, and for sharing her knowledge.

Introduction

THIS BOOK IS FILLED with places to eat, from roadside take-out stands to elegant restaurants that won't let you make a shadow in the doorway without a jacket. Some have long descriptions, others just a line or two. But each place in here I can recommend as a place worth visiting, where you can find something fresh and enjoy the fruit of someone's skill in the kitchen.

The last line of the information block for each restaurant provides a quick read of what the place does. The price of the entrées should convey the cost of dinner. The hospitality line in each restaurant description indicates that I went to the restaurant myself. The staff's ability to make me feel welcome and comfortable ranks high as a qualification for a place at which I want to dine.

I've included some places that I criticize but that had good food to offer. Others aren't in here at all because I can't recommend them, or because it just didn't seem necessary. I can't tell you the number of places I visited that were overwhelmed with tourists, where the food was ordinary or substandard, and where the staff were too busy to answer questions. Those places will do just fine without me anyway.

I included many restaurants and lobster shacks on the recommendation of people I trust. Please let me know if your experience mirrors mine. Write to the publisher, The Countryman Press (P.O. Box 748, Woodstock, VT 05091; or e-mail countrymanpress@wwnorton.com), to let me know if you think a place I have included isn't good. I want to hear about it. If I missed a good place, I'd like to know that too. If there is a restaurant that you believe should be in here, please let me know why, and I will try to follow up with a visit.

I plan to keep visiting the places I have included, as well as to take note of new or improved places, writing and updating new editions every few years. Restaurants pop up on the horizon, flourish, and flare out as fast as shooting stars, so there may well be one in here that vanishes soon after the book is published.

So be warned. Call the places you're heading to first, and make sure they are open. They might have closed for the season, or for good. Also, business hours are always changing, and the ones I listed may have altered.

I did not impose a rating system on the restaurants in this book, but a few meals remain in my memory as some of the most pleasant I have ever had. It is a real privilege to eat in a restaurant that has a great chef, as I have a few times. But the best meals I ate were wonderful for a variety of reasons. The restaurants don't fit in a narrow category, so they can't be easily compared. You'll encounter my finds in the descriptions of XYZ, Anneke Jans, and the Dip Net, among many others—places that range from linoleum to linen.

I *can* rate crabcakes, however. The best crabcakes I've ever eaten are still served at the elegant Back Bay Grill in Portland. Close, in second place, are the fine versions served at Tall Barney's in Jonesport.

Comparing all the lobster rolls you can buy on the coast of Maine is the work of a lifetime, but I am getting that work under way. One delicious example, and also the largest I have eaten with freshly picked lobster meat, can be found at the Pemaquid Fisherman's Co-op's Harbor View Restaurant.

It is difficult to discern whether you are eating freshly picked lobster meat.

In spring, when lobsters are still barely awake, nobody has enough lobsters to steam, cool, and shuck their own. According to my expert, even in summer, when lobster is plentiful, most places use lobster meat that has already been taken out of the shell by a shellfish company. There just isn't time to do that work when the line is stretched out the door, and the customers are hungry.

Red's Eats in Wiscasset, for instance, does not pick its own lobster meat.

At those places that do cook fresh lobsters and pick their meat, you must wait for it. Harraseeket Lunch and Lobster in South Freeport has a wait every day of the week. Their lobster roll is full of big pieces of lobster.

Cheaper rolls have less lobster.

Four ounces of lobster is the typical quantity at the places best known for a good roll, and those places stretch from Kittery to Calais, with every town boasting about its own. One easy-to-visit place is Scott's Place, in Reny's parking lot in Camden, the favorite of Joseph Barber, manager of the Owl & Turtle Bookshop in Camden.

The Lobster Pot in Ellsworth makes a good roll too, with a place to enjoy it along a scenic river, and the staff here are fully responsible for picking hundreds of pounds of lobster throughout the summer to fill these rolls.

The processed lobster meat that is packed and frozen in the United States is required by law to be rinsed, which strips it of its salty juices. The kitchen has to add salt to the thawed meat when it goes into a roll. But Canadian frozen lobster retains the creatures' cooking juices and tastes better. Try asking where the lobster meat originates.

Readers are welcome to tell me which Maine lobster roll they think is best.

Restaurants have changed for the better in the last 20 years.

Now, I want them to take a few steps backward.

The cheapest restaurants would do us all such a big favor if they could go back to making every part of their meals from fresh ingredients, and stop buying frozen boxes off the back of the tractor trailer. A few are out in front, like Jonesport's Tall Barney's, already noted for making terrific crabcakes and serving sublime pies. There's one off the coast, the Brookside Restaurant in Smyrna Mills, not listed in this book but too good not to mention, with its turnips and new potatoes and peas side dishes. I thank the staffs at these restaurants for going to the trouble of working with good vegetables, fruits, and fresh meat.

Too many others make food that is slovenly, with processed ingredients masquerading as real food. We should all be in revolt—and taking ourselves off to the places written about in this book that make things right.

Enjoy.

CHAPTER 1

Kittery to Kennebunk

FOUGASSE

SNUG WITH THE SOUTHERN BORDER OF MAINE and traditional vacation destinations of long standing, the towns on this end of the coast support dozens of good restaurants. Many are a summer's-night destination for people in Boston with a little wanderlust and only a little time.

The towns, starting from the southern border and traveling north, are Kittery, York (Cape Neddick), Ogunquit (Perkins Cove), Wells, Kennebunk, and Kennebunkport, which includes Cape Porpoise and Goose Rocks Beach.

Kittery has its own "food alley," a collection of great food shops, on Route 1 near the bridge to New Hampshire. From the first interstate exit in Maine, merge into the Kittery rotary and head south on Route 1 to find Mayan chocolates, freshly made ravioli, and wine from southern Italy.

York has many places to eat, fun to go to as much for the view—especially at Cliff House—as for the food.

The view always competes with what's on the plates in a restaurant perched over the sea, like MC Perkins Cove, on the southern end of Ogunquit.

Downtown Ogunquit, as quiet in winter as a midwestern town, becomes a place without parking in July and August, when tourists crowd the sidewalks and take the free trolleys to the beach. That long, beautiful, sandy beach was a source of inspiration for painters who started this town's career as a summer colony, as artists have been known to do elsewhere along the Maine coast.

Wells, right alongside Ogunquit, has been the middlebrow neighbor, but new restaurants opening there are changing that description.

Kennebunkport, the flaunting sister of plainer Kennebunk, lords over all with its vast array of places to eat. I've included many Kennebunkport restaurants that have good reputations, but the criticism "overpriced" could be applicable. It depends on your preferences. For some of us, the silverware and the quality of the linens don't really matter. For others, all the expensive accoutrements of fine dining are what make an evening out worthwhile.

Yankees are stubborn, suspicious people, and anyone who lives in Maine is influenced by the land's long-enduring skepticism. It must come into our systems from the earth itself, growing fine vegetables in its brief summer, but austere under the winter sky for so much of the year.

You may be one of those in sympathy with local history, preferring a paper plate of freshly shucked fried clams to gussied-up lobster.

But there are places for all tastes, here as everywhere, on this friendly, accommodating, and eagerly commercial coast.

Kennebunk

Federal Jack's Brew Pub
(207) 967-4322
8 Western Avenue (before the bridge)
www.federaljacks.com
Hospitality—Brusque and busy in-season
Open daily for lunch, dinner, and late-night food 11:30 AM–1 AM, Sunday brunch
10:30–2
Entrées $12 to $22

☛ *A great place to try new beers and ales*

This is a favorite place for people who love casual dining and good beer. Seafood pasta with shrimp, calamari, and mussels in marinara ($16.95) could find a good match with one of the ales brewed here, and so could roast salmon, clam chowder, or a boiled lobster. So could a Pepper-Jack Burger, with jalapeño-Jack cheese and sautéed onions ($7.95). Our good waitress at the Wayfarer (see page 15) made this her destination on her night off.

Grissini Trattoria
(207) 967-2211
27 Western Avenue, Lower Village
www.restaurantgrissini.com
Hospitality—From an Italian greeting at the door to the quick, silent attention throughout the meal, service here is excellent.
Open for dinner daily from 5:30–9, Saturday until 9:30
Entrées $19 to $29
Handicapped accessible, reservations recommended

☛ *Northern Italian dishes on a generous scale that are sometimes too complicated*

Owned by Laurence Bongiorno, a Kennebunkport entrepreneur who also owns Stripers and the White Barn Inn, this high-ceilinged restaurant with a huge stone fireplace opened in 1996, serving simple pizzas and grilled fish and pasta from away. The linguine *con vongole,* with minced clams, capers, and garlic, and garnished with whole clams, brings the sea along with the pasta. *Carpaccio,* thin-sliced raw beef served with arugula, Parmesan, and a truffle vinaigrette, is a classic dish, as is the *caprese,* fresh tomatoes and fresh mozzarella, with oil and balsamic vinegar and a piece of flatbread.

Pizza Margherita, with tomato sauce and mozzarella, could keep the rest of the meal simple. An entrée such as Tonno, grilled tuna with fresh corn, sun-dried tomato, and chorizo salsa on arugula rev up the flavors. On one visit, an entrée of scallops in puttanesca sauce sat on too sweet puff pastry under frisée. But a seafood risotto with tender Maine shrimp showed fine restraint and admirable skill. Wines from Italy, like a Borgogno Barolo, are of course featured, but several from California vineyards, including Distant Bay Pinot Noir from Monterey County, can also be ordered.

Kennebunk Inn

(207) 985-3351
45 Main Street
www.thekennebunkinn.com
Hospitality—Affable and knowing, and still swift to take an order and bring it along
Full menu available Tuesday through Saturday 5–9, lunch Monday through Friday 11:30–2, pub menu daily 4–9
Entrées $8 to $30
Handicapped accessible, reservations recommended for the dining room

☛ *Yes, really good food that is moderately priced*

Shanna Horner O'Hea, chef-owner, operates this inn with her husband, Brian O'Hea, delivering on their motto—"affordable class." But it's the food that makes it work.

With prices ranging from $4 to $15, an evening out with a glass of Le Cigare Volent (a Rhône blend with earthy strength that is usually pricier than $11 a glass) and a pizza isn't too much at all. The grilled, thin-crust pizza represents one item of American regional cuisine served here.

The menu changes with the season. A ginger–butternut squash soup steamed from bowls here in late September, and dessert featured caramel apple cheesecake.

A s'more, created with a graham cracker–almond crust filled with a chocolate pâté made with Grand Marnier, topped with a homemade marshmallow browned in the oven before serving, delivers a powerful chocolate surge. The homemade marshmallow on top is unctuous and smooth, far better than the store-bought variety. Available in both the dining room and tavern, all desserts are made by Horner O'Hea, who, like her husband, has a degree from the Culinary Institute of America.

Black truffle gnocchi ($12) with ragu and mozzarella, and a crabcake sandwich ($14), were on a recent menu. A more substantial entrée was the braised beef short rib ($19) with smoked fig and ricotta cheese ravioli.

Fifty-five wines, with eight reds and six whites by the glass, fill the wine list, and most are moderately priced.

On the Marsh
(207) 967-2299
46 Western Avenue, Lower Village
www.onthemarsh.com
Hospitality—Elegance in a fancy décor feels luxurious. (There is a dress code, but jackets and ties are not required.)
Open for dinner at 5:30 Wednesday to Saturday, Sunday brunch with live music 9–2

☛ *High-style meals in cushy dining rooms overlooking the marsh*

Start with crunchy gulf shrimp with leeks and lemon saffron aioli ($13) or venison carpaccio with capers and truffle oil ($15) at this place, where the ambience is all about spoiling you. Jeff Savage is in the kitchen grilling up his fine Quebec foie gras—perhaps with roasted cippolini onion ($17).

Lobster here is easy, with two tails and claws from 1½-pound Maine lobsters served with wild rice and lemon beurre blanc (market price). La Crema Pinot Noir from California ($34 a bottle) is recommended by the restaurant to pair with the grilled pork tenderloin ($29) with roasted asparagus. A roasted garlic and wild mushroom ragout ($26) in a puff pastry shell with asparagus and pumpkinseed oil is perfection when you veer away from meat and fish.

A less expensive bar menu also is offered, with mussels and a lobster BLT among the possibilities.

Windows on the Water
(207) 967-3313
Chase Hill
www.windowsonthewater.com
Hospitality—The owner, John P. Hughes, is almost always here, making sure the evening runs smoothly, whether that means mixing a perfect Manhattan or clearing the table. He succeeds.

The entrance of Windows on the Water

Open daily for lunch 11:30–2:30, dinner 5:30–9:00 April through December;
closed Monday and Tuesday January through March
Entrées $22 to $48
Handicapped accessible, reservations recommended

☞ *Casual elegance is the motto here, with food that inspires praise.*

Twenty-two years of serving dinners have kept the skills here polished, and crab-cakes with Meyer lemon and mustard crème fraîche prove the point. The Maine shrimp "Poke," a southern tradition, presents fried, tender shrimp with a maple soy sauce jazzed up by red onion, dried red cranberries, and pine nuts.

Windows on the Water uses high-quality ingredients, such as chicken from the Amish Country fed with organic corn, which I savored roasted ($22), and freshly caught striped sea bass ($33), which was perfectly cooked and served on a round of purple Peruvian fingerling potatoes, mushrooms, and sautéed leeks. I wouldn't want to resist the Meyer lemon soufflé ($7), topped with good whipped cream, for dessert.

More than 100 wines, stored in a special cellar, are served, from modestly priced and good Salena Estate Shiraz from Australia to amazing Monterey Chalone Pinot Noir ($53).

Bakery, Breakfast, and Fish

Cherie's (207-985-1200), 7 High Street.

Open for breakfast Monday through Friday 7–11, Saturday and Sunday 7–1; lunch Monday through Saturday 11–2, deli service until 6 except Sunday. The bakery has been operating for 12 years, making blueberry pie, strawberry-rhubarb pie, all kinds of pie—and pastries, cakes, tarts, and tortes. We recommend the Key lime pie. The house granola is available for purchase, as customers who ordered it for breakfast demanded some to take home.

The breakfast menu lists eggs any style with home fries and toast for $4.50. The Breakfast Burrito combines scrambled eggs, black beans, jalapeños, cheddar cheese, and steak in a tortilla ($8.50). Three pancakes ($4.75) or one for a child ($1.50) make this the right spot for a family. Lunch and takeout operate throughout the day, and sandwiches and soups are always fresh.

The Clam Shack (207-967-2560 for takeout; 207-967-3321 for the seafood market) is right at the bridge that spans the river between Kennebunk and Kennebunkport.

At this beloved landmark, fried fish comes through the take-out window from Mother's Day to Columbus Day, when the seafood market next door sells lobsters, clams, and fish.

The Kennebunk Farmer's Market runs from May through October, Saturday 8 to noon, in the municipal parking lot off Route 1 behind the Kennebunk Inn.

Kennebunkport

Alisson's
(207) 967-4841
11 Dock Square, P.O. Box 344
www.alissons.com
Hospitality—Good, experienced service
Open daily for lunch 11–5, dinner 5–9, closing at 10 on Friday and Saturday
Entrées $14 to $23
Handicapped accessible through rear door

☞ *A neighborhood tavern serving the standards*

Right in the middle of town, Alisson's is an old hand at taking care of people and keeps the things most popular with visitors at the top of its good menu. Some plain, standard dishes, like chicken Parmesan, are made very well. The Conden family has been in charge for two generations. Lobster pie, lobster rolls, lobster bisque, and clam chowder are all here, and you can also order grilled salmon, baked haddock, or seafood fettuccine ($21.95), with the Parmesan cream sauce that makes scallops, shrimp, and lobster even better, for some. But the hamburgers make a good case for dropping the seafood for a night—the Deedee burger has blue cheese dressing, sautéed mushrooms, and onions ($6.95), and it sent me into a small ecstasy one winter night. The brownie sundae has a similar effect.

Bandaloop

(207) 967-4994
2 Dock Square
www.bandaloop.biz
Hospitality—Fast service with a friendly attitude
Open for dinner daily in summer, off-season Wednesday through Saturday
Entrées $15 to $25
Handicapped accessible, reservations recommended

☛ *Informal doesn't mean anything less than delicious.*

Experimentation on the menu raises interest in diners jaded by the same old, same old—like a fried egg roll full of Gorgonzola, walnuts, and red onion and served with a reduction of port. Even if I didn't entirely love it, I welcomed the innovative spirit.

Fried tofu ($15) was perfectly done and made enticing with peanut sauce. Thai green curry was another sauce choice among five on the menu, offered to accompany a variety of entrées, from the fried tofu to pork chops and grilled sirloin ($22).

But I really lucked out with a special—pistachio-crusted salmon ($22) with a blood orange and jalapeño glaze that held just enough acidity to work with the tender fish.

Bartley's Dockside

(207) 967-5050
By the bridge in Kennebunkport
www.bartleysdining.com

Hospitality—Casual and quick
Open daily for lunch and dinner 11–10
Entrées $14 to $24

☞ *Casual and traditional, with fish delivered fresh daily*

A long-standing refuge from the Kennebunkport sidewalks, this casual restaurant makes some fine dishes, like crabcakes with scallions, topped with a little Dijon cream. The baked haddock ($16.95) is promised fresh, never frozen. Bouillabaisse ($19.95) tops the price list, except for the heavier lobsters. The pie is coveted by all who make its acquaintance and is sold by the slice. Some customers reserve a slice when they sit down to make sure there's a serving left when it's time for dessert. Wild blueberry pie, made by Mrs. Bartley herself, goes for $4.75. "We just added an extra oven, we're selling so many," said Brian Bartley, owner, heading into the restaurant's 30th year in 2007.

The Belvidere Club at Tides Inn By-The-Sea
(207) 967-3757
252 King's Highway
Goose Cove Beach
www.tidesinnbythesea.com
Hospitality—Casual, with no attitude but friendliness
Open daily mid-May through mid-October for dinner
Entrées $19 to $34
Reservations suggested

☞ *Ambitious dishes in a Victorian dining room on the sea*

The Belvidere Club had been offering tavern food for years, but in 2004 it forged a higher path, rustling up elegant dishes that draw an eager following.

Patrons have always particularly enjoyed drinks at the bar, with its mahogany top from the demolished Shawmut Inn in Kennebunkport. Eastlake molding around the bar shelves also adds character to the decor selected by owners Kristen Blomberg and Marie Henriksen, who treasure their classic John Calvin Stevens shingle-style inn.

Pan-seared veal sweetbreads with wild Maine ramps ($11) starts dinner ambitiously, and grilled foie gras with a wild mushroom terrine ($14) is another classic worthy of another taste.

Moulard duck breast with French beans and grilled asparagus ($25) or Maine lobster ravioli with baby bok choy and *guanciale* ($34) are among the fabulous dinners anyone deserves after a long walk on the endless beach across the street from the inn. A very good vegetarian entrée is always on the menu. The wild mushroom stuffed Swiss chard ($19), its mushrooms collected by a Scarborough forager, revealed a full range of flavors, from earthy to delicate.

Almost all of the 26 wines are offered by the glass for about $7.

With a menu for the kids, and lots of space for them to enjoy themselves, even a young family could enjoy a great dinner here.

Cape Arundel Inn
(207) 967-2125
208 Ocean Avenue, P.O. Box 530A
www.capearundelinn.com
Hospitality—Wonderful service, with an emphasis on cordiality
Open March through New Year's Eve at 5:30 for dinner, daily in the summer; closed Monday off-season
Entrées $24 to $34
Reservations recommended

☞ *The dinners here rival the quality of the beautiful view.*

The dining room of the Cape Arundel Inn has incorporated what was once a porch, filling two walls with windows that seem to float above the blue expanse of ocean just across narrow Shore Road. Walls paneled with cream beaded board warm the room and sustain the inn's traditional atmosphere, where the very good waiter served us generous pieces of butter with silver tongs shaped like a chicken's feet. Tired of olive oil, I loved the butter on my bread.

We had the best table in the house, in the southern corner at the window, and watched the sea and a rising moon with pleasure, noting the lights coming on in the house at Walker's Point, where George H.W. Bush and his wife live.

The crabcakes took up our pleased attention a moment later, crisp and sweet with a little sautéed onion, red pepper, and a squiggle of creamy rémoulade. The bottle of Pouilly-Fume my companion chose made a pleasant contrast. The list itself started out in both red and white categories with some high-priced wines, and settled into a good selection priced between $30 and $40.

Another visit two years later, when I encountered the same polished service and superb meals, brought an encounter with the same waiter, one of several who have worked for years with owner Jack Nahil, here since 1997.

Broiled swordfish steak with roasted tomato salsa ($32) came from a very fresh fish to make the best piece of swordfish I'd had in years.

Rely on Cape Arundel Inn for elegant dinners with a view of the moon rise over the ocean.

My friend's duck "duo," duck leg confit and a grilled duck breast in a raspberry honey demi-glace, was another work of excellence, just like a rack of lamb ($35) with gamey intensity, accompanied by fried parsnips and garlic mashed potatoes.

The sautéed Maine lobster and wild mushrooms in a whiskey and herb beurre blanc looked spectacular at a nearby table. Filet mignon with blue cheese, wasabi vinaigrette, and garlic whipped potato also was on the menu ($34).

The profiterole with French vanilla gelato, Amaretto chocolate sauce, and whipped cream made me want to proclaim, as I hereby do, "We have a winner!" We should have ordered two.

This restaurant deserves to be called romantic, with the meals shedding love, the shaded candles glowing around the room, and the conversation and piano just noisy enough for us all to feel very much alive.

The Colony Hotel
(207) 967-3331, 1-800-552-2363
140 Ocean Avenue, P.O. Box 511
www.thecolonyhotel.com
Hospitality—Rough edges can come at the beginning of the season, when the staff are learning the ropes.

Open daily mid-May through late October for breakfast and dinner, lunch poolside Monday through Saturday in summer
Entrées $14 to $34
Dinner reservations recommended

☛ *Modest comfort food that's appealing because of the lovely surroundings*

Enjoyment in the big dining room has everything to do with feeling comfortable with children, who play outside on the putting green and sit nearby on the porch with its water views. The twin lobster dinner with the lobster meat already picked from the shell is a straightforward temptation for a visitor who needs to keep her hands clean in case they are needed by a restless kid.

There is a reason not to take the fancy food route, with a dinner of twin tournedos of beef ($25.50) with tomatoes and crabcakes likely to be starchy. One experience with the scallops that were described as "lobster stuffed" ($21.50) disappointed with just two small pieces of lobster and an abundance of crumbs.

But this place excelled at the simple classics, serving a clam chowder that tasted of fresh clams and the sea, and an excellent blueberry pie with a flaky crust.

This old hotel was built in 1914 and has 124 rooms on 11 acres. It is full of old-fashioned charm, but new directions have earned it praise from environmentalists for green practices, like composting all the kitchen scraps.

Mabel's Lobster Claw
(207) 967-2562
124 Ocean Avenue
Hospitality—Takeout, and a restaurant used to a fast pace
Open daily April through October for lunch and dinner
Entrées $13 to $30
Reservations recommended

☛ *A casual local favorite for fish and lobster*

Along the section of Ocean Avenue that follows the Kennebunk River, this place is within walking distance of the busy shops and first on the lists of innkeepers' recommended spots for lobster and fish. It offers lobster stew, clam chowder, and steamed clams, along with alternatives, including hot dogs and hamburgers. Might as well make a reservation for dinner.

Nunan's

(207) 967-4362
Route 9, Cape Porpoise
Hospitality—These folks have been doing this for years and handle the crowds like pros.
Open weekends in May, daily from Memorial Day to mid-October for dinner 5 to closing
Entrées $3 to $26
No credit cards (there's an ATM at the grocery store around the corner)

☛ *The classic lobster shack, intact in all its glory*

This place looks tiny from the front but extends deep through four rooms full of small and large picnic benches, all inside a raftered barn hung with generations of lobster buoys. Its charming exterior—black clapboards with yellow and red trim—and the sturdy tables inside have been welcoming nightly crowds for years. While she was filling up a coffeepot with water, I met Bertha Nunan, who said she had been working at Nunan's since it opened in 1953. She's now fully retired, and her two sons and their wives are running the place. One wife, Terri Nunan, has been working here for 33 years, since she was 14.

The place is always popular. "You can't change something when it's good," Terri Nunan said. "We stay the same; that's what people come for."

The paved area in front of the door (two parking lots just around the nearby house provide all the parking) is called the pasture. By 5:15 the place is often full, and the customers waiting for a table stand out there.

Two boiled 1⅛-pound lobsters—for one person only—cost $25.95. A large cup of clam chowder is $5.50. The cheapest meal is the peanut butter and jelly sandwich for $2.95. Hamburgers, hot dogs, and grilled cheese sandwiches are available for the anti-seafood customers, along with an open-faced grilled chicken sandwich ($6.95) and a Delmonico steak dinner ($18.95). A lobster roll is $9.95, and beer and wine are available.

Pie, cheesecake, and brownies are on the dessert menu. Although Nunan's does not take credit cards, you can pay with a personal check or traveler's checks.

Pier 77

(207) 967-8500
77 Pier Road, Cape Porpoise
www.pier77restaurant.com
June through September open daily for lunch 11:30–2:30, dinner at 5 in-season;

October through December, and March through May, open Wednesday through Sunday; closed January through St. Patrick's Day
Entrées $17 to $32
Handicapped ramp, but call about bathroom in planning stages; live jazz most nights

☞ *A beautiful setting and terrific professional cooking create lovely dinners.*

Oysters Bingo ($14), with garlic, spinach, Parmesan, and cream is one of the best baked oyster dishes I've had, the spoonful of cream light and rich and the rest of the flavors delicate and not overwhelming. Gumbo ($25), with crayfish, shrimp, scallops, sliced okra, and broccoli rabe, is substantial and wonderfully flavored. Baseball Steak ($32) is a thick cut of top sirloin. But the presence of a simple spaghetti dish with tomato sauce ($17) on the nine-item menu shows consideration for customers who may have a taste for something simple and not too heavy.

If you want to be right next to the windows, a reservation is probably necessary, but water views are possible from most tables.

Chef Peter Morency, 1973 Culinary Institute of America graduate, also presides over a lunch item called Pete's Pulled Pig, a North Carolina barbecue sandwich ($8), fish-and-chips ($12), and seafood stew ($14).

With myrtle topiaries on the dark wood tables and a few Victorian pieces upstairs, plus an informal downstairs bar called the **Ramp,** where you can dine simply at night amid sports memorabilia, this spot at the end of Pier Road is ready to nourish all its visitors.

Stripers Waterside Restaurant
(207) 967-5333
131–133 Ocean Avenue
www.thebreakwaterinn.com
Open daily in-season for lunch and dinner
Entrées $18 to $32
Handicapped accessible, reservations recommended

☞ *Upscale seafood and steaks in a beautiful dining room*

Stripers has ringside seats on the Kennebec River. The long, pale blue dining room is as elegant as possible. A long aquarium fills one end with more blue light, while the cobalt fish inside it flash their scales.

After tossing out a simple menu that forced an awkward marriage between casual fish shack food and upscale surroundings—according to reports it had worked at the original location, but did not when I tried it out in 2004—Stripers now features cuisine that reads like the script from most high-end fish places, with an innovation in its list of carpaccio dishes. Beef carpaccio ($13) is thinly sliced, raw beef served with arugula salad; lamb carpaccio ($10) is rolled in pesto and served with sun-dried tomatoes and balsamic vinegar. Salmon carpaccio ($11) has been cured in vodka and jasmine tea.

Yellowfin tuna ($28) is served with spinach and tomato confit, and cod ($26) comes with Israeli couscous and pea foam. You can also order tempura-fried cod ($25), shrimp ($23), and scallops ($24) served with fries and a vegetable. Steaks include a venison loin ($32).

The Wayfarer
(207) 967-8961
Pier Road, Cape Porpoise
Hospitality—Friendly women take care of you in this casual, pretty place.
Open Tuesday through Saturday for breakfast, lunch, and dinner; breakfast on Sunday from 7 to noon
Entrées $11.50 to $21.95
No credit cards

☛ *A simple, well-kept restaurant for good chowder, fine lobster rolls, and a relaxed meal*

Our lobster rolls fit the classic mold: lots of sweet fresh lobster on a buttered and grilled hot dog bun, with a little mayonnaise and a lettuce leaf. The mayo was a generic brand from the SYSCO truck, one waitress said. The lobster roll went for $13.95 in 2006. Melissa Gilbay, a waitress, said, "Nothing's changed here in 30 years."

Maybe, just maybe, you've had enough lobster. This is just the place for a very good chicken salad sandwich. The chicken was fresh, in good-sized chunks, and the toasted wheat bread gave the sandwich a nice crunch. Both the roll and the sandwich were served with potato chips and a good sour dill pickle spear on a big white plate.

The striped wallpaper and white wood booths make this a pretty place, with tables and a counter. When offered blueberry, strawberry-rhubarb, or raspberry-peach pie ($3.95), we chose the last and enjoyed the sweet filling without a worry in the world.

White Barn Inn

(207) 967-2321
37 Beach Avenue
www.whitebarninn.com
Open for dinner Monday through Thursday 6–9:30, Friday and Saturday
5:30–9; closed most of January
Prix fixe menu for $89 per person
Dress code: jackets required, ties optional; no jeans or sneakers, no athletic
wear allowed
Reservations are required, along with 24-hour cancellation notice. If the
reservation is canceled with less than 24-hour notice, the full amount is
charged to the credit card used when the reservation was made.

☛ *The king of the mountain for formal restaurants in Maine*

This is one of the highest-ranked restaurants in New England.

The silver is real, the tablecloths are linen, and the barn sure doesn't hold any
farm animals anymore, unless they've been roasted and sauced to perfection.

This immaculate, elaborate restaurant is designed for those of us who love
formality and special arrangements. There comes a time in our lives when all
this makes sense, when some of us want to really go all out and be floored by the
ambience, the flowers, the swift service on silent feet.

The changing menu has included seared foie gras and quail breast on a croissant galette, pecan-crusted scallops, or a lobster spring roll to start; iced watermelon and cherry soup as a "intermezzo"; and then main courses of salmon with
sweet corn and chorizo ragout, lobster on fettuccine with cognac butter sauce,
or Rice Paper Cannelloni with garden vegetables. You can opt for wines that fit
the menu, already picked out for you, for another $48 per person, or buy one of
the 7,000 bottles stored in the wine cellar.

Peach and lime charlotte with roasted pepper and peach salsa mixes a little
savory into dessert. And obviously there's an army of dessert wines, ports, and
liqueurs.

The 2006 summer tasting menu ($125, with wine for an additional $65)
looks yummy, starting with yellowfin tuna with sweet chili sauce, then "scallop"—possibly just one—with red beet sorbet, goat cheese and yogurt sorbet,
lamb cutlets with morels in Madeira sauce, cheese, and best of all, chocolate
soufflé with mint chocolate ice cream.

Farms, Fish, Wine, and Treats

Blackrock Farm (207-967-5783; www.blackrockfarm.net), 293 Goose Rocks Road.
This innovative nursery features an organic vegetable stand with wonderful varieties from its 1-acre garden full of heirloom tomatoes and special vegetables often served at local restaurants. The stand is open on the honor system, and the nursery is open daily in the summer.

Cape Porpoise Lobster Company (207-967-4268; www.capeporpoiselobster.com), 15 Pier Road.
Open year-round. Fresh fish, lobsters, and clams are sold. "Everything that we have is local" and comes right off the boat that caught it, the manager said. In the summer cooked seafood is available for takeout. **Cape Pier Chowder House** is at the end of the pier, serving chowder and seafood for lunch and dinner from April until November. On weekends it also serves breakfast.

Cape Porpoise Kitchen (207-967-1150; www.kitchenchicks.com), 12 Mills Road.
This charming store sells wine and cheese, and Coffee By Design coffee. From the kitchen come twice-baked potatoes, Caesar Salad, flank steak, quesadillas, barbecued baby back ribs, and lasagna. Crabcakes and the wildly popular meatloaf are local favorites. For breakfast, croissants, muffins, and coffee cake taste wonderful with coffee at one of the two tables or at the bar by the windows.

Port Lobster (207-967-2081; www.portlobster.com), 122 Ocean Avenue (before the Colony Hotel).
Live or cooked lobsters packed to travel, and chowders, lobster, and crab rolls to go. Retail sales of a wide range of fresh seafood and frozen items.

Kittery

Anneke Jans Restaurant
(207) 439-0001
60 Wallingford Square
www.annekejans.net

Hospitality—Showing grace under pressure, and very attentive
Open Tuesday through Saturday from 5 PM
Entrées $14 to $26
Handicapped accessible, reservations recommended

☛ *Chic and sophisticated. Both the décor and the fabulous food beckon customers to make the trip and make it often.*

Anneke Jans *(ANN eh ka Jahns)* is the kind of place that makes me feel like the night is special, the people are brilliant, and my own wits are sharp—something to be grateful for indeed.

Its casual feel rises from a funny mix of spare décor employing branches and Spanish moss, a semicircular bar, black-painted cork-lined walls, and a brightly lighted stainless steel kitchen visible over a high counter.

Turnbull Sauvignon Blanc from Napa Valley, Oakville Estate, 2004 ($9) was sweetly scented and balanced alongside grilled calamari ($10), with its thin, tender rings of squid set on mashed potatoes with arugula. Mussels with bacon and Great Hill blue cheese ($8, or as an entrée with fried potatoes $14) proved terrific, even taken home in the black Asian take-out container.

A thick pelt of crushed black peppercorn spiced up slices of rare yellowfin ($23) alongside a pile of chickpea "fries," but the best thing on the plate was the "melted spinach," with its fusion of butter and leafy green. Grilled swordfish ($23) came with broccoli rabe and a crunchy round of risotto.

Valrhona chocolate soufflé cake ($7.50, as are all desserts) put me in a frenzy of pleasure, the dark, thin-textured cake charged with chocolate and set in a moat of raspberry puree. Steamed lemon pudding is a house favorite, and there is always a tarte tatin, sometimes apple or pear.

Bob's Clam Hut
(207) 439-4233
315 Route 1
www.bobsclamhut.com
Open year-round, summer Sunday through Thursday 11–9, until 10 on Friday and Saturday, one hour earlier closing off-season
Seafood entrées $8 to $29

☛ *The first place to eat Maine seafood; open in the winter*

An old establishment with a great new attitude, Bob's gives people 60 and older 15 percent off on Tuesday. Order the unthickened cream-and-milk-broth clam chowder, or the basket of fried oysters ($12.50), for a cold winter day. You can eat lobster stew, lobster rolls, and lobster salads here, but plain boiled lobsters are not on the menu. The restaurant prides itself on the freshness of its clams, and the frequently changed oil, a brand named Crystal that contains trans fats. It's "100 percent partially hydrogenated soybean oil," according to the manager who read the label to me when I called. (In fact, anywhere on the coast of Maine, unless a place advertises that their oil has no trans fat, you can be pretty sure it contains trans fat.)

The clams served at Bob's come from the Ipswich area in Massachusetts.

In good weather, there are tables outside along Route 1 and around the corner of the restaurant. That's when you could try to snag a picnic table in the back by a little garden, and definitely finish up with **Ben & Jerry's** ice cream, available at their own window. If you drive up the coast frequently, take one of their five-punch cards. After it's full you get a free small cone.

Cap'n Simeon's Galley

(207) 439-3655
90 Pepperell Cove (on Route 103 between Kittery and York Harbor), Kittery Point
www.capnsimeons.com
Open daily in summer 11:30 AM through dinner, Sunday brunch 10 to 2; call for hours in the off-season
Entrées $11 to $19

☛ *An old building on the sea, originally a store that opened in 1828, serving seafood and burgers*

Broiled haddock and broiled scallops are the most popular entrées, with fried oysters (often from Prince Edward Island, $11.95), clams from Ipswich, and many other fried dinners served here year-round along with steamed lobsters galore. Thirty-five tables seat 120 diners in the old, beamed dining room, which overlooks the ocean and two lighthouses—Whaleback Light and the lighthouse at Fort Constitution, a Coast Guard station in Newcastle, New Hampshire. Fort Foster and Fort McLeary are also visible through the big dining-room windows; you may have to wait for a window seat on a summer weekend.

Chauncey Creek Lobster Pound

(207) 439-1030
16 Chauncey Creek Road, Kittery Point
www.chaunceycreek.com

Hospitality—Counter service, often with a wait in the busy summer months; the meal is brought to you at a sheltered or outdoor table.
Open daily from Mother's Day to Labor Day 11–8, Tuesday through Sunday until Columbus Day
Entrées $1.95 for a hot dog; upwards of $20 for lobster
BYOB

☛ *An authentic lobster pound, with the basics and more, at outdoor picnic tables*

One of travel writer Chris Tree's favorite lobster shacks in Maine, this place has been serving up boiled lobster, steamers, chowder, and mussels for more than 50 years. You find a seat first at one of the more than 40 blue, pink, or orange picnic tables, because you need to put down the wine and glasses, salad, or whatever else you brought along to supplement the menu—not chips and soda, management asks, because they are sold here. Order at a window, and the staff bring your meal out to you at the table number you gave them. Some of the tables are under shelter, convenient if you visit on a day with iffy weather. They also have screens to keep out the bugs.

Like Miller's farther Downeast, there is no fried food. But you can get raw shellfish, like oysters ($7 for a half dozen), and clams on the half shell, as well as steamers. Make that bottle of wine a muscadet, and drink in the river view.

There is a chicken dinner ($7.95), and you can also order a hot dog. But the main event is the lobster, in a range of sizes, because it was lobster that got things going in the 1940s, when this place was a lobster pound only. Now people have such a good time here, you are asked to stay no longer than two hours.

Warren's Lobster House
(207) 439-1630
11 Water Street (Route 1)
www.lobsterhouse.com
Open Sunday through Thursday 11:30–8:30, Friday and Saturday 11:30–9
Entrées $13 to $17, more for lobster

☛ *A longtime lobster shack with a giant menu and lots of tables*

Look for the big sign when you cross into Maine from Portsmouth, New Hampshire. This place has a big salad bar with more than 50 choices ($8.99), just like the sign says, and could be a southerner's first chance to crack open a Maine lobster. Around since the 1940s, when it had six stools and served only clams and lobsters (at 25¢ a pound), the long menu will now please just about anyone, and the staff know how to take care of crowds. The restaurant can seat 350 and bakes its own breads and cakes. Every party that sits down gets a key to the Captain's Treasure Chest in the gift shop, where they are encouraged to see what their luck can bring.

Food Markets, Bakeries, and Fish and Wine Stores

It's enough to make anyone wish they lived in Kittery: a whole neighborhood of high-quality places to get dinner, from artisan bread to fresh fish to ground beef and fresh pasta, with a bottle of the best southern Italian wine and the freshest salad.

Beach Pea Bakery (207-439-3555), 53 State Road (Route 1).

Open Monday through Saturday 7:30–6. *Fougasse*—made from rosemary dough, brushed with olive oil and sprinkled with sea salt and formed like a fat pretzel-shaped leaf—is the bakery's most popular bread. All are hand-formed, European-style breads, according to Mariah Maher, who co-owns the business with Tom Roberts. Open since January 2001, this place is hopping, with cakes, croissants, coffee cakes, and cookies, all made with high-quality natural ingredients. Sandwiches are made with meats roasted on the premises; soups are offered in the fall, winter, and spring; and salads are now on the menu.

Sandwiches are a mainstay for lunch at Beach Pea Bakery in Kittery.

Cacao Chocolates (207-438-9001; cacaochocaltes@aol.com), 64 Government Street.

Open Tuesday through Friday 12–6, Saturday 10–4, closed Sunday and Monday and the month of August until the Thursday after Labor Day (because it's too hot for chocolate). *Cacao* (pronounced ka-COW) is the Latin name for the cocoa bean plant. Homemade chocolates are always taking exciting new directions here, with ingredients like chèvre, bergamot, and juniper. Dense, pure, luscious flavors fill your mouth. The 80 truffle varieties (but only 18 to 24 are in the case on a given day) include strawberry with balsamic vinegar, and black pepper and chèvre with cognac.

The ginger-buttermilk truffle was inspired by ice cream at Arrows (see page 24), as was the fennel. The habanero pepper line is popular, and herbs and flowers like bergamot are infused for yet more nuances of taste and scent.

Caramels with French sea salt made another kind of bliss. English toffee is a "killer" that no one seems able to resist, but be forewarned: In the worst summer humidity it's not available.

"It almost doesn't matter what we put in the case," Susan Tuveson, the owner, said. That's because her customers leap to try any new invention, sure to enjoy the highest-quality chocolate with whatever she devises as the latest twist in flavoring.

Carl's Meat Market (207-439-1557), 25 State Road (Route 1).

This custom butcher shop is run by a man who grinds his own hamburger. You can order however much you want, from any cut you like. All natural beef can be cut to order at this real butcher shop, which also sells venison and duck.

Enoteca Italiana (207-439-7216), 20 Walker Street, off Route 1 before entrance to Navy Yard.

Open Tuesday through Saturday 10–7, Sunday 12–4, closed Monday. Antipasto platters and lots of Italian wine. Many small house wines, from Sicily and other regions, are sold here. Ninety percent of the store's offerings are Italian wines. Importers out of New York, including Via, allocate wines to this shop. "I'm able to tap into the New York market; I can get $10 bottles of wine that are absolutely phenomenal," said Chris Souder, who owns the store with his wife. He admires the southern Italian ethic that has kept prices low while boosting quality. The Puglia region, the heel of the boot, makes wine with the *primitiva* grape, called the original zinfandel grape. Salice Salentino, a favorite wine area within Puglia, is the source of some of the best wines, along with Sicily and Sardinia. Meat lasagnas, made with five layers of hand-rolled pasta, are prepared by a woman from Abruzzo who lives in New Hampshire. Twenty kinds of olives; antipasto like grilled artichoke hearts and roasted tomatoes from Italy; fresh ricotta from New Haven, Connecticut; cheeses; many salamis; and different hams, mortadella, and pancetta are also for sale. Fresh sausage from Manhattan typically sells out quickly after Thursday deliveries.

The Golden Harvest Produce Market (207-439-2113), 47 State Road (Route 1).

A long-standing market that features local produce in-season, and specialty items, like ramps, when they can be found at the wholesaler, in business since 1960.

Loco Coco's Tacos (207-438-9322), 36 Walker Street.

Open Monday through Saturday 11 to 9, but closed every day from 3 to 4. Terrific tacos are made here, near the shipyard—they are "crazy good," according to Enoteca Italiana owner Chris Souder (see above). "You're the first place up here with real food," say visitors from San Diego, according to manager Mona Materese. Luis Valdez, the owner, opened Loco Coco's in October 2004. Burritos, enchiladas, quesadillas, tacos—fish and shrimp tacos are especially good—and taco salads fill the menu. For breakfast try huevos rancheros and steak and egg burrito ($7.25). Everything is authentic and made from scratch. All the meats are grilled in front of your waiting eyes. Loco Coco's seats only 20 but has a huge to-go business.

Sue's Seafood (207-439-5608), 33 Old Post Road (Route 1).

Open Memorial Day through Columbus Day daily 10 to 6; closed Tuesday in winter, but otherwise open the same hours. Premade entrées and side dishes are available to take home. Lobster rolls and crabmeat rolls are sold for takeout. Fried fish may become available when space becomes available. Much of the fish sold here comes from local fishermen, when they have what Susan Allen accepts. She opened in this location in 2005, after operating another fish store nearby. "I have refused so much stuff that they won't send me what's not fresh." Two kinds of tuna (locally caught bluefin and big-eye from Hawaii), fresh haddock, cod, sea scallops, and an array of other shellfish (shucked if you want) were available when I visited. Bait and tackle are for sale for sportfishermen, and recommendations for charter boats can be had here too.

Terra Cotta Pasta Co. (207-475-3025), 52 Route 1.

Open Monday 10–6, Tuesday through Saturday 9–6:30, and Sunday 10:30–4. A 2-pound bag of fresh egg linguine is the most popular item here; the pasta is made in Dover at the owner's other store and always fresh. Raviolis range from roasted garlic with three cheeses to sweet potato and butternut squash to wild mushroom with roasted shallots in a lemon thyme pasta. Pumpkin, cranberry, and cheddar cheese ravioli is available in the fall. Lasagnas, other meals to go, and a variety of cheeses are offered. A deli case contains other prepared foods. A lot of samples are available on Saturday between 12 and 5. You can always try something from the deli case, or whatever soups are on the menu. Let the clerks know if this is a first visit and you will be offered the grand tour. Refillable bottles of Greek olive oil and balsamic vinegar are sold—the olive oil is delicious and priced right.

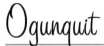Ogunquit

Arrows
(207) 361-1100
Berwick Road, P.O. Box 803, just inside the Cape Neddick–York line
www.arrowsrestaurant.com
Hospitality—A staff trained to fold napkins and whisk away crumbs hovers sweetly
Open for dinner Tuesday through Sunday July through August; Thursday through Sunday in October; weekends in November and December; closed January, February, March, on weekends in April and May, and Wednesday through Sunday in June
Entrées $41 to $44
Reservations very necessary

☛ *The height of elegance, where dinner is all about dozens of different tastes, Arrows caters to lovers of refinement.*

This handsome old dining room, decorated with an arrangement of dozens of orchids ascending tree branches in vases on the night of my visit, is the destination of customers eager to taste new varieties of foods in a wide array of creative invention. Arrows' owners and chefs, Mark Gaier and Clark Frasier, and their *chef de cuisine,* Justin Walker, are masters at curing ham, growing produce, making cheese, and even laying by an occasional bottle of hard cider, all to add to the elaborate meals served here on plates that are compositional extravaganzas. An appetizer of five dumplings came with five sauces, for instance, and lettuce from the lovely, orderly gardens came in four varieties with four vinegars. Entrées are multiplicity on a plate: perfectly grilled snapper and a square of pork belly accompanied by apple foam and apple fondue, along with a tart of black truffle béchamel on sliced parsnips (which didn't give the parsnips any room to shine); or duck breast, smoked duck, and a duck egg with grapes, grape sauce, fried basil, and sautéed greens. Best of the night was the Blini Service, with teensy pancakes we topped with crème fraîche (made here, of course), honey, wine-soaked cherries, and other condiments for a mouthful of sweet magnificence. Wine by the glass is expensive (most $10–16); there are reasonably priced bottles on the big beautiful wine list.

If you love elaboration and don't mind the expense (one person's tab here in 2006, with two glasses of wine and tip, was $132), this can be a lot of fun.

Barnacle Billy's and Barnacle Billy's Etc.
(207) 646-5575, 1-800-866-5575
Perkins Cove
www.barnbilly.com
Barnacle Billy's Original opens for lunch and dinner at 11 daily; Etc. opens daily at noon, May through October
Entrées $2.50 to $7

☛ *A classic lobster shack with a view, and some ambition in the menu*

You have to get over the fee for parking and enjoy the view after you make it to this classic lobster shack on the water, started in 1961. The Grande Lobster Shack, perhaps, the place you get whisked away to from Boston. Pricey, of course, but knowledgeable about lobsters, with perfectly portioned 1½-pound lobsters for $23.95 in 2006. A 2-pounder sold for $31.95. You get your steamed clams with butter and broth for $16.95, and cheeseburgers for the know-nothing kids are $4.35 (but you are grateful they can't stand lobster and keep the bill from achieving orbit). The onion rings have been known to be soggy, but a seat on the outside deck over the water makes all things seem right. Two fireplaces warm things up when the cove is fog-bound.

A bowl of lobster stew ($16.95) and corn on the cob round out the proper menu for a city slicker out for a Maine meal.

Maple syrup comes with the scallops wrapped in bacon ($8.75).

Cliff House
(207) 361-1000
Shore Road, P.O. Box 2274
www.cliffhousemaine.com
Hospitality—Competent service
Open daily late March through December for dinner

Entrées $24 to $38
Reservations recommended, handicapped accessible
Dress code: "Relaxed proper attire" and no athletic wear at dinner

☛ *A sea of tables overlooking the sea, with some good dishes and others that miscalculate*

We came into the dining room from a side door that had led us past the new "vanishing edge pool," an impressive sight curved on the top of a terrace overlooking the sea. The scale of things at the Cliff House matches its exalted location on top of the cliffs at the edge of the sea, and its new spa looms above when you park in the parking lot.

The big dining room, with corporate carpet and drop ceiling, is furnished with cream swags over the wide windows and reproduction Queen Anne side chairs at the tables.

A first course could be classic clam chowder ($6) or lobster bisque ($9), crabcakes ($12) with red pepper and Meyer lemon aioli, steamed mussels with andouille sausage ($11), or raw Maine oysters ($16). The list is simpler now than in past years.

There is no longer a house or Caesar salad served with dinner, but if the Caesar on the menu resembles the one we ate, it will be a success.

Seared Maine blueberry halibut ($28) comes with a warm blueberry compote and jasmine rice. An earlier version was too sweet, but this one could have tweaked out the excess sugar.

Blueberries show up in the chicken entrée ($26) too, which combines sage butter and blueberry barbecue sauce, and sets it all on top of fennel–San Andre cheese risotto.

Herb-crusted lamb ($38) with Asiago polenta sounds more palatable, but I tend to prefer simpler dishes.

Fisherman's Catch
(207) 646-8780
134 Harbor Road
Hospitality—A casual place with experienced owners, good service
Open May through October
Entrées $6 to $19
Handicapped accessible

☛ *A fish place with some imagination, especially off-season*

This weathered, shingled building stands in a salt marsh. You can eat at outdoor picnic tables or head indoors for casual dining. Customers like the mussels and steamers combo (about $11) when the place is focused on its homemade chowders, lobster dinners, fried oysters ($10.25), and seafood platter with haddock, shrimp, scallops, and clams ($19; for two people $29).

Fried jumbo shrimp ($12) come with french fries, homemade coleslaw, and roll with butter. For dessert people get a little wild about the bread pudding with whiskey sauce ($4) and the Key lime pie ($4).

Mussels in garlic wine ($9), one special that is served more off-season than on-, is just another reason to visit the area in September and October.

Five-O Shore Road

(207) 646-5001
50 Shore Road
www.five-oshoreroad.com
Hospitality—Fabulous service and great bartending
Open daily for dinner 5–10 in summer, Thursday through Sunday in winter
Entrées $20 to $29

☛ *A cool interior, an up-to-date menu, and good drinks at the bar*

Wood and terra-cotta-colored walls give the bar a warm glow and make it a good place to start an evening. Bar manager Gary Pucciarelli calls the cosmo the signature drink, but in the summer of 2006 the pomegranate martini was holding strong. On the interesting wine list, the Joseph Phelps Pastiche ($9.50 a glass) joined dark fruit to tannins with panache. Baracchi Italian olive oil in bottles on the table is a special touch, its fruity green a good taste on the crusty bread; the restaurant plans to serve wines from the same family.

On my visit the outstanding dish was an appetizer of beef tenderloin brochette ($11) with a beefy sauce and a small nest of rice noodles tossed with black sesame and apricot. But the foie gras mousse ($12) was too meager and too overset by pear-ginger chutney.

A tangle of frenched bones on the rack of lamb ($32) looked like the elephant graveyard in *The Lion King,* but that didn't stop thorough enjoyment of the wonderful medium-rare meat with a hazelnut crust. Wild salmon sat in a bowl of *tzatziki* ($25), soupy but good.

Baked chocolate pudding on the dessert menu sounds like the old favorite, chocolate soufflé, and anytime sounds like the right time to find out if it is. If you go in the spring or fall, you can enjoy a great atmosphere of peace and quiet.

Gypsy Sweethearts

(207) 646-7021
30 Shore Road
www.gypsysweethearts.com
Open June through September for dinner Tuesday through Sunday at 5:30,
weekends only in spring and fall
Entrées $17 to $27

☛ *An established business with some Caribbean dishes, good wine,
and a happy staff*

"The menu is definitely going a little more Caribbean," said Tony Tarleton,
chef-owner Judie Clayton's business partner. The meals served in the pretty old
rooms have been pleasing customers for more than 22 years. Whole wheat pizza,
potato gnocchi, scallops with garlic aioli, or crabcakes with lime mayonnaise
make starting dinner festive.

Entrées in 2006 included seared sea scallops ($23) over field greens with
Mandarin oranges and pineapple, served with lemon risotto.

Shrimp Margarita ($22) came with poblano cream with tequila and spicy
rice. Poblano *rellenos* ($17), roasted and stuffed with corn, *tetillo* cheese, and
currants, was accompanied by smoky tomato salsa. You don't have to order the
rack of lamb ($29) to get the roasted garlic bread pudding, which comes as a
side for $4, but why not?

The desserts are homemade and have included ice cream, cappuccino crème
brûlée, and chocolate mascarpone tart (all $7).

Things are not changing a lot here, and that makes the days run smoothly.
Tarleton still employs the restaurant's original hostess, who started in 1982. "We
don't have much turnover." He said most people are happy here, and joked
that he paid them more than he paid himself. He was funny in a Rodney Dan-
gerfield kind of way about the entrées he gets to eat—like the ones that fall on
the floor.

This is one of the first restaurants to receive the *Wine Spectator* Award of Excellence, for a reasonably priced wine list with 80 wines, 21 available by the glass.

MC Perkins Cove

(207) 646-6263
Perkins Cove
www.MCperkinscove.com

Hospitality—Smooth competence oversees all in this well-run space.
Open daily for lunch 11:30–2:30, dinner 5:30–9:30 or 10, bar menu until 11; closed January
Entrées $19 to $34
Handicapped accessible, reservations recommended, for lunch also

☛ *The view triumphs, and with Arrows owners Mark Gaier and Clark Frasier in charge, the flavors sing out with equal glory.*

"MC" stands for the first names of the owners, who also own the extravagant restaurant Arrows. Their meticulous ways are in action here in the skill of the cooking and the smoothness of the operation.

MC Perkins Cove is a casual, fast-paced place that fits into its environment, both the surging water out the wide windows of the back of the building and the swarming crowds of summer visitors on a narrow street of Perkins Cove in front. Customers are asked not to wear bathing suits to eat here; any other casual wear is fine.

The $44 Grand Shellfish "Tower" with oysters, littleneck clams, shrimp, tuna sashimi, mussels, and Maine lobster would be a grand way to finish a day at the beach, but a half-dozen oysters ($17) might suffice. A cone of fried oysters ($13) was perfectly done here, and served with chive and chili mayonnaise, but it has gone off the menu.

There is reason to be circumspect about the appetizers because the entrées can be so compelling, including a November special of beef short ribs ($29)—an enormous serving of rich, flavorful meat on mashed potatoes and chopped Swiss chard.

Regulars on the list in 2006 include "Beijing Style" duck confit with orange, ginger, and star anise ($29) and house-made sausages ($25) that you can be sure are made with all kinds of attention to the right meat, the right spices, and the right proportion of fat to lean.

But the mainstays here are grilled steaks and fish paired from lists with sauces, "Evil Carbos," and vegetables. "Choose me" the menu directs—olive and sage hollandaise, for instance, with perhaps the shrimp brochettes ($28), onion rings, and Beijing-style cabbage. Hmmm, that doesn't sound quite right. How about Clark's Mom's Sauce, with Worcestershire, soy sauce, balsamic and red wine vinegars, olive oil, rosemary, and mustard, on a hanger steak ($25) with Mark's Mom's Corn Custard and grilled asparagus?

Comfort Night, Wednesday, offers a three-course meal with a bottle of wine for $49, and live jazz is played at Sunday brunch (same as lunch, from 11:30 to 2:30).

These choices are far from ordinary, and any questions would receive clear guidance. But when the lists are short enough, like the six options presented here in each category, they make dinner fun.

Jonathan's Restaurant
(207) 646-4777
92 Bourne Lane
www.jonathansrestaurant.com
Open daily for dinner from 5 to 10 in summer; check for hours off-season
Entrées $18 to $24

☛ *A longtime presence on the restaurant scene, with a big menu*

After a five-year absence, Jonathan West returned to his eponymous restaurant in 2006 and made some changes. The farm-raised lamb from his South Berwick farm is back on the menu, along with beans grown by his father in his vegetable garden. The menu begins with a daily chowder and includes Boursin-stuffed mushrooms ($8), fried calamari with sweet-and-sour sesame sauce ($8.50), and four oysters served with both cocktail sauce and wasabi and ginger ($10). Salads come with the entrées here.

West decided he would go back to simpler entrées and drop the fancier stuff, and as much as possible use local food, vegetables from his own garden, and Maine products like goat cheese.

Fresh garden tomatoes come with buffalo mozzarella in late summer and fall. Elderberry nectar makes a fine addition to the dressing, as well as to the Maine Martini ($8) with Cold River Vodka.

A mainstay from both his earlier years as owner and chef and during his five years away is the caramelized salmon filet ($23), marinated in triple sec and orange juice, dusted with sugar and black pepper, and sauced with lemon beurre blanc. Mediterranean Pasta ($19) included the farm-raised-lamb sausages, with garlic, mushrooms, shallots, and tomato on pasta with Maine goat cheese. Grilled steaks, fish-and-chips, and fried scallops fill simpler dishes.

Warm bread pudding, brownie sundaes, and homemade ice cream end the meal. Cantaloupe and watermelon sorbet will last for a couple of months in the fall.

Tom Rush, Patty Larkin, and others appear here in concerts through the summer and into the fall. The concert schedule is on the Web site.

Lobster Shack

(207) 646-2941
Lower End of Perkins Cove
Hospitality—Counter service for lobster, with a short menu
Open daily for lunch and dinner at 11, mid-April through mid-October
Entrées $2.25 to $20

☞ *All that's needed for a fine lobster dinner is here.*

This simple little restaurant holds only 12 tables, each made of one solid pine slab. Built in 1963, they are refinished every year and fill the small space with honey-colored light.

Lobster rolls are made from fresh-cooked lobster meat with a little mayo on the classic toasted hot dog bun, absolutely no lettuce or celery.

Lobster is the big thing here, from 1 to 3 pounds. There's a sink in the dining room for washing up at after you crack the shells.

The house chowder, a combination of haddock and clam with potatoes and onions, comes in a milk-and-cream base, without any flour thickening. Jason Evans, the owner, is stepping into his father's shoes (his father bought the place in 1986) and said he'd grown up on the unthickened chowder in Portland.

Desserts, from Bread and Roses Bakery (see page 35), are apple and blueberry pie. "Just plain and simple," Evans said.

98 Provence

(207) 646-9898
262 Shore Road, P.O. Box 628
www.98provence.com
Hospitality—Great service with minimal fuss
Open for dinner Wednesday through Monday in summer, with fewer hours in the off-season
Entrées $26 to $38
Handicapped accessible, reservations recommended

☞ *Classic delicious food from southern France, prepared with an artist's eye for color*

Late August is a great time to visit Provence—the restaurant—when nearby farms are finally harvesting food that carries the rich flavors typical of the region of France for which the restaurant is named. A yellow-tomato gazpacho, with a mound of avocado mousse in the center, came freckled with paprika and was the richest saffron yellow. It was ready to have its portrait painted, but was too delicious to stare at for long.

The wine list is dominated by French labels, and there are a few $26 bottles from both the United States and France. Some, like the Château des Annereaux Lalande-de-Pomerol, are available by the glass. That wine ($10 a glass, $48 a bottle) filled my mouth with its silken heaviness, reminding me of the sophistication of the French palate and its dedication to flavor.

Who else could have bred geese and cultivated them—in a way that many believe does not hurt them—to make the exquisite foie gras, served at 98 Provence on our visit in a little herb-crusted cylinder with small buttered, toasted baguette rounds ($20)? A later menu offered foie gras grilled with cherries poached in port ($16).

For dinner, veal mignon ($28) cooked with bacon came with wild mushrooms, and boneless quail ($25) came with chorizo and Moroccan couscous.

98 Provence offers diners both a prix fixe and an à la carte menu, and if you can be content with the choices on the fixed-price menu, they seem less expensive. For $35, for example, there were mussels with Bleu de Basque and lemon, salmon in a potato crust with watercress salad, and for dessert, apricot curd profiteroles with chocolate sauce—a tempting invention.

The priciest fixed menu ($43) started with arugula salad with figs and prosciutto, followed by snapper with a *pistou* vegetable fricassée, and ended with nougat glace with almonds and honey.

People who vacation in Ogunquit depend on the great food here, including sorbets like mango, coconut, and raspberry; or a glassful of berries in cream; or the banana *clafoutis* we obediently ordered with our entrées so it could be ready in time—and that was accompanied by coconut ice cream.

Oarweed Restaurant
(207) 646-4022
Perkins Cove
www.oarweed.com
Open daily at 11 for lunch and dinner from May to Columbus Day
Entrées $12 to $32, full bar

☛ *A personal touch and local owners keep this casual spot perfect for good Maine seafood.*

This business started in 1963 as a restaurant. Now four people own the business, but the property is still owned by the original family that built the building.

Jeff Fitzgerald, one of the owners, extols the lobster and steamed clams. "There are not many restaurants you go to that have steamed clams done the right way," Fitzgerald said. They are part of the soup-to-nuts Shore Dinner ($32). Beguiling menu items include haddock with lobster stuffing ($22.50), and a lobster salad plate with 5 ounces of lobster meat and just a touch of mayonnaise ($25.50), a fabulous way to eat lobster. There is no fried food.

Chowder and burgers race out of the kitchen. Lobster rolls ($16), made with fresh-picked lobster meat either cooked in this kitchen or right next door, are another best seller.

The windows overlook Oarweed Cove and the Atlantic beyond, and the first steps of Marginal Way pass by the building. This beautiful walk along the ocean's edge is the foremost attraction of this area.

Ogunquit Lobster Pound
(207) 646-2516
504 Main Street
Open daily June through October at 5, April and May weekends only
Entrées $11 to $30

☞ *A log building that's seen 80 years of lobster cooking*

You can pick your own lobster and watch it cook in the big outdoor cookers, or relax with a beer at an outdoor picnic table with some steamers without worrying about the dripping butter. In 2006 lobster sold for $16.95 per pound. People who want other items can find them on the big menu. Although one local called this place "incredibly expensive," it does have the beauty of its history and a deep understanding of how to take care of the season's hordes of tourists. More than 300 people can dine here at one time. Other favorites on the menu include the ribs, steaks, and sandwiches, like a chicken Caesar wrap.

The pies are made by Linda, a woman who lives right next door and who has been baking here almost every day for 20 years.

Poor Richard's Tavern
(207) 646-4722
125 Shore Road
www.poorrichardstavern.com

Open Monday through Saturday for dinner 5:30–9:30
Entrées $17 to $25
Reservations suggested

☛ *New England comfort food*

This business started nearby in 1958 and keeps its food tied to its roots. Yankee Pot Roast Jardiniere ($17.95) is a standard on a menu that features New England classics. Another is the lobster stew dinner ($21.95), which also holds crabmeat and haddock in its creamy depths. Richard's Lobster Pie ($23.95) is always a favorite with visitors.

Every day salmon is served in a different way. Capon is served with apple sausage stuffing.

You also can find a filet mignon with béarnaise sauce ($23.95). Everything is served with buttermilk biscuits.

Desserts are homemade, all $6, and include strawberry rhubarb cobbler and Key lime parfait.

Breakfast, Takeout, Wine, Bakeries, and Ice Cream

Amore Breakfast (207-646-6661, 1-866-641-6661; www.amorebreakfast.com), 178 Shore Road.

Open early spring through mid-December 7 AM–1 PM, closed Wednesday and Thursday. The friendly ambience of this favorite breakfast spot, with its knotty-pine paneling and white wooden chairs, is enhanced by the good smells. Maybe they come from the Mama Mia Omelet, with sausage, onions, green peppers, basil, and provolone ($7.50), or the Oscar de la Renta Benedict, with asparagus and crab on an English muffin with dill hollandaise ($8.95).

No—it's from the pecan-coated, cream-cheese-stuffed French toast, with a side of sautéed bananas in a rum syrup; $7.95 for a full order, but the half order ($5.95) is just fine. Plenty of free parking.

Beach Plum Lobster Farm (207-646-7277), Route 1, across from Beach Plum Farm.

Open from mid-April to New Year's Day; usually 9 to 7. This place sells only lobsters and clams, boiled, steamed, or raw. If you bring your own butter and paper towels, you could eat the creatures outside on a fine day, at one of the picnic tables or by the little pond next door. One of the three gas-fired cookers sits outside the door, simmering all day long.

Bread and Roses Bakery (207-646-4227; www.breadandroses bakery.com), 28A Main Street.

Open daily at 7 AM (the retail side opens later in January and February). Mary Breen started this thriving business in 1989. Fabulous cakes, pies, cookies, brownies, and cinnamon-raisin and whole wheat bread are all made with high-quality ingredients. Beware the dreadful temptation of the cinnamon puffs—muffins that have been rolled in melted butter and sugar. The very friendly, helpful staff numbers some who have been here for many years because although Breen is very demanding, she rewards good work well. Carpe Diem coffee, and tables at which to enjoy it. The breads are made with Sir Galahad King Arthur unbleached flour; some are vegan or kosher. Salads, sandwiches, panini, and fresh homemade pizza.

Cove Café (207-646-2422), Perkins Cove.

This sweet little café, open daily at 7 AM from May to the end of October, is set in a white cottage with a blue-and-white-striped awning and serves good variations on the standard breakfast menu, like a tomato, basil, and mozzarella omelet ($8.95), or a crabmeat, cheddar, and asparagus omelet ($10.95). Try the cinnamon roll French toast ($8.95) topped with strawberries. "People love it," said Cheryl Churchill, a waitress here since 2001.

Fancy That (207-646-4118; www.villagefoodmarket.com), Main Street (at the corner of Beach Street and Route 1).

Open daily mid-April through mid-October, 6:30 AM–11 PM in summer, closing earlier in spring and fall. Promising strong coffee, baked goods, and bagels, and sandwiches and chowders for lunch. This place advises you to call in a lunch order before 11 AM so you won't have to stand in the long line that forms at noon in the summer; the sandwich menu is online. The Italian Pavilion is an amazing sandwich creation: baked ham, bacon, provolone, Boursin, black olives, and green peppers with more veggies on French bread (large $6.99). Chicken salad is chopped fine, and the lobster rolls are not on hot dog buns and include lettuce, tomato, red onion, and sprouts. Hmmm—sounds like heresy!

Perkins and Perkins (1-877-646-0288; www.perkinsandperkins.com), 478 Main Street.

Open in summer daily 11 to 8; call for hours off-season. Ample parking. Wine and more—cheese, mustard, salsa, olives, and pâté. All of it to buy and much of it to try at the adjacent wine bar, **Vine,** open at 4:30 from the end of May to Labor Day, with outside dining on a heated patio.

Maine lobster bruschetta ($10) starts a meal. Crab and shrimp casserole ($10) with crab chunks and shrimp mixed can be paired with one of more than 30 wines by the glass, like the suggested Foris Pinot Noir ($9). Shrimp and Portobello Mushrooms ($18) is one of the four entrées served at night.

The food store makes its own line of chocolate, jam, and candy. Caribou Crunch, a combination of popcorn, caramel, chocolate, pecans, and spices, is the top seller.

Scoop (207-646-2122; www.villagefoodmarket.com), 230 Main Street.

Open 6:30 AM–11 PM daily in-season, closed from the end of October to April. Twenty-six flavors of delicious Maine ice cream, frozen cappuccino, and frozen fruit slushes.

The Village Food Market (207-646-2122; www.villagefoodmarket.com), 230 Main Street.

Open 6:30 AM–11 PM daily in-season, closing earlier off-season. Sandwiches include Italian, chicken, and cheese grinders, premade in the summer. There are 2,500 bottles of wine, a large array of cheeses, and a prepared-food case with pasta dishes and prepared meats for bringing dinner home. In summer it goes upscale with grilled marinated fresh vegetables, like zucchini and red peppers, paired with grilled sirloin or chicken. Baked lasagna survives year-round, as do other Italian dishes from the Italian chef. Bagels are from Massachusetts and are baked fresh every day. The bakery makes pies, cakes and tortes, cookies, and bars; many are sold to local restaurants.

Wells

Joshua's Restaurant and Bar
(207) 646-3355
1637 Post Road
www.joshuas.biz
Hospitality—Swift, intelligent service
Open for dinner 5–10 Monday through Saturday, closed Sunday
Entrées $19 to $28

Handicapped accessible, reservations recommended

☛ *Ambitious meals made with local food, worthy of a long drive*

Set in an old building just north of the junction of routes 109 and 1, Joshua's has undergone renovations that have transformed this old private home. The handsome old fireplace, pumpkin-colored walls, and bamboo flooring in some sections make it charmingly old and conveniently new.

The bar is charming and a good place for a drink or glass of wine from the good list.

One of the owners, Joshua Mather, former executive chef at Five-O, works with meat and produce from local farms, some from his parents' farm. His parents also are partners in the restaurant. Seafood is caught on local boats. Mather makes his own bread at the restaurant and has been doing so since his first season in 2004.

Fabulous Maine crabcakes ($10) are among the best starters, served with freshly made lemon-dill aioli. A beef tenderloin brochette ($9) is grilled and basted with roasted garlic marinade, but the fried artichoke hearts with chipotle aioli ($9) on a fall menu sound the most appetizing of all.

Pork tenderloin ($21) is jazzed up with barbecue sauce and fresh ginger-plum chutney, and duck breast ($25) is glazed with honey orange and comes with port wine sauce. On an earlier visit, the roast duck was served with the skin roasted to dark brown, utterly crisp and delicious along with the tender meat, vegetables, and mushrooms. Even so, we wished we'd ordered the rack of lamb ($28), with a Burgundy reduction and mashed potatoes, off that fall menu.

Fudge pie with Joshua's own vanilla ice cream ($6, as are all pies), maple walnut pie, or Key lime pie make fitting endings.

Wine, Fish, Farms, and Ice Cream

Chick Farm (207-985-2787; www.chickfarm.com), 19 Waldo Way (2 miles from Route 9A).

Organic vegetables and strawberries, fresh eggs year-round, which can be bought on the honor system at the farm. Call for hours. Chick Farm also sells at the Wells Farmer's Market; see below.

Congdon's Doughnuts (207-646-4219), 1090 Post Road.

Open daily 6 AM–3 PM in summer; closed Tuesday in the shoulder season; open

Friday, Saturday, and Sunday from November to April. Rumor has it that the delectable doughnuts sold here are cooked in lard, but management, which called the doughnuts an old family recipe, said, "We're not giving all our secrets away." These are the doughnuts to eat, however, when it is time to eat a doughnut. One blogger calls them the best in the USA.

Scones, muffins, elephant ears—puff pastries with cinnamon or raspberry—and sticky buns also are all out front. A full-service restaurant in back features a variety of Benedicts and hashes, along with the usual eggs and pancakes.

Moody Cow (207-646-1919), 259 Post Road.

Ice cream, and a deli that makes standard cold-cut and salad sandwiches.

Pine Tree Place Home & Garden (207-646-7545), 411 Post Road.

A farm stand here sells produce from local Maine farmers in-season. The farm stand opens May 1 and stays open until the end of October. A deli, selling locally made pies and breads, also operates in the summer, making sandwiches with a Maine theme from its own baked meats, as well as salads and soups. Carpe Diem coffee from a Maine entrepreneur is ready to pour, and wine is for sale too. This gift store and farm market is one of the oldest in southern Maine, in business since 1928. The tagline "from apples to zinfandel" fixes their business in customers' minds.

Scoop Deck (207-646-5150), 6 Eldridge Road, just off Route 1.

Open daily late May through September; 11–11 in July and August; 11:30–9 or 10 after Labor Day. The ice cream comes from Thibodeau Farms in Saco. You order inside a handsome white-clapboard barn, where Doug Erskine, the owner since 1985, can scoop up one of more than 60 flavors or give you a frozen yogurt or sorbet. "What's Triple Chocolate Ecstasy?" a customer asked when we were there. She sat on the outside benches with her cone and found out.

Seafare Market (207-646-5460), 231 Post Road (Route 1).

Open daily 10–7:30 in summer, closing Tuesday and earlier in the off-season. Fresh seafood. Everything from up and down the coast, from haddock to swordfish, sole, and tuna to shellfish, from oysters to littlenecks to soft-shell clams. Sandwiches and fried seafood are sold for takeout and eat in, at inside tables or outside picnic tables or tables on the deck. The lobster rolls contain 4 ounces of lobster meat picked here—most of the time—with mayonnaise on a toasted hot dog bun (usually about $13). Clam chowder and lobster bisque too.

Pine Tree Place is one-stop shopping for meals and gardens both.

Spiller Farm (207-985-2575; www.spillerfarm.com), Route 9A, 4 miles west of Route 1 at 1123 Branch Road.

The farm store is open year-round, and pick-your-own strawberries, peas, raspberries, beans, apples, and pumpkins are available in-season. The phone number gives a recorded message about picking availability. Tours given.

The Wells Farmer's Market runs from the end of May to the end of September on Wednesday from 2–6 at the Wells Town Hall parking lot on Sanford Road (Route 109), a half mile from Route 1. Applegate Deer Farm, from Newfield, sells venison, and Liberty Fields Farm, Saco, sells fresh goat cheese that Chick Farm owner, Marilyn Stanley, said is "very good."

York, Cape Neddick, York Beach, and York Harbor

Arrows Restaurant is just within the borders of York, but because it is accessed from Ogunquit, the description is listed there.

Cape Neddick Lobster Pound
(207) 363-5471
Shore Road, Cape Neddick
www.capeneddick.com
Open daily in summer for lunch and dinner; closed some days off-season; closed December through mid-March
Entrées $15 to $24

☛ *A local hangout because of its popular seafood and dinner menu*

A sea of vehicles fills the parking lots here on summer nights, when the outside deck is warm enough for an alfresco lobster. The big inside dining room is always ready for customers hungry for seafood. There's plenty of other things to feed kids, but for many of us the Shore Dinner, with steamers or mussels and a hot boiled lobster, is all you can desire.

Lobster Stew ($12.95) has a touch of sherry along with butter and cream, and lobster salad ($16.95) contains the lobster meat from 1¼-pound lobster on mixed greens. Steaks and several curries made with coconut cream are options aside from seafood, but the fried clams here have earnest supporters.

The lobster pound opened in 1958 and grew until now it seats 225. In summer you can sit outside where you can see the Cape Neddick River move in and out with the tides.

Russell's lobster shack, covered with old lobster buoys, stands behind the building. Russell Seaver sells fresh lobsters here when he is not out fishing.

Clay Hill Farm
(207) 361-2272
220 Clay Hill Road, Cape Neddick
www.clayhillfarm.com

You can buy lobsters here from a local fisherman, next door to the Cape Neddick Lobster Pound.

Hospitality—The incredibly well-trained staff seem to know what you want before you do.

Open daily for dinner at 5:30 mid-May through the end of October; closed Monday in November and December and from April to mid-May; closed Monday and Tuesday in January, February, and March

Entrées $18 to $28

Handicapped accessible, reservations recommended

☞ *Fine dining in the old-fashioned style in a warm, plush environment*

The 30 acres that surround this building foster trees and wildlife. The National Wildlife Federation praised the business for making its land a bird sanctuary.

Many customers find their own civilized refuge on arriving here. Early birds will get a special dinner for $18.95 from Sunday to Friday at 5:30 PM.

The cushy, old-fashioned ambience has a correlative in the lobster bisque ($8), a thick, smooth, rather bland, but certainly warming, bowl of soup.

Shrimp wrapped in bacon ($7.75), shrimp cocktail ($8), and crabcakes ($8) are on the appetizer list. I loved my house salad ($6), with baby spinach, dried cranberries, and pistachio nuts.

One night's salmon dish ($19.50) held a sauce that was described as wasabi cream, but wasabi was indiscernible in the blanket of white sauce, and the roasted asparagus had been roasted into dark brown sticks. Veal saltimbocca ($21) proved to be a veal cutlet under a heavy blanket of cheese and a thick layer of salty prosciutto, not at all delicate.

But peach melba ($6.50), the classic dessert recommended by our wise waiter, seemed to throw all previous disappointment to the winds. Devouring this delight of tender peaches in raspberry sauce on vanilla ice cream, with whipped cream, was like feeding on ambrosia.

Fazio's
(207) 363-7019
38 Woodbridge Road, York Village
www.fazios.com
Open for dinner Tuesday through Saturday 4–9, closed Monday
Entrées $15 to $19

☛ *Classic Italian meals, a pizzeria next door, and homemade pasta*

This place has won a lot of praise for its good Italian cooking, great marinara, and homemade pasta. Located just outside of York Village, the yellow dining room makes a fine destination on any night of the year. You can start your meal with *arancini,* a Sicilian rice ball stuffed with ground beef and peas, served with tomato sauce ($6).

The entrées are reasonably priced and wide ranging, with the option of simply enjoying the pasta with a sauce ($6 for a small serving, $9 for a large), a perfect choice for the child tagging along.

Linguine with clam sauce, garlic, and a little hot pepper ($11), meat lasagna ($12), and manicotti with ricotta filling and tomato sauce ($11) are classics from southern Italy. Seafood Tecchia ($16), scallops and shrimp cooked in a white wine and lemon-garlic sauce and served on linguine, would go over well with someone who simply cannot eat enough seafood; and the daily ravioli, the veal *piccata,* or the *bistecca* could take care of anyone else in the family. Or order an eggplant Parmesan sub next door at **La Stalla Pizzeria (207-363-1718).**

Flo's Hotdogs
No phone
Route 1, Cape Neddick
Open for lunch
Entrées $1.50

☛ *Hot dogs served with a secret sauce and mayo in a low building*

A recipe available on the Internet for Flo's special sauce calls for yellow onions, molasses, white vinegar, brown sugar, crushed red peppers, and hot sauce. Boil it up and slather it on, or stop at Flo's, where they do it for you. Flo, who ran this eatery for 41 years, died in 2000 at the age of 92; her daughter-in-law Gail carries on. Schultz hot dogs, soda, milk, chips, long lines, and discipline.

Flo's now operates other branches, including one in Wells on Route 1.

Frankie & Johnny's Natural Foods
(207) 363-1909
1594 Route 1, Cape Neddick
www.frankie-johnnys.com
Open Wednesday through Sunday 5–9 in July and August; open Thursday through Sunday 5–9 April through June, and September through November
Entrées $17 to $27
No credit cards, BYOB

☛ *A healthy food place with vegan options and great meat*

Kari's Cajun Crab Cakes ($6.95) are served with a minted rémoulade sauce, and fried calamari ($6.75) comes with coconut curry dipping sauce. Many vegan and vegetarian dishes, like the bean curd satay ($5.75), make this place a natural for non-meat eaters.

But others will be happy to find Lydia's Lamb ($26.75), a grilled rack of lamb accompanied by mashed potatoes. Grilled salmon ($19.75) tastes great with mango-pineapple salsa. The pasta is homemade for several concoctions, including a vegetarian harvest special that changes with the seasons. Private parties are hosted in the winter.

Stonewall Kitchen Café
(207) 351-2719
Stonewall Lane, York
www.stonewallkitchen.com
Open for takeout and for dining in the café Monday through Saturday 8–6, Sunday 9–6; order at the counter
Entrées $11 to $14

☛ *Popular for its great food, this is the place everyone is talking about.*

Stonewall Kitchen was already famous for wonderful jams and other condiments, made since 1991, as well as an ever-growing list of mixes, desserts, and

This pretty Stonewall Kitchen store has every kitchen category covered.

other foods. It was already a popular tourist stop, because so much of what it sold was offered as free samples in the stores, here in York, in Portland, and in Camden, to name just those few. The café opened in 2004 at its present head-quarters in York and serves many dishes made with the mixes and jams, vinegars, mustards, and other delicious things you can now buy, after a meal, next door.

A lobster salad BLT, on toasted brioche with basil aioli and served with coleslaw, was on the fall café menu ($14). The Stonewall burger ($10) pairs grilled Angus beef with cheddar cheese, lettuce, tomato, and roasted garlic onion jam on a toasted roll, with a choice of a small salad or french fries.

Brunch here is spectacular, especially if you start with a split of Domaine Chandon ($9.50) and try the Linzer waffles with raspberry and hazelnut butter sauce ($12). The good, short wine list is a real plus.

Rum raisin bread pudding, or bananas Foster with vanilla ice cream, sounds right for just about anytime.

Wild Willy's Burgers
(207) 363-9924
765 Route 1, York
www.wildwillysburgers.com

Open for lunch and dinner year-round but closed Sunday; closed January and February
Entrées around $6
No credit cards

☛ *Beloved for delicious burgers and freshly made french fries*

The menu has focus. Burgers. Fries. Some of the burgers come with sautéed onions, others with barbecue sauce, but every one has withstood the test of customer satisfaction to stay on the menu and to bring customers back again and again. Order at the counter and wait for your number. Enjoy. Among the 6-ounce burgers the Wicked Good ($5.95) is well-liked, with cheddar, sautéed onions, and mushrooms. Fresh-cut Maine potatoes, mostly Green Thumb potatoes from Fryeburg, go into the fries ($1.95 small, $2.95 large). A chicken sandwich and Angus steak chili are two variations from the burger theme. Wine and beer are served, and vanilla, chocolate, strawberry, and coffee frappes ($4) are made with Gifford's ice cream.

Breakfast and Lunch, Bakeries, and Nigerian Pygmy Goats

Food and Co. Gourmet Market and Café (207-363-0900; www.foodnco.com), 1 York Street, York.

Open Monday through Saturday 8–6, summer 7–7, closed Sunday. Cheese, olives, sandwiches, take-out dinners, and wine. The café serves lunch from 11 to closing. Join the club and get your 10th sandwich free. Salad plates with hummus, falafel, or Caesar, also are served, or you can order a serving of any of the prepared foods, like roasted chicken, heated up.

Old Mountain Farm (207-361-2126; www.oldmountainfarm.com), 60 Old Mountain Road, Cape Neddick.

Nigerian pygmy dairy goats for custom-ordered milk; call first.

Pie in the Sky Bakery (207-363-2656), 1 River Road (Route 1), Cape Neddick.

Open Thursday through Monday 9–6, closed Thursday October through early May; closed two weeks after Thanksgiving and the first six weeks of the year.

Thanksgiving is the biggest week, when Nancy Stern sells as many as 600 pies. Custom orders from holiday special menus and regular menus are available. Blueberry, apple, and pumpkin are top sellers. Variations include pumpkin-pecan pie, sour cream blueberry, jumble berry (blueberry, blackberry, and raspberry), and chocolate pie. Prices about $25 for a 10-inch pie that serves eight.

The York Farmer's Market runs mid-June through mid-October, Saturday 9 AM–1 PM, and is located at the Greater York Region Chamber of Commerce near Exit 7 (York) off I-95, next to the Stonewall Kitchen Factory on Route 1.

CHAPTER 2

The Portland Region

THIS BIG CHAPTER COVERS THE COAST from Biddeford to Freeport, with Maine's largest city, and its varied assortment of places to eat, right in the middle.

One of my predecessors in this line of work, Cynthia Hacinli, who wrote about Maine restaurants in her 1991 book *Down Eats,* reported that the city fathers said Portland had more restaurants per capita than San Francisco. Not true, many others have since argued.

But that conveys the gist of our enthusiasm.

A lot of Portland's residents go out to eat or have something to do with making dinner for others—growing, selling, or preparing the food, serving it up, eating it, and always talking about it. Some restaurants, like Street and Co. and Back Bay Grill, have been serving dinner since Hacinli wrote about them. Fore Street, too, is an institution, a revelation to newcomers and a pleasure that the rest of us rely on, especially in the cold winter.

Even the city's best places shun dress codes, having chosen to welcome all their customers, while those diners who like to dress elegantly can outfit themselves to the nines, more for their own pleasure than to conform.

In the last couple of years a rash of new places has spread from one end of town to another, and many are thriving and expanding. Bar Lola serves small plates, The Front Room serves big ones. Caiola's on Pine Street fills plates with ever-changing pleasures and has brought back the feeling of neighborhood to a section of the West End.

Up in Yarmouth, SeaGrass Bistro has made a name for itself with inventive arrangements of the finest fresh ingredients.

Everyone involved in making these places work, from the dreamers who sink their money into a new design to the chefs who insist on high-quality ingredients to the customers who praise and criticize to the servers who can suffer both the kitchen and the dining room, are trying for the Holy Grail of a night out: the bliss of a perfect meal.

May they get it right, just like Mrs. Dalloway.

Bar Mills

Snell Family Farm 207-929-6166, 207-929-5318; www.snellfamily farm.com), P.O. Box 326, Route 112 (or 1000 River Road in Buxton). Open 9–6 daily in-season. Produce from this big farm comes to Portland and Saco farmer's markets Saturday and Wednesday mornings, but visiting the farm is fun, and you can pick your own apples. The pumpkin selection in the fall is huge. Stop in on Maine Maple Sunday, a Sunday in late March, for a glimpse of sap-boiling operations.

The late-fall bounty at Snell Family Farm.

Biddeford

Bebe's Burritos
(207) 283-4222
140 Main Street
Hospitality—Friendly counter service for takeout, and full table service

Open for lunch and dinner Tuesday and Wednesday 11–7, Thursday and Friday 11–9, Saturday 12-9
Entrées $4 to $12

☞ *Good burritos and other basics with fresh ingredients*

This café is the most colorful spot in downtown Biddeford. The wall on the left as you enter is decorated with a desert scene. The order counter lies in the back, past red walls with blue green trim and exposed brick. I ordered a guacamole tostada ($6.95), two corn tortillas topped with guacamole, mango salsa, lots of lettuce, and a hot chili sauce. But a fine choice is the roasted stuffed poblano peppers ($8.95) with rice, black beans, corn, and salsa, served with guacamole and sour cream. My friend had the chicken burrito ($6.95), filled with the soft stewed chicken we'd encountered at the Mexican Restaurant in Harrington (see page 283), a touchstone of authenticity. The rest of it—beans, cheese, lettuce, tomatoes, scallions, and sour cream—made it taste good. Aluminum foil and tins with plastic cutlery sit by the cash register for takeout. Thursday to Saturday from 6:30 to 8:30 you can hear live music, sometimes from Chris Humphrey, jazz professor at the University of Southern Maine, who brings a big crowd, and the Billy Billy Band, playing roots blues.

Buffleheads
(207) 284-6000
122 Hills Beach Road
www.buffleheadsrestaurant.com
Hospitality—Wonderful friendly atmosphere and staff
Open daily in summer for lunch 11:30–2, dinner 5:30–9; closed Monday from Labor Day through October and also from April until Memorial Day; closed Sunday and Monday and serving dinner only November 1 until the beginning of April
Entrées $9 to $25
Handicapped accessible, reservations recommended

☞ *A family-run restaurant with quality food and a place in locals' hearts*

Watch the sea through almost every window, and if it's winter you'll probably spy buffleheads—ducks with a white patch on their heads that call the cove home.

In summer enjoy the outside patio.

I recommend the onion rings ($4.95), some of the best I have had. Spinach salad with bacon, mushrooms, and warm blue cheese vinaigrette ($4.95) was perfect too.

One night's special, scallops with leeks in a red pepper sauce ($16.95), was cooked perfectly and lovely in that creamy, sweet sauce. But best of all was a dish off the menu, Fried sole with Creole meunière sauce ($17.95), finished with pecan butter. The moist fish, spicy crust, and zingy sauce all added up to a terrific dish. Roast turkey dinners in winter, and pizza, burgers, and other Italian classics like baked manicotti ($11.95), are also on this family-friendly menu, which does well by its delightful brownie sundae, too.

Directions are provided on the restaurant's good Web site, and signs are up on the road to guide you down to Hill's Beach, a little off the beaten track, and entirely worth seeking out.

Breakfast and Lunch

Cole Road Cafe (207-283-4103), Cole Road.

Open Wednesday through Saturday 7 AM–1:45 PM, Sunday 8 AM–1:45 PM. Joyce Rose, chef-owner, started this business in 1992. "It's always been pretty busy," she said, "our breakfasts are rather unusual." She means the omelets with chorizo and Muenster, or stuffed French toast that changes weekly, perhaps banana walnut brown sugar, or strawberry Amaretto cream cheese (both $6.95; most lunch specials are also at this low price).

For lunch you might find a blueberry-chive chicken salad sandwich, on homemade wheat bread (half whole wheat and half unbleached flour). Another possibility is the fresh crabmeat and onion quiche with dill Havarti, mozzarella, and provolone.

"We make everything fresh here every day," Rose said. The business seats 68; Rose won't renovate, she said, because the size now is "perfect. I can't handle any more."

Cape Elizabeth

The Audubon Room, Inn by the Sea
(207) 767-0888
40 Bowery Beach Road
www.innbythesea.com
Hospitality—Welcoming and attentive to every wish

Open daily for breakfast, lunch, and dinner year-round
Entrées $22 to $29
Reservations recommended

☛ *A special-occasion place with good food*

Arrive a half hour before your reservation and sip a gin and tonic while sitting in deep cushions on a couch in a wide landing on the stairs, overlooking this big inn's pool and lawn. That was my strategy with a friend. After a few minutes we carried our drinks outside and strolled past the gardens, with their dark purple lettuces tucked in amid the bedding plants, to a boardwalk that takes you down to the sea, still bitter cold in June.

With our hands chilled a half hour later, it felt good to retreat to the dining room with its Audubon prints and surrounding porch. The peach walls and a carpet patterned with small scrolls of leaves cocooned us while we looked at the lawn and its tidy parterres, and the ocean filling the horizon, from a more comfortable distance.

Our sharpened appetites made a wide bowl of Atlantic surf clam and parsnip soup ($8), a smooth buttery puree with a zigzag of sorrel cream across the top, perfect. Lobster bisque ($10) gets its lobsters from Alewives Farm just down the road, and is flavored with tarragon and sherry.

There is nothing to dislike in that comfortable room that has offered menus of marinated flank steak with wild mushroom port demi-glace ($24) and a changing fresh fish. Alex Tumidajski is the executive chef; he also serves halibut with grapefruit beurre blanc and rack of lamb with fig demiglace.

The Good Table
(207) 799-4663
527 Ocean House Road (Route 77)
Hospitality—Informal and friendly
Open for three meals Tuesday through Saturday 8 AM–9 PM in summer,
11 AM–9 PM in winter, Sunday 8–3 year-round
Entrées $10 to $19 (twin lobsters $24), lunch up to $11
Handicapped accessible

☛ *A local institution, for families and visitors, with Greek specialties*

A fire that burned the old Good Table down in summer 2001 brought such love and encouragement from the community that the restaurant owners needed only seconds to decide to rebuild.

Their new, larger building, just south of the left turn to Two Lights Road, is a restaurant families depend on for good food that pleases kids and grown-ups. It's a great place for lunch, with specials like hot pastrami and Swiss on rye, or hummus with fresh vegetables on a tomato tortilla, as well as standard temptations like the gyros sandwich of spiced beef and lamb, onions, tomato, and *tzatziki* in a pita ($5.75). There's spanakopita, of course, and fish-and-chips. The last item, big succulent pieces of fried haddock with french fries and coleslaw ($10), always reliably well-made, is a favorite. We also like to get the Greek salad, with a ton of crunchy lettuce topped with feta and olives ($6.50). A breakfast menu lists the expectable, along with a few foreign takes like Greek soul food, incorporating feta, onions, tomatoes, and peppers with the scrambled eggs ($7 if you add Greek sausage).

Dinner offers up lots of fried fish and clams, baked haddock, grilled meat, and salads, all low key and fresh.

But keep your eye on the specials board, where beet salad with pumpkin seeds and goat cheese ($7.50) might be found, or swordfish with ginger sweet potatoes ($19), the fish moist, the sweet potatoes tender and brilliantly flavored with ginger, and green beans that were fresh and perfect. The owner said that as many as half of the meals she serves come off that board, and it's clear why. They are well-made, straightforward recipes that are delicious.

But everything on the menu is solid too, and the chicken chunks ($5) ordered for a child are made with fresh chicken.

The screened back porch would be a good spot to enjoy a dessert like the too-good bread pudding with caramel sauce, flaky apple pie, or ginger pound cake with peaches.

Winter nights inside the main dining room, with its old pictures, collection of women's hats, and light wood wainscoting, are almost as nice. And if you're Greek, there are parking spots reserved just for you to the right of the front door.

The Lobster Shack at Two Lights
(207) 799-1677
225 Two Lights Road
www.lobstershack-twolights.com
Hospitality—Line up at the door for counter service; eat inside or out.
Open from the end of March through October daily for lunch and dinner 11–8
Entrées $4 to $22

☛ *One of the best sites for outdoor lobster dinners, with fried seafood and hamburgers too*

A winner for most spectacular setting, the Lobster Shack has been around since 1968 and is now run by members of the Porch family, grandsons of the first owner. The beautiful site, at the end of Two Lights Road next to a lighthouse, overlooks rocks that tumble down to the surf from the edge of the picnic table area, but there isn't a lot of room for cars. Crowds at lunch and dinner can jam the parking lot. Try to arrive early or late to avoid the problem—and drive slowly through the little neighborhood as you wind toward the point, so the year-round residents can relax.

You order and pay for your food through a door on the right of the small building, using the time you wait in line to decide between the bowl of lobster stew ($9.95), the lobster salad, the lobster roll, the lobster dinner, or the lobster dinner with an extra lobster ($28 on our visit but always changing with market prices).

Of course you can also eat the good fried clams, fixed with crumbs and cooked in soybean oil, as is all the fried food, according to the sign outside. A cheeseburger goes for $2.50, hot dogs are $1.50, but everyone adds in the french fries or onion rings for a few dollars more. A veggie burger is available. A glass case by the cashier shows off raspberry cream turnovers, mini blueberry pies,

A summer day is the perfect time for fried seafood or lobsters at the Lobster Shack at Two Lights, in Cape Elizabeth.

and other desserts. Once you have your receipt with your order number, it's time to explore; a loudspeaker can reach your ears within a fair distance of the building.

A leading cause of tension for families here are the same rocks that make such a beautiful foreground to the sea. Figure on anyone under the age of 35 taking off on those rocks and decide beforehand if you can handle it. The cries of parents in full-throated panic attacks—"Don't go any farther! Come back right now!"—are common.

Of course, once your kids are grown up, you don't need to watch them so closely. Or do you? Storms that bring huge waves to this shore also attract spectators of all ages who like to creep as close as possible, and people have mistaken the safety range. Although it happens rarely, people have died here. So watch out for your parents, and your friends too, and don't let yourself tempt the sea either, when it has such an unimaginable strength in its stormy moods.

Bakery

The Cookie Jar (207-799-0671), 554 Shore Road.
Open 6–6 Monday through Saturday, 6:30–5 on Sunday. Just across the South Portland line, this little place does a big business, offering local residents with a sweet tooth everything they could desire. Among the many cookies, the raspberry-filled and the macaroons stand out. The little tables in the shop's windows are a perfect place to enjoy a cream horn, or another favorite, the Bismarck, a raspberry-and-cream-filled sugar doughnut. Cakes are made to order, and cupcakes are ready at hand.

Farm Markets

Alewives' Brook Farm (207-799-7743), 83 Old Ocean House Road.
Open daily 9–6. Lobsters are sold here, as well as corn on the cob. The lobster season is longer, as is the season for soft-shell clams and the whelks, or "snails," that the owner sells to the local Asian market. The whelks come up in the lobster traps along with the lobsters. Strawberries, beets, radishes, lettuce, and other vegetables are available in-season.

Maxwell's Farm Market (207-799-2940; strawberry hotline: 207-799-3383; www.maxwellsfarm.com), 185 Spurwink Road.

Open May through November, Monday through Saturday 9–6:30. Produce from the fields just outside the building is picked and sold inside—a particular virtue during the spinach E. coli scare of the fall of 2006. Tomatoes with a ripe, juicy flavor can be found from July until October, as hoop houses give them a long Maine run.

The market sells loads of sweet corn, great lettuces, and all the pumpkins you can imagine. There's also a field of flowers where you can cut your own bouquet, after checking in at the store.

Big pick-your-own strawberry fields ($1.60 a pound in 2006, and no credit cards in the strawberry fields) are a short drive away on Two Lights Road. The season can run between mid-June and mid-July, but call to see if the market is open: A cold spring can make the season late, and a hot June can end it fast.

Takeout and Counter Service

Kettle Cove Take-out and Dairy Bar (207-799-3533), Route 77 (south of the Two Lights Road turnoff).
Open Memorial Day through Labor Day.

Everyone relies on this place in the summer for homemade ice cream, especially after going to Kettle Cove or Crescent Beach. The fried haddock sandwich and other take-out standards are good too.

Two Lights General Store (207-347-7165), 517 Ocean House Road (Route 77).
Pizza and sandwiches for lunch, and coffee and breakfast dishes, can be enjoyed at tables inside or at picnic tables outside, or taken to the beach.

Cumberland and Great Chebeague Island

Chebeague Island Inn
(207) 846-5155
61 South Road
www.chebeagueislandinn.com
Hospitality—Congenial and unpretentious—a comfortable seaside inn
Open for dinner daily 5–9 from Memorial Day to Columbus Day

Entrées $20 to $40
Reservations recommended, especially on weekends

☛ *Great meals in a beautiful classic island inn that's relaxed and refined*

Martha Dumont has transformed the Chebeague Island Inn, and its best days are just getting under way. The wide porch looking over Casco Bay toward Yarmouth has a timeless quality—tempting me once to forget about time altogether. Under its pastel, robin's egg blue ceiling, I sat with a friend on a wicker couch and drank a glass of merlot. On a rapidly cooling Monday evening in July, with the insistent wind turning the corner of the porch a few feet away, we decided against eating on the screened porch and walked into the dining room a while past our reservation time, after relaxing indeed.

The room's dark, beaded-board paneling placed the atmosphere in the eternal summer of Maine summer cottages. But white linens and handmade leather chairs make this dining room sumptuous.

The executive chef, Terry Foster, started cooking here in 2006, and earlier worked at the Harraseeket Inn in Freeport. He was head chef from 1990 to 1998 at Pilgrim Inn in Deer Isle.

Start with lobster, corn, and leek stew ($11) with basil oil, or baked Bangs Island mussels ($10) with preserved lemon-caper butter, two appetizers from the changing local-food-focused menu.

Entrées in the fall might be roasted halibut with summer-vegetable succotash and fingerling potatoes ($26) or roasted Maine lobster in chardonnay, tarragon, and chanterelle mushroom butter ($33 and up depending on market price). If the weather is cold the cabernet-braised beef short ribs with Parmesan polenta in thyme pan sauce would suit the appetite ($25).

Ice creams like ginger are homemade and always freshly made, and one star on the dessert list is the glazed lemon cake with blueberry compote, served with lemon sorbet ($6).

Getting here without your own boat is possible by ferry, either in 15 minutes from Cousins Island or an hour and a half from Portland. Parking at a lot on Route 1 for the Cousins Island Ferry cost $15, and round-trip tickets were $12 in 2006, so this might work best as a day trip, with a visit to the island golf course or a bike route.

The food is worth it.

Apples and Farmer's Markets

Sweetser's Apple Barrel and Orchards (207-829-3074), 19 Blanchard Road (just off Route 9).

Open August through November 10–6 daily. Connie and Dick Sweetser are the present owners of this orchard that has been bearing fruit since the 1880s. Their open-air fruit stand sells all the apples as they ripen, including Connie's favorites, the Red Gravensteins, crisp and complex in flavor, that last just a couple of weeks in September. By October you can find the winter apples here, the ones that keep well in the refrigerator and can be used to make a pie or a baked apple, like Northern Spy and Wolfe River.

A variety native to this orchard, the Rolfe, or Rholfe-Sweetser, has been grafted and cultivated by Fedco Trees. New trees are growing that will fruit in a few years, keeping alive another rare tree from Maine's 18th-century orchards. Cider, squash from nearby farms, and dried beans from up north are also sold here.

Cumberland Farmer's Markets

happen in two locations. The one in Cumberland is in Cumberland Center at Greely High School on Route 9, every Saturday 8:30–noon. The same farmers go to Falmouth's Shops at Falmouth Village on Route 1 every Wednesday 2–5. The season is from late May until mid-October. You will likely find Sally Merrill, whose Sunrise Acres Farm grows beets, lettuce, heirloom tomatoes, and all the greens you can eat along with the meat from its farm-raised chickens, lambs, and beef cattle.

This apple finder in front of Sweetser's Apple Barrel shows what's ready in the orchard.

Falmouth

Harmon's Lunch (207-797-9857), 144 Gray Road (Route 100).

First owner Marvin Harmon died in 2003 at age 83; he opened in 1960. But he retired in 1985, and no one can taste a difference. Is it something in the meat? The hamburger with everything (red relish, sautéed onions, and mustard, $1.75) is perfection. Customers are obsessed with them, and that's good because that is all that's on the menu, except for hot dogs and fresh-cut french fries. Don't go on a Saturday or during the Cumberland Fair, farther down this road. Our friend Steve Hirshorn (catch his radio show 6:30–8:30 AM Thursday on WGBM FM radio, 90.9) said he couldn't get in, it was so packed.

Ricetta's Brick Oven Pizzeria (207-781-3100), 240 Route 1.

This is a good spot for lunch, because they serve a pizza *and* a Caesar salad buffet. Among the many combinations, apple pie pizza stands out for dessert. (They also have a location in **South Portland at 29 Western Avenue; 207-775-7400.**)

The Falmouth Farmer's Market is held on Wednesday 3–6 late May through mid-October at the Shops at Falmouth Village at Route 1 and Depot Road.

Freeport and South Freeport

Conundrum
(207) 865-0303
117 Route 1, Freeport
Hospitality—Welcoming and outgoing
Open for dinner until 10 and late-night eats Tuesday 4:30–10, Wednesday and Thursday 4:30–11, and Friday and Saturday 4:30–midnight
Entrées $12 to $15 (one steak entrée for $25)

☛ *With more than 600 wines and modest prices, this is a place to try something new.*

The server offers a free splash of any wine you want to try. A more unusual red might be the Allegrini Palazzo della Torre ($7), a blend of varietals common in

Fidel Velasquez cultivates astonishing heirloom tomatoes in the greenhouses of Sunrise Acres Farm in Cumberland—they are sold at both the Falmouth and the Cumberland farmer's markets.

amarones from the Veneto. Owner Vincent Migliaccio sells more than 60 of his 600 wines by the glass at this comfortable place on Route 1. You can drink tastes, half glasses, or regular ones, tasting your way through many wines or settling in with a favorite.

And from a menu that keeps it simple, with fettuccine and meatballs ($10.95) to warm you up in the winter, or a Wolfe's Neck Farm burger ($8.95) served with spears of sweet potato, you can enjoy a simple meal while you try wine, because wine always tastes better with food.

The outside deck is tented and heated year-round for overflow from the small dining room.

Migliaccio said his place has the longest wine list in the state of Maine. He said he charges less so people can try things out—as they certainly did when we visited. He said he pays the wholesale price for a bottle with the sale of two full glasses, unlike most restaurants, which pay for a bottle with the sale of one glass.

What's more, you can go to the store next door and buy bottles of many of his selections. Many of the wines he serves are for sale on the shelf in neighboring Old World Gourmet (see page 63), a deli and wine store owned by Migli-accio's parents.

I can say from experience that the Portuguese Barros 20-year-old port that Conundrum sells is $2 to $3 more expensive per glass at Hugo's and at Fore Street in Portland.

Harraseeket Inn—Maine Dining Room and Broad Arrow Tavern
(207) 865-9377, 1-800-342-6423
162 Main Street
www.harraseeketinn.com
Hospitality—Well-trained and on top of things
Maine Dining Room—open daily for breakfast 7–10:30, dinner 5:30–9 (till 9:30 Friday and Saturday), Sunday brunch 11:45–2
Broad Arrow Tavern—open daily 11:30 AM–10:30 PM, until 11 on Friday and Saturday, lunch buffet every day (except Sunday) 11:30–2
Entrées $26 to $38

☞ *Buffet-style dining and more formal dinners in two dining rooms that keep the local farmers' produce on their plates*

The Harraseeket Inn is what one lover of fine food I know calls a solid restaurant, for both its more formal dining room and the dark green Broad Arrow Tavern.

We admire their posted philosophy, which advocates the use of local ingre-dients, from farm vegetables to oysters and mussels. On busy Sundays, when the drawing room turns into the setting of an elaborate brunch buffet, you can enjoy poached wild salmon and know you'll be avoiding the farmed variety. The Wolfe's Neck Farm meat a carver is slicing according to your preference is also raised without hormones or antibiotics. The pale dining room with antiques and fireplaces is handsome, with a view of the perfectly groomed gardens.

This is a good place to bring a large group, because they do not faze the staff.

The Sunday brunch, and the evening meals, are more gourmet in the old-fashioned sense of the word. You can get a chateaubriand for two with bordelaise sauce for $75. For $58 you can also enjoy the recommended Rhône wine, an E. Guigal Gigondas, one of many on a fine list.

But more adventurous meals on a summer menu included a marinated ostrich loin ($31) grilled with blueberry-thyme barbecue sauce. Crispy-skin salmon ($28) came with Peruvian purple potato salad, shaved green beans, and arugula in a dressing of creamy goat cheese.

Many good chefs have made their way through this business to others in the area, like Sam Hayward, whose Fore Street is at the top of the list, as is Lee Skawinski's work at Cinque Terre. It's a place to look out for the next surge of talent, as the menu changes with the seasons.

Harraseeket Lunch and Lobster
(207) 865-4888
36 Main Street, South Freeport
Hospitality—Counter service with clear directions and clean picnic tables
Open daily 11–8:45 from Memorial Day until Labor Day, until 7:45 last weekend in April to May and after Labor Day to Columbus Day
Entrées $9 to $19; lobster rolls $14; no credit cards accepted, but there's an ATM inside

☛ *Pretty waterside spot for well-made lobster rolls, lobster dinners, and seafood*

When things are hopping at Harraseeket Lunch, as they almost always are, the attendant in the parking lot will give you fair warning—"There is a 40-minute wait on all orders," she told us one sunny Wednesday in July. Even for a lobster roll? Even for a lobster roll. That's because they steam and shuck and mix the lobster meat right before they put it in the roll and send it out for you to eat.

But with everyone around you waiting for his or her order, this can be a convivial scene. A seat at one of the clean red picnic tables under the blue-and-white-striped awning has the shade you need, and the drink orders can be filled right away.

"Is number 133 almost ready?" a 12-year-old boy who couldn't take the wait asked plaintively at the order window.

When the lobster roll came, in exactly 40 minutes, it was in a white paper bag and wrapped in a white napkin—a buttered and toasted roll that still felt warm, full of big pieces of fresh lobster in a light mayonnaise dressing. It tasted great, even though the others at the table groused about the small size. This one cost $14, and I thought it had everything going for it.

The location on the water allows you to watch the latest crate of lobsters being unloaded, and at another order window steamed lobster dinners are available. A friendly worker inside volunteered to show off a lobster for a woman with a camera, and a child reached out to touch the mysterious creatures that attract visitors from around the country and the world. It's summer in Maine.

Breakfast, Lunch, and Informal Dinners

Isabella's Sticky Buns Café and Bakery (207-865-6635) 2 School Street, Freeport.

Open daily at 7 AM, closing at 5 PM in summer, 3 PM in winter. Isabella's makes the good-for-you and so-delicious food you need to save your soul along Freeport's outlet-lined Main Street. Around a corner a block north of L.L. Bean, you can order a wrap made with a chicken salad that includes chicken, grapes, and Gorgonzola; or the popular You Ham ($6.99), a panini warmed on a panini grill, with roasted red peppers, sliced ham, cheddar, and cilantro pesto.

Breakfast includes signature sticky buns, of course, and croissants, cinnamon swirls, muffins, and scones, or the eggs Benedict with portobello mushrooms and roasted red pepper substituted for the ham ($6.95).

Many of his customers are local people, but according to owner Alex Caisse, "It's hard to not get the tourists in this town. You close your eyes and they appear." The tourists who come here are the lucky ones. Napkin art—"The napkin art is huge," said an enthusiastic manager named Ryan—covers a bulletin board on one wall, and you're welcome to add to it. Messages tacked up come from all over the country, and the best artwork is saved in napkin-art books you can look at during a visit.

Morrison's Chowder House (207-865-3404), 4 Mechanic Street.

If a company can come up with superbly flavored frozen lobster stew, as Morrison's has, surely the fresh chowders and lobster stew it serves in its chowder house will be just as good. Seafood salads, rolls, and a children's menu, as well as the chowders that are making a name for this company.

Old World Gourmet, Deli and Wine Shop (207-865-4477; www.oldworldgourmet.com), 117 Route 1, Freeport.

Open Tuesday through Thursday 10–5, Friday and Saturday 10–6. The big selection at this deli means you can come here for a fancy sandwich assortment to throw a party, with chicken salad, Mediterranean and Greek salad roll-ups, and Genoa salami. It would be the perfect stop for a house guest who offered to provide lunch. I recommend the Mediterranean roll-up (half, $3.25; whole, $5.50), with its fresh tortilla and spicy contents, from the hummus to the roasted red peppers and Havarti. Grilled panini come hot from the grill and can be enjoyed here at one of the tables in the front of the store or wrapped to go.

Soups, chowders, salads, and baked goods, from pizzas to macaroons and chocolate chip cookies, complete anyone's dream picnic, along with a bottle of great wine. This place is located by the tall statue known locally as the Big Indian, north of I-295's Exit 17.

The Village Store (207-865-4230), 97 South Freeport Road, South Freeport.

A great sandwich place that also makes picnic lunches to order. Deli manager Mandi Krauthamer's favorite sandwich is the Thanksgiving ($5.50), with lettuce, cranberry sauce, turkey, and stuffing; she likes it on the plain wrap. "We bake all kinds of pies and goodies here, and then we have 25 different sandwiches for lunch," she said.

Old Orchard Beach

Joseph's By The Sea
(207) 934-5044
55 West Grand Avenue
www.josephsbythesea.com
Hospitality—Low-key, friendly service, from the upstairs deck to the downstairs dining room
Open daily at 5 mid-May through Columbus Day; open Thursday, Friday, and Saturday until Christmas and from March to May; closed January through mid-March
Entrées $18 to $29
Handicapped accessible, reservations recommended

☛ *Alongside the amusement park is this idyllic spot on the sea with exceptional cooking.*

Off to a formal start in 1968, the ambience of this restaurant has mellowed. But the food retains its high standards, even if you don't have to dress up to eat it.

Paul Dussault is the chef and the son of the first owner, 82-year-old Joseph Dussault, who still unlocks the building in the morning. Louise Lesperance, Paul's sister, runs the dining room. Under their management this remains a real refuge, a great place to shake off the frantic hurly-burly of Old Orchard Beach, or at least enjoy an interlude of calm—and careful cooking.

A few second-floor tables look out across sand dunes to rolling waves, and you sometimes see a rising moon above the horizon of the sea.

Especially impressive was a fairly simple dish, a crowd-pleaser that has probably been on the menu for ages—pasta maison ($22), a heap of al dente angel-hair pasta with Maine shrimp, mussels, scallops, and two tender pieces of salmon, each cooked perfectly, in light cream. Try the Special Catch, which could be grilled mahimahi ($24), with cubes of fresh mango, spinach, yellow squash, and a mild cabbage. Braised pork shanks ($21) with fennel, and Delmonico steak ($27 for 20 ounces of beef), are other possibilities.

One drawback here were supermarket strawberries in the Pavlova ($6.60, as are all desserts) at the height of strawberry season; but otherwise this dessert of real whipped cream and crisp meringue was a pleasure, as was the chocolate espresso torte, with mocha mousse and a sweetened espresso sauce.

Portland

Back Bay Grill
(207) 772-8833
65 Portland Street
www.backbaygrill.com
Hospitality—Warm, inviting, swift, and competent
Open at 5 PM for bar service, seating at 5:30, Monday through Saturday
Entrées $18 to $35
Handicapped accessible, reservations recommended

☛ *A premier place to treat clients and make your friends really like you*

The big mural on the wall, painted in the summer of 1993 when this restaurant opened in its down-at-the-heel neighborhood, sets a tone of pleasure and animation. The people depicted in the mural are eating steak and quiche, talking up a storm, hitching up a skirt, and grabbing hold of friends. In the real dining room, taupe walls and amber sconces share the scene with an ornate gold mirror and carpeting patterned with swirls of leaves.

Back Bay Grill has been feeding its appreciative customers for all the years since, enduring flush times and the dot.com bust. Larry Matthews is the chef-owner who worked in the kitchen and decided to buy it in 2002. He has been running this thriving kitchen with a perfect touch, choosing to simplify and not overcomplicate meals. Another of his innovations is the take-out menu—almost all of what is on the regular menu—and also packaging veal demi-glace, red wine sauce, and duck stock, perfect for making dinner at home suddenly fabulous.

A bar offers room for people looking for a cocktail, but dinner, or just an appetizer or dessert, can be enjoyed there if reservations are unavailable.

I recommend everyone at least try the crabcake, the best I've ever had, but it is not always on the menu. Sitting high and wide, a dark golden brown, in a liquid coaster of lemon-pepper crème fraîche, the marvel elucidated crab to the exclusion of almost all else. A bite of the cucumber salad in between mouthfuls of the hot crab fixed me up for bite after wonderful bite.

If it isn't available, perhaps you'll find the "butter-warmed" lobster with Jester tomato salad ($16), a perfect end-of-summer combination.

The wine list holds stellar, ever-changing wines, many sold by the glass, like Shottesbrooke Sauvignon Blanc 2005 from Australia ($8.50), or a splurge, Ferrari-Carano Cabernet Sauvignon 2002 ($14). If you ask, the fine bartender is sure to have a few original cocktails up his sleeve, like the Back Bay Grill Rum Punch ($10). You can snack on truffled popcorn while you enjoy your drink.

Veal sweetbreads, another appetizer, revealed a dense, smooth white texture, so toothsome under a thin crust. The red grapes had been thoughtfully, if maniacally, peeled, removing any chance of an acid interruption to all the rich pleasure of the sweetbreads and parsnip puree enriched with a dark meat jus and bits of bacon.

A romaine salad was served with the leaves layered on top of each other like a pagoda.

A Scottish salmon entrée paired with a lobster citrus salad ($24) gave one of us an appropriate reward for reaching her tenth wedding anniversary (her plate of fresh berries with crème fraîche had "Congratulations" written in chocolate on the rim, a friendly touch on the restaurant's own initiative). She called the thick piece of tender fish fabulous, and added that her husband loved the Vidalia onion soup.

Someone on a budget could dine deliciously on wild mushroom and goat cheese *agnolotti,* little half moons of stuffed pasta ($18).

For dessert, a hazelnut praline made a cylinder for Champagne sabayon and berries, and a pyramid of different sorbets included ginger and lemon, orange and poppyseed, and limpid watermelon. Caramel ice cream with bourbon-caramel sauce, another possibility, demands to be enjoyed.

Bar Lola

(207) 775-5652
100 Congress Street
Open for dinner Wednesday through Saturday 5–10
Entrées $12 to $14, but this is a place that specializes in multicourse dinners
Handicapped accessible, reservations recommended

☛ *Small plates with perfect ideas on them in this welcome change of a restaurant*

The idea for Bar Lola was to have a place that was giving little tastes of whatever was most fresh, most seasonal, most delicious. Say, for instance, that the season's first lettuce had just arrived in the kitchen. Why not present it with the simplest vinaigrette all on its own, and not in the chronic restaurant salad composition of greens, cheese, nuts, and fruit? Not that I don't like those elaborate salads, but Bar Lola would be a place dedicated to flavors on a small scale, each showcased on a small plate.

Bar Lola has been packed by people glad to give this concept their business. A summer night here with a family of friends showed the only weakness—when the perfect little taste of chocolate needed to be ordered repetitively, until everyone had eaten it. That can add up even if the plate itself cost only $5 or $6. Sharing is also more difficult when you want to be able to eat your whole small serving yourself.

A fall menu included chicken *piccata* with a rosemary scone ($13); one big free-form ravioli with fresh herb-ricotta filling, served in a broth of roasted tomatoes, garlic, and thyme ($12); grilled lamb chops with figs, and lentil and olive salad ($14); and a pork loin rolled with Maine apples, goat cheese, and brandy sauce, roasted with fresh applesauce ($14). "We haven't repeated ourselves yet," said one of the three owners, Guy Hernandez.

So perhaps none of these dishes will reappear.

The One Fifty Ate Spinach Salad, warm spinach, bacon vinaigrette, and a fried egg ($6), is one classic that may be a menu staple. One Fifty Ate in South Portland (see page 110) is the mother ship of this dinner restaurant.

Toffee chocolate cake ($5) makes its own toffee sauce when you bake it; soft and gooey with a little ganache.

A medium plate, a salad, and a large plate will be a good meal for most of us, plus dessert or a small beginner. Although some customers resist the idea of eating multicourse meals except on special occasions, Bar Lola's owners believe their meals can convince their enthusiastic customers that a four-course meal should be the new norm. The restaurant's prices are reasonable, averaging $30 for a three-course meal. When you make a reservation here, the table is reserved for a long time. "It's not the place to come for a quick meal," Hernandez said.

Bibo's Madd Apple Café
(207) 774-9698
23 Forest Avenue
Menus posted at blog.myspace.com/bibosmadapplecafe
Hospitality—Informal and responsive
Open for lunch Wednesday through Friday 11:30–2, for Sunday brunch 11–2, and for dinner Wednesday through Saturday 5:30–9, on Sunday 4–8
Entrées $15 to $19
Reservations best during the theater season

☞ *Inventive, good entrées in an arty environment*

Bibo's Madd Apple Café sits next door to the Portland Stage Company and gets most of its business during the weeks shows are performed there. That makes it a good place to go off-season to escape the summer crowds farther downtown, and its food will delight anyone with an appetite.

Lately, a little more focus on local products keeps dishes more tied to Maine, but eclectic is the theme. ("Madd Apple" is the old English spelling of a name for eggplant.)

Bibo's wine list features domestic bottles and offers a reserve list in the back for pricier bottles like a 1998 T-Vine Syrah ($60). Thirteen wines can be ordered by the glass; over 60 wines are on the wine list, and new varieties are added all the time.

A hot goat cheese "medallion," a disk of smooth cheese inside a thin crisp crust, accents that tart cheese's creaminess. Another menu stuffs shrimp with herbed goat cheese, on a salad of greens with roasted pepper puree.

All the servings here are very big. Two people with regular appetites could share one entrée and be satisfied, like the white bean and sweet Italian sausage risotto ($15.95), or pan-roasted haddock on mashed cauliflower, with sautéed fresh corn, spinach, and tomatoes ($16.95).

Although I faced two courses that surpassed my appetite, I can't explain why I ate dessert with no difficulty. Truly, appetite is irrational.

The lemon tart ($6) was a rectangle of gelled lemon curd surmounted by a cumulus of whipped cream and lots of blueberries. On the plate red raspberry and orange-mango purees were used to create a design of four striped crowns on each side and gave the dish elegance. The crème brûlée ($6) met with approval by an expert, who called it the best in the state of Maine (Pier 77's crème brûlée is right up there).

With its cantaloupe walls, fuchsia trim, and blue-and-green tablecloths, Bibo's is an exuberant setting for its well-made food—and the quantities may be more welcome in the winter, when appetites grow sharp.

Blue Spoon
(207) 773-1116
89 Congress Street
Hospitality: Businesslike and competent
Open for lunch 11:30 to 3 and dinner 5-9 Tuesday through Thursday, 5-9:30
Friday and Saturday
Entrées $8 to $19
Reservations for parties of 6 or more only

☛ *Elegant meals for modest prices*

This popular restaurant's small dining room runs along its storefront at the top of Munjoy Hill, along with a short marble bar, and a happy mood is usually fizzing in the yellow room, with local artists' paintings and photos on the walls.

Owner and chef David Iovino opened the place with the idea of making high-quality food without charging a ton of money. He told us he was taking morels off the menu, for instance, because they were getting too expensive; but they'd worked well earlier in the year.

With a background at Savoy in New York City, a restaurant that emphasizes green market, seasonal produce, Iovino is intent on finding local sources for his good food, like artisan bread from One Fifty Ate, a bakery and café in South Portland (see page 110).

On one visit my companion, a pasta hound from the age of six months who was forking rigatoni, cheese, and marinara into her entranced mouth, bitterly regretted the four fat slices of oil-soaked country white she'd already eaten.

Sicilian fish stew, mussels, cod, and salmon with tomatoes, basil, and grilled garlic bread ($17), wafts an aroma like incense of the sea.

A party of four skinny women beside us, two in their 50s and two in their 20s, relished the big hamburgers and large bowls of mussels with lemon and garlic. Other customers who are salad hounds say they could live on the green apple, goat cheese, and red onion with mixed greens in a vinaigrette ($6 small, $8 medium, $10 large, which is the size of an entrée).

For dessert look for the bittersweet chocolate custard ($6, as are all desserts), flan, and dishes that change with the seasons. Apple crostada and pumpkin panna cotta were on a fall menu.

Caiola's
(207) 772-1110
58 Pine Street
www.caiolas.com
Hospitality—A wonderful welcome is the usual at this fine neighborhood place. Open for dinner Tuesday through Thursday 5:30–9:30, Friday and Saturday 5:30–10
Entrées $13 to $23

☛ *Terrific cooking and friendliness combine to woo everyone who dines here.*

In 2006 chef-owner Abby Harmon, after 15 years of honing her skills at Street and Co., opened this fine restaurant with co-owner Lisa Vaccaro, who runs the dining room and greets new and return customers with equal courtesy. They have created a great new business appreciated deeply by folks who live nearby and find dinner here a favorite night of the week.

Shrimp Romesco ($17.95) on one Friday-night menu pleased with its onion polenta, juicy sautéed spinach, and crisp snap peas. Crispy duck, and scallops and mussels in saffron sauce, were other delectable entrées, all well matched by a range of wines that include inexpensive finds worthy of a purchase after you try them here, like a Costières de Nîmes from Château La Beaume ($23).

The highlights of two evenings at Caiola's were ramps in a savory pudding, with smooth custard full of the pungent scent of ramps, and some tart ramp pickles ($7.95), a perfect modest portion evoking the spring woods. For many the Caesar salad with fried oysters is the perfect small supper or beginning dish. The six hot oysters hold both spice and crunch, and a depth of ocean flavor inside. Another regular favorite is the thick hamburger ($12.95), with melted cheese and bacon, accompanied by a signature version of Tater Tots, the size of small eggs, crunchy outside and packed with silky potato puree. Families seem to have no trouble finding something for everyone.

Wonderful homemade ice cream can come in mocha chocolate chunk ($6) with chips the size of dominos, served on a disk of meringue, and the brownies in raspberry sauce are magnificent. A cheese course includes local cheeses, probably some from the Silvery Moon Creamery, in Westbrook.

Cinque Terre

(207) 347-6154
36 Wharf Street
www.cinqueterremaine.com
Hospitality—Good natured and enthusiastic
Open daily for dinner at 5 PM; may be closed first week of the new year (for a scouting trip to Italy)
Entrées $18 to $25, but multicourse Italian meals are encouraged
Reservations recommended

☛ *A place to experience the soul food of northern Italy*

Cinque Terre is another reason living in Portland is so delightful. The northern Italian meals executive chef Lee Skawinski puts together here, from the dreamily light gnocchi to the tender fresh *pappardelle* to the roast quail and the roasted sea bass, make dinner a lyrical pleasure.

But Italian meals of many courses, with pasta, risotto, or gnocchi always preceding the meat or fish and the antipasti before that, are distinctly foreign and a hard sell when your customers want one or at most two courses. Cinque Terre offers pasta portioned in appetizer and entrée sizes, with the waitstaff still gently encouraging guests to try a few dishes and giving insight into the long, entirely Italian wine list.

An antipasto of grilled red onions, roasted peppers, zucchini, and cheese ($9) could be followed by handmade gnocchi with Maine venison Bolognese ($10 for a small portion, $18 for large), and culminating in a third course of salmon with sautéed spinach ($19).

On our last of several visits, the fungi appetizer, sautéed summer mushrooms on crostini, made us happy, and the crispy Montasio cheese with potato, onions, and white truffle oil caused a sensation.

The woman who ordered it, a new Portland resident, said, "I'm beginning to believe Portland is the undiscovered gastronomic center of the East Coast."

Ecco la.

Dogfish Café

(207) 253-5400
953 Congress Street
Hospitality—Friendly and quick
Open for lunch at 11:30 Monday through Saturday, with dinner specials Wednesday through Saturday 5-9

Entrées $9 to $17

☛ *A café with uneven cooking*

The Dogfish Café is on the verge of being a restaurant. Sitting at a busy inter-section in the midst of parking lots and truck traffic, the back outdoor space is not appealing.

Inside, the place is hip, like its name, with brown paper covering the tables and sage green wooden booths under an indigo ceiling. But the wine list is limited to old standbys, the chicken is overcooked, and the bread is too white.

Side salads ($3.50) were plain, and that made them fine. Fresh greens, sim-ple vinaigrette, and some modest grated cheese were all they needed to be good.

But meals off the night's specials board, served from 5 to 9, also disap-pointed. This popular place is always hopping on weekends, possibly because the main interest is a drink; but a glass of Baroncini Chianti Colli Senesi ($5.75) tasted a little musty, as if the bottle had stood open too long. It was better than the Four Vines Zinfandel ($5.50), however, which tasted like a vanilla Coke because of intrinsic problems.

Swordfish ($14.50) had been cooked perfectly, full of good juices, and a coating of roasted tomato aioli was a rich accompaniment, but the sugar olive jam on top of that was too much, and the couscous alongside was mushy. Chicken cacciatore ($13.95) had fine pasta in a thin sauce with overcooked chicken on top.

five fifty-five
(207) 761-0555
555 Congress Street
www.fivefifty-five.com
Hospitality—Perfect service
Open for dinner 5–10, until 10:30 Friday and Saturday, Sunday brunch
10:30–2:30
Entrées $20 to $27
Reservations recommended

☛ *A chef about whom other chefs are talking, serving great food*

When a restaurant like this thrives and grows, you know its dinners have become the favorites of many loyal customers. five fifty-five added a lounge next door to its original space in summer 2006 and plans to remain open daily year-round, serving inventive, careful dishes that don't hesitate to seduce.

Don't miss the meals at five fifty-five, focused on great taste, local products, and inventive intelligence.

Steak and Cheese ($9.95), a small plate or appetizer, combines thinly sliced Angus beef with shaved Parmesan, arugula—wild for a little more bite—and truffle oil to make you think you are lost in the woods. A "green plate" from the list might be Two Blues ($8.95), Maine blueberries with Maytag blue cheese and organic greens in a blueberry-champagne vinaigrette.

One main dish, grilled organic Irish salmon ($21.95), is served with Fishbowl Farm fried green tomatoes and bourbon-soaked corn bread.

.5 Lounge is open similar hours, with food served at the same hours as the restaurant. Mussels from the main menu are one of the crossover dishes, available in both spots, and were prepared with house-pickled cherry peppers and chive butter one fall ($11.95). The french fries might come with basil aioli or rosemary vinegar. A burger with changing accompaniments is available only in the lounge. One version, the Huntsman's, is served with a blue cheese biscuit and Vermont cheddar, along with hand-cut potato chips. The Truffled Mac & Cheese ($11.95) is enriched with béchamel and artisanal cheeses, with hand-rolled *torchio* pasta, and a dash of white truffle oil with slivers of black truffle, fresh if available.

The dessert menu is the same as in the restaurant, and here no holds are barred. Chocolate Paradise is a chocolate-caramel *pot de crème* with chocolate-coated macaroon and coconut ice cream ($9). The ice creams are served in endless, crazy variations like saffron-honey and rosemary-lime. Garlic ice cream could arrive here soon, and I imagine we will like it, all of us putty in the hands of the mad genius in the kitchen.

Fore Street

(207) 775-2717
288 Fore Street
www.forestreet.biz
Hospitality—Great service without a rush, despite the crowd
Open daily for dinner weekdays 5:30–10, weekends until 10:30
Entrées $17 to $34
Handicapped accessible, reservations almost always a necessity. If you arrive early you can get your name on a list for the tables kept open for walk-ins, or you can eat at the bar.

☛ *Go here for the best evening out, with an exciting dining room and wonderful meat and fish.*

Chef and part owner Sam Hayward has presided over the kitchen since 1996. In 2006, *Gourmet* magazine included Fore Street among the top 50 restaurants in the country, just as it had five years earlier. Hayward's great recipes have been written up in the *New York Times.* I rated his restaurant with five stars, the maximum in the reviews I write for the *Maine Sunday Telegram.*

The big dining room with its high rafters and exposed bricks centers on the open kitchen and its fires. Servers leap to pick up meals when they're called, while a cook shoves roasting pans deep into the wood-burning oven and another cuts apart turnspit-roasted loins of pork with triumphant exuberance. This hearth draws all eyes, not just for the flames dancing inside the wood-burning oven, but more particularly to watch the chefs, like dancers, turning, stooping, sliding dish after dish and plate after plate, making dishes for hundreds, among them oven-roasted mussels with a large scoop of almond butter scented with garlic, and a splash of vermouth.

Hayward has been buying the best local produce for years, and some of it sits on display like the art it is in the restaurant's glass-windowed produce closet. Wild Maine chanterelles foraged by Rick Tibbets, one of Maine's best foragers, might arrive at the table in a soup with spinach ($8.50), or in a side dish with opal basil butter ($12). Fore Street moved its side dishes into a separate list in 2006; a close comparison with other years' menus shows no significant change in prices, especially when a side of house-rendered lard roasted red potatoes ($4) serves two generously.

The restaurant serves pizza and a pasta dish that could suit any reasonable child while her parents are rooting in their big bowls of fish and shellfish stew, or platters of wood-oven-roasted wild king salmon or whole lobster. Some children have become roast pork fanatics after a taste of the pork loin ($21), even though they might skip the house-pickled onions.

While some dishes are costly, the juicy roast chicken and roast monkfish are not, something to remember when a dinner at Fore Street seems out of reach. In 2006 a friend and I ate here for $106 with tip.

Dessert is astonishing—if you feel you can't taste another bite, consider your figure blessed.

Warm chocolate soufflé cake ($8) has been toppling diners' resolutions since Fore Street opened in 1996, and the peach tarte tatin ($7.50) is just as effective, with its silk fruit and tender, flaky puff pastry. A warm plum and peach cobbler ($7) had a tanginess of warm fresh fruit that makes one of the best endings to a meal.

The Front Room
(207) 773-3366
73 Congress Street
www.thefrontroom.com
Hospitality—The place can get mobbed, and takes no reservations, so prepare to wait at peak hours.
Open 5–10 daily in summer, brunch daily 8–2:30, but call in off-season for reduced hours
Entrées $9 to $18
Handicapped accessible

☛ *A noisy, energetic spot for a rich, good brunch and reliably good dinners with some standout specials and menu items*

There is room here for those awaiting payday, with a meatloaf dinner for $12, or macaroni and cheese with a side of vegetables for $9. But if payday has come around, try the fancier fare, changing with the seasons, like a soft-shell crab special ($16) on a rich mound of saffron rice, peas, and leeks. Tender as butter (and just as rich), braised short ribs ($16) were even more delectable.

People seeking peace and quiet, though, should avoid this sometimes raucous place.

The interior has been handsomely renovated; tabletops and columns are crafted of mahogany. Tables will be set outside for alfresco dinners in summer, when a glass of the wine, from a generous selection, would go nicely with the salmon pastrami appetizer ($9) or a special salad full of pristine local arugula and Sunset Acres Farm goat's-milk feta ($9).

But I must describe the inevitable eggs Benedict, here made with lavish paprika hollandaise, buttery biscuits, and tender ham under those poached eggs. Beware the richness of everything on the breakfast menu, like a fried egg sandwich with blue cheese and bacon ($6) that can satisfy the appetite in a few bites. I can vouch for the fact that this is no time to add the apple coffee cake ($1.75) to your order, however attractive and delicious it is.

Hugo's
(207) 774-8538
88 Middle Street
www.hugos.net
Hospitality—Unobtrusive and flawless
Open for dinner Tuesday through Saturday from 5:30
Prix fixe four-course dinner, $65 (varies with changing menus)

☛ *Magnificent, inventive food by one of the best chefs in New England*

Dinner at Hugo's nourishes more than the body, and I don't exactly mean the soul. Rob Evans is so spirited, his menus read like the leaps of a dancer, or the section of a symphony that gives the orchestra the direction, furioso. Some of these skills Evans learned—starting at Maine's Goose Cove Lodge in Sunset, then on to the Inn at Little Washington, and the French Laundry in California's Napa Valley. But I think most of the ideas here are original.

Open in 2000, Hugo's is owned by Evans and his partner, Nancy Pugh, who makes perfect tomato martinis and oversees miraculously ordered service. The whole staff seem to work every table, with one main server and seamless attention. The fine wine list is generous, offering less expensive bottles mixed with the higher priced.

Small, perfect portions make up the four-course dinners that might start, if Evans ever repeated menu items, with summer vegetable soup filling a third of a small bowl holding a few round-shaped pieces of zucchini, turnip, and fresh greens, along with a slippery ravioli in a clear, salty prosciutto broth. Swordfish tartare was served in a slender porcelain canoe with dabs of Tabasco sabayon and a little scattering of crunchy saffron-dusted popped rice.

Next up was the crisp, golden-crusted pork belly, a small square of tenderness, with poached apple and pear pieces and anise hyssop, an herb with an anise flavor that was just a faint presence. A small fried Scottish salmon cake was a cylinder of brilliant coral tenderness, its center moist with pink grapefruit and a little heap of shaved fennel salad alongside to brighten the rich flavor.

Every dish is a balance of elements, nothing outsize and all harmonious. In the third course, for instance, a cappuccino cup held a foamy serving of oyster stew, only one tender just-cooked oyster in the salt-intense broth. Little "puffs" of crispy crackers the size and shape of oyster crackers but utterly original, tender, and full of finely minced oysters were lined up in a short row flanking the small golden cube of roasted, delectable cod. And a smoked tomato added a rich dark sweetness to the other tastes.

The pan-fried trout remains in memory for the utter tenderness of its flesh and the rigid crunch of its skin, a marvel, while its accompanying fried little pickles, the tart note on the plate, made a funny surprise with the first bite.

Desserts were exemplified by the Delices de Bourgogne cheesecake, smooth, slightly salty, and just sweet enough; its creamy substance was matched by peppery slices of date and a little black pepper graham cookie.

The bar menu allows tastes of a plate from the main menu, and other ideas not on it, for someone interested in dipping a toe in this pool before taking the plunge.

Katahdin

(207) 774-1740
106 High Street
www.katahdinrestaurant.com
Hospitality—A little haphazard when it's packed
Open for dinner Tuesday through Thursday 5–9:30, Friday and Saturday 5–10:30
Entrées $20 to $26

☛ *A popular neighborhood restaurant and hangout*

The martinis and Manhattans come with a dividend in a little jug at this corner spot known for its great drinks and its good bartender, Winnifred Moody. But the wine list is on the expensive side. On the positive side, glasses of wine are very large, and perhaps that explains the $8 average price. Another drink possibility is any of the seven beers on tap, like Czech Pilsner Urquell or local Bar Harbor Blueberry.

Winterpoint oysters from West Bath make a good first course, along with crabcakes with *pasilla* chili-lime aioli ($9), or lobster ricotta tart with arugula and pecorino ($12).

A salmon entrée with pistachio crust ($22) came with a tart, lively vinaigrette. Shrimp with arugula, pancetta, and pecorino was full of rich saltiness.

But a vegetarian entrée was heavy and unappetizing.

As chefs change and menus shift, the meals here will undoubtedly evolve. This is a great spot to meet friends for drinks, and is worth checking out for a casual dinner.

Local 188
(207) 761-7909
188 State Street
Hospitality—Congenial and ready to elaborate on the choices
Open for dinner Tuesday through Saturday, Sunday brunch
Entrées $15 to $19, tapas under $10

☞ *A hip place with phenomenal food*

Open in 1999 and featuring ever-changing art, Local 188 likes to surprise. One show featured drawings that from a distance resembled illustrations from a children's book. But close up we found that the bush the goat was munching on was not planted in the ground. Another displayed reconfigured letters that began life by forming the sign for Miss Portland Diner, and returned to life as "Show Love."

Red Japanese lanterns hang from thick black cords suspended from the olive green ceiling, between an exposed brick wall and a wall painted the color of unsalted butter, in a long room with three rows of tables.

Start with a little dish of shrimp and garlic ($5.75). The small oval bowl of Maine shrimp, served with a tiny bit of red pepper and a lot of garlic, did stimulate appetite without sating it. Ripped-up chunks of salted, chewy bread from One Fifty Ate (see page 110) are served with a dish of olive oil, tempting a hungry customer to overindulge, they taste so good.

Rioja, several of the 15 reds you are likely to find here by the glass, might include the butch Scala Dei Priorat Negre ($6), and the house sangria ($4.50), for a lighter, fruity but not insubstantial drink, is also worth a try.

French lentil salad ($9) sent my friend, a chef, into surprised pleasure, it had been made so well, with thin shavings of Manchego a salty contrast to the nutty little lentils.

The changing art at Local 188 vies with the good meals for your attention.

Little dishes, the tapas like that shrimp dish, graduate to *raciones,* or medium-sized plates, possibly a mahogany clam, chourico, and bean Portuguese stew ($11), and then comes *ensalades,* salads like the lentils.

Next up are the *comidas grandes,* which reasonable customers skip entirely, but I don't. The seafood paella ($19) differs every night, and is certainly good with mahogany clams, mussels, salmon, and Maine shrimp, along with green beans and long grain rice in a saffron broth. Sweet-and-sour glazed pork tenderloin ($16) cured that insipid meat of its blandness with thyme, hot grape tomatoes, and juicy sautéed spinach.

A simple flan ($6, as are all desserts) or a more complicated three-citrus cheesecake, baked by Trent Harris, are well-made finales.

Mim's Brasserie
(207) 347-7478
205 Commercial Street
www.mimsportland.com
Hospitality—Efficient and friendly, fast-paced
Open daily for breakfast and lunch 7–3, for dinner 5–9:30
$7 to $15 for à la carte dishes, sides extra

☛ *Classic, simple French food, with regional innovations*

Mim's took over a curved-front brick building on Commercial Street in spring 2004 and has been filling its small upstairs and downstairs dining rooms since. There's no chance the two terraces, also up and down, will go begging on a sunny day, since the address is tourist central.

Initial grumbling about prices has been overcome by consistent quality and straightforward good food. Mim's uses ingredients as local as possible, featuring cheese and eggs from Sunset Acres Farm in Brooksville, and seafood from markets on Commercial Street. Brunch dishes, like their classic eggs Benedict ($10), cannot be improved, with fresh eggs and tender Maine ham on a thick fresh slice of toasted sourdough bread. Plain eggs and bacon will be the best of their kind, and the orange juice is fresh squeezed. The iced coffee was superb, the darkest of dark roasts undefeated by its ice.

Lunch salads might be too plain, as my friend said, regretting ordering the romaine salad with slivered almonds, grapes, and *grana padano.* The upstairs dining room, a curved wall lined by a bench with a few shag pillows and a row of little tables, is a cool environment for such substantial things as onion soup with melted Gruyère ($7) and organic chicken with roasted pepper and olive tapenade on crusty bread ($8.50).

Dinner can be a tender local pork loin with prunes and spiced red wine ($18) or braised short ribs with fava beans ($20), with a side of spinach sautéed with garlic and olive oil ($5) shared by two.

A list of cocktails includes a Metropolitan ($8.50) made with Calvados, dry vermouth, and a dash of bitters.

Rachel's Osteria
(207) 774-1192
496 Woodford Street
www.rachelswoodgrill.com
Open for dinner Wednesday through Saturday from 5
Entrées $17 to $25
Handicapped accessible, reservations recommended

☛ *An Italian theme with delicious, rustic meals in large portions*

If you know the astute preferences of older women, then you know their favorite spot to dine is one you can trust to be satisfying—comfortable, friendly, casual, and certain to offer lots of pleasure on its plates and in its glasses. Rachel's emphasizes the basics like garlic and extraordinary olive oil, and in the bruschetta, a simple thing often mangled, you can recognize the skill. The bread is grilled and crisp, the tomatoes have flavor, and the basil is packed with summer.

Owners Robert and Laura Butler take off for Italy often to keep in touch with the source and learn about another great wine to offer—one customer extols Robert Butler's ability to pair dinner choices with a wine she leaves up to him. There are 250 bottles available.

Porcini-dusted diver scallops on angel-hair pasta ($23) and a full rack of lamb with cabernet balsamic glaze ($27) show off a range that keeps customers eager to find this outpost just off Brighton Avenue. Pasta *vongole,* with clams in a white wine garlic sauce ($21), is another reason to go.

Homemade chocolate pudding with white chocolate chips, like a rich mousse or ganache ($8), is a favorite end to the meal. The Portal, a tawny port, and Sandeman Vintage Port 2000 (both $7) could be another.

Street and Co.
(207) 775-0887
33 Wharf Street

Hospitality—Brisk and capable in a busy atmosphere
Open daily at 5, seating for dinner at 5:30
Entrées $17 to $29
Reservations recommended

☞ *The best place in Portland for great fish*

This restaurant fits snugly into three brick-lined rooms off cobblestoned Wharf Street. Before you go inside, you can stand a moment and watch the cooks through a middle window; they always seem to be working frenetically. That's why you need to call first for a reservation, although the bar is pleasant and you can order some food there. Street and Co. has been in business for a long time and fills its seats with people who have eaten there over and over, confident they can get great grilled fish, or spicy lobster *diavolo* for two ($39.95), or classics like scallops in Pernod and cream sauce, or shrimp and garlic on linguine.

The restaurant offers regular appetizers, including mussels, and oysters on the half shell, that can come from the coast of Maine or Washington. A "taste" of rare tuna with chickpeas ($4), just a couple of bites, started off the menu one night in fall, as did spiced Gorgonzola-stuffed fig ($3.50).

Crabmeat sautéed in brown butter with mushrooms and greens over puff pastry ($12.95) is a frequent item on the menu. Sole *francaise* ($22.95) is lightly battered sole with butter and capers—and has been on the list for 17 years. Scallops in Pernod and cream ($24.95) is another long-timer. Street and Co. also makes mussels marinara ($18.95) and shrimp with tomato and capers ($20.95), both served over linguine.

But choose specials, because, according to a local chef, that's where those Street chefs show off their chops. A whole fish is always offered, always special; and one evening's roast branzino ($25.95), a Mediterranean fish, was splendid, its fine-grained white flesh perfect under a cloud of tapenade and over a bed of chopped garlic, spinach, and white wine butter sauce.

Fennel-crusted monkfish ($25.95) turned that local fish into something almost elegant, and scallops in a white wine sauce on linguine ($22.95) were tender and the pasta al dente.

Desserts like chocolate sin ($6), a flourless chocolate soufflé, usually exact allegiance.

The copper-covered tables at Street and Co. are small, the rooms full, and the noise level high. That jacks up the excitement, yet none of the busy staff lose their cool.

Uffa

(207) 775-3380
190 State Street
www.uffarestaurant.com
Hospitality—Impeccable service and attention to young and old
Open for dinner Wednesday through Sunday from 5:30, Sunday brunch 9 AM–1 PM
Entrées $23 to $30
Reservations recommended

☛ *Elegant meals in a small restaurant with a good reputation and a lot of charm*

Slices of just-baked wheat bread, buttered from a tiny blue-rimmed white tub, and a glass of Eola Hills Pinot Noir from Willamette Valley in Oregon ($9) made anyone feel right at home.

The rough wooden booths hark back to an earlier incarnation, but white tablecloths and candles burning in bottles on the top edge of the white beaded-board wainscoting create a charming atmosphere, comfortably formal, just as the skilled work of the kitchen transforms meat and fish into fine dinners without any pretentiousness.

Not that chef James Tranchemontagne won't pick up a dusty classic like

The smart surroundings have nothing on the good dinners at Uffa.

mushroom vol-au-vent ($13) with spinach in a light creamy sauce and make it intriguing all over again.

Full-sized entrées run from $18 to $25, but you can also enjoy items from a bistro menu with smaller portions and more variety.

You might start by sharing organic beet greens ($8) with roasted beets and Berkshire Blue cheese, a salad from that list, go on to a strudel ($13) of chanterelles with a drizzle of truffle oil, and finish with a 7-ounce lamb steak ($18), grilled and served with *tzatziki*-influenced cucumber-yogurt compote.

The Chocolate Tower ($8) is a mind-boggling cylinder of chocolate on a bed of milk chocolate crème anglaise, plain crème anglaise, and raspberry coulis with milk chocolate mousse piped into the "tower."

Baby Cakes, thankfully, is a section that offers smaller desserts ($6).

Two scoops of ice cream ($5) can be ordered with possible toppings. The homemade ice cream here startles the tongue with its fullness, so different from even the most expensive store-bought. Nectarine and sun jewel mango are lovely flavors—and if you want an experimental dish, call ahead and the kitchen will try to make it for you.

Vignola

(207) 772-1330
10 Dana Street
www.vignolamaine.com
Open daily 5–midnight
Entrées $16 to $20

☞ *The casual offshoot of Cinque Terre (see page 71), this place focuses on fresh seafood, pasta and pizza, cheeses, and cured Italian meats.*

Popular from the start, Vignola is another great resource for Portlanders hungry for Italian food with high standards. Pork and lamb meatballs served with polenta in a porcini mushroom sauce was a fall menu item. Many kinds of pizzas are served. Four regular pizzas ($10–13) are on the menu, with changing specials, and each one is cooked in a stainless steel oven with a stone interior heated to about 700 degrees Fahrenheit. Noah Tipton, who works here making pizzas or washing dishes as the business needs, said his favorite pizza is made with prosciutto, truffled pecorino cheese, and buffalo mozzarella. This one has lasted on the menu since Vignola opened in June 2006.

The menu adjusts to what is seasonal. Skate wing, roasted cherrystone clams, and Winterpoint oysters on the half shell are among the potential seafood choices. Some are breaded and fried, but most are grilled.

The late hours and the cheese plates with local and European cheeses make this a really good wine bar, with more than 20 wines by the glass. A plate of cured Italian meats—or one of the pizzas, of course—is another perfect nosh with a glass of wine.

The bar sits over the dining room, serving drinks like a basil-orange *mojito* ($10). Portuguese-style port cocktails using white port, like a white port tonic with a twist of orange, are served.

Five Japanese Places

Restaurant Sapporo (207-772-1233; www.sappororestaurant.com), 230 Commercial Street.
Open for lunch Monday through Friday 11:30–2, and Saturday and Sunday from 12 (open all day); dinner Monday through Thursday 5–9, Friday and Saturday until 10 with late-night sushi and lower prices on rolls, with music videos, until 11:30.

Sapporo is the Grand Dame of Portland's Japanese restaurants, and loyalty runs high for many who learned to love sushi at these tables, and at an earlier location in the Old Port. Standards also have been kept high, and the exceptional sushi proves it.

Yosaku (207-780-0880), 1 Danforth Street.
Open Monday through Thursday for lunch 11:30–2; dinner 5–9:30, Friday and Saturday until 10:30; lunch Saturday and Sunday 12–3, and dinner ends Sunday at 9. Yosaku offers live music some nights and always high-quality sushi and sashimi. It could be said to have the classiest decor.

Benkay (207-773-5555; www.sushiman.com), 2 India Street, at the farthest eastern end of Commercial Street.
Open for lunch Monday through Friday 11:30–2; dinner Sunday through Thursday 5–9:30, Friday and Saturday 5–10, with late nights Friday and Saturday 10 PM–12:30 AM. Benkay makes a Rock 'n Roll ($11) that wraps up eel, avocado, tuna, cream cheese, *kanikama,* grilled salmon, scallions, and cucumber. The octopus salad dressed fried octopus, lettuce, spinach, and radicchio with sweet soy dressing ($7.50).

Fuji Restaurant (207-773-2900; www.fujimaine.com), 29 Exchange Street.
Open Monday through Thursday 11:30–9:30, Friday and Saturday 11:30–10:30, and Sunday and holidays 12–9:30. The hibachi downstairs opens Tuesday through Sunday at 5, and daily from June to August. Fuji serves excellent sushi and several cooked Japanese dishes like Unaju ($14.95), broiled eel on rice, but we miss the Yaki Soba. Korean cuisine is another specialty, like Bulgoki, sliced marinated beef ($15.95), or Chop Chae, noodles with beef and vegetables in sauce ($11.95).

Newest in town is **King of the Roll (207-828-8880), 675 Congress Street.** Open for lunch Monday through Friday 11:30–2:30, dinner Sunday through Thursday 4:30–9:30, Friday and Saturday 4:30–10. The fanaticism about fresh fish is laudable at this sushi bar, where the chef-owner is eager to tell you what the best things are. Trust him on the sushi, sashimi, and all the fish and vegetable rolls, regulars say—but cooked dishes are not the focus here.

Three Thai Places

Bangkok Thai (207-879-4089), 671 Congress Street, across from the statue of the poet Longfellow.
Open Monday through Saturday for lunch 11–2:30 and dinner 5–9:30, Bangkok Thai has the good location in town. People cram in, but there's more room with an addition, and the brightly painted walls jazz up the atmosphere. We liked the Pik Khing Scallops, mixed with green beans, carrots, and sliced lime leaf. The coconut rice pudding is addictive.

Suwanna Truong runs **Sengchai Thai (207-773-1001; 803 Forest Avenue).** She's serving the freshest dinners; and the most refreshing Tom Yum Koong ($2.50). This savory soup with lemongrass, lime juice, and fresh mushrooms, and the most delicious curries, is full of clear flavor and only the freshest shrimp, chicken, or pork. Open daily 11–10, this is a friendly place. Truong came to the United States from northeast Thailand when she was 34, in the mid-1990s, learned English as she worked in a restaurant, and got herself out front once she could handle a few English phrases. Her restaurant is worth the trip to taste the herbs and spices that Truong oversees and mixes herself.

Siam Restaurant (207-773-8389), 339 Fore Street.

Open for lunch Tuesday through Friday 11:30–2, dinner 5 to closing Tuesday through Sunday. Siam presents Thai and Thai-inspired meals in a more elegant restaurant than is typical. Chef-owner Thomas Yordprom said he cooks from his Thai grandparents' recipes, with curries made with galangal, lemongrass, lime leaves, and the rest of the many ingredients that are ground fresh to create the elixir that draws us back to Thai dinner over and over.

A lemon Cosmopolitan ($8) from the bar here is a fine way to get under way, as was a fruit salad in a miso vinaigrette ($5). Seafood curry ($17) was only slightly sweet, rich with coconut milk and full of shrimp, scallops, and lobster. Roast asparagus, yellow pepper, and onion introduced their own crunch and savor. Crisp-skinned Thai basil duck ($14) held a brown sauce vibrant with ginger and hot chili.

Bangkok Thai tempts its customers with vibrant flavorings of Kaffir lime and lemongrass.

Breakfast, Lunch, and Informal Dinners

Artemisia (207-761-0135), 61 Pleasant Street.

Open Monday through Friday 11–3, Saturday and Sunday 9 AM–2 PM. Dinners Thursday, Friday, and Saturday 5–9. This place excels at great grilled sandwiches and inventive combinations, like roast beef with Gorgonzola mayonnaise, tomato, and red onion on grilled French peasant bread.

But the menu's Tuscan Grill, with grilled portobello mushrooms, pesto, goat cheese, and roasted red peppers on grilled Tuscan bread ($6.50), made my day. The grilled bread saturated with melting pesto and oozing goat cheese was heaven. The coleslaw beside it was made in the 1950s style, creamy with mayonnaise, and was a pleasure as well.

Huevos rancheros with spicy ranchero sauce ($8.50) and pesto frittata ($7.25) with melted provolone and fresh tomatoes are fine brunch dishes, but the Mango-Mosa isn't so hot—they'd taste better with a glass of decent wine from the short wine list.

The iced coffee was, as the server announced, "The Real Stuff—I wouldn't still be here working otherwise." It vied with Mim's French roast for darkness honors.

Dinners change every week, but often the moist roast pork with pineapple-mango chutney is on the menu. And any hour of the day the blond wood tables and the deep colors on the walls make this simple room attractive.

The Bayou Kitchen (207-774-4935), 543 Deering Avenue.

Open Wednesday through Saturday 7 AM–2 PM, Sunday 8 AM–2 PM, closed Monday and Tuesday. With blues on the stereo, red chili lights around the windows, and the heat from Cajun food off the grill keeping the atmosphere at a simmer, it's just possible to feel elsewhere. As the pierced delivery guy hoisted a box of potatoes on the cook's shoulder, and a trio of 20-somethings played poker while awaiting their 1 PM Monday breakfast, the smoky scent of my red beans and rice ($5.95) kept me focused. Four of the other customers were over 75—this is a place for anyone with a taste for crawfish, gumbo, and andouille. The corn bread comes browned from the grill and buttery, ready to accompany the jambalaya ($6.50) or with chicken and crawfish ($8.95) added to the andouille sausage, onions, peppers, garlic rice, and "our Jamba juice." Weekends can be jammed. And be warned—they do not accept credit cards.

Becky's Diner (207-773-7070; www.beckysdiner.com), 390 Commercial Street.

Open daily 4 AM–9 PM. The world-famous Becky's Breakfast is served from 4 AM to 4 PM, without home fries until closing. Breakfast is the focus here, drawing in so many tourists on a rainy morning that the line is out the door even in the middle of the week. The center of this universe grew from a little business started by a woman looking for a way to support her kids. She's come up with a way to buy their sneakers, pay for college, and keep them employed, too.

When we were talking about Becky's in a local law firm's waiting area, the receptionist praised the oatmeal—"cooked to order" according to the menu. Okay, but the rest of us go for the fluffy eggs, the big bowl of fresh fruit salad, always different, or whatever is on the white board for that day's special. The long row of coveted red booths is always full, and a $2.75 slice of pie—apple, blueberry, coconut cream, and peanut butter covered half the list one day—is the best way to end a meal, even breakfast. Customers vary from thick-necked fellows with tattooed heads to older Mainers on Social Security treating themselves. Dinners like meat loaf ($9.25), roast turkey ($9.25), or fried clams

($12.95) were introduced to feed fishermen who were hungry and not in the mood (or the wardrobe) for an Old Port restaurant, but now everyone is going.

You can rely on fast, good, cheap food out of this bustling kitchen on Hobson's Wharf, at the very bottom of High Street, where the biggest challenge is finding a place to park.

Bintliff's American Café (207-774-0005; www.bintliffscafe.com), 98 Portland Street.

Open daily year-round for breakfast, brunch, and lunch 7–2, dinner Wednesday through Saturday 5–9. Since there is inevitably a line here on weekend mornings, why not have a more pleasant (because less crowded) breakfast during the week? The eggs Benedict ($8.95) comes with heroic portions of home fries, cut in big chunks and darkly browned, and a slice of homemade bread along with the English muffin under the poached eggs, Canadian bacon, and light hollandaise. A Georgia pecan caramel waffle ($9.95) comes up the stairs to your table, rich with toasted pecans and caramel syrup. You can order a single pancake as a side for $2.95, and find real maple syrup here too. Wraps, burgers, big salads, and chowder fill the brunch menu, and are also available for lunch.

Dinners cooked by chef Justin Cross show off more skills here, from the lamb burger with goat cheese and *tzatziki* ($12) to the Maine cod in roasted tomato beurre blanc ($17), perfect in late summer to follow the now classic beet salad ($8) with chèvre in orange vinaigrette. Dinner is the undiscovered treasure of this spot besieged by brunch goers, so skip the weekend-morning lines and enjoy the calm attention at night. The specials are always jumping on what's fresh. In warm weather you can sit on a back deck in the open air.

The Brea-Lu Café (207-772-9202), 428 Forest Avenue.

Open 7 AM–1 PM weekends, 7 AM–2 PM weekdays.

Brea-Lu combines short-order cooking with a friendly, relaxing atmosphere. Now that it has air-conditioning, the summer-weekend breakfast crowds will be more comfortable.

Breakfast standards offer a huge quantity of spicy home fries, fried eggs, and toast. Specials on the board often include eggs Benedict, and under new management this came with hollandaise laid on with a trowel. Enormous pancakes engulf the plates; kids are hard-pressed to finish just one. Breakfast burritos and omelets are also served. Lunch is available Monday through Friday—burgers and sandwiches and a couple of salads. One of Portland's best waitresses,

Debbie Thibodeau, is now the manager; she makes a meal swift and friendly, and also sells her pretty jewelry here when she's on her shift. You can score a friend's birthday present when you're at the register paying for your eggs and toast.

Federal Spice (207-774-6404), 225 Federal Street.

Open Monday through Friday 11–9. For a fusion of Mexican, Asian, Southwest, and Caribbean, this small lunch place (with lots of outside tables) concocts the best. Locals stream here during the business lunch hour for the ginger-lemongrass rice and Asian slaw with curry coconut chicken and peanut sauce wrap—and many other choices. Daily specials might include a pumpkin rice wrap with Asian slaw and Asian barbecue sauce. The bright yellow walls and blue bench enliven the dreary location under a parking garage. You can have a local beer to go along with the sweet potato jalapeño corn bread and chili when winter blows into town.

Flatbread Company (207-772-8777), 72 Commercial Street.

Open Monday through Thursday 11:30–10, until 11 Friday through Sunday. In fall open Sunday through Thursday 11:30–9, Friday and Saturday 11:30–10. Ever since it opened its doors, Flatbread has drawn in big, enthusiastic crowds that enjoy its wood-oven-baked pizzas. A long bar has a lot of stools for people waiting for a table, but even they are often all taken on weekend nights. The big room full of light thrown in off the water through the windows is festooned with banners proclaiming, simply, GARDEN HERBS, or MAINE LOBSTER, or WHOLE-MILK MOZZARELLA. A hobbit-hole-shaped beehive oven with a fire inside attracts everyone's attention, and the children like to gather close while the young man with the long paddle slides the pizzas around to keep them baking evenly. This is a children's restaurant, and for the most part that does not mean it's a place to avoid if you don't have any toddlers of your own.

The flatbreads, as the restaurant calls them, are offered in several versions; there is a vegetable and a meat special every night, like roasted local scallops, smoked bacon from Sunset Acres Farm, organic scallions, mozzarella, Parmesan, and herbs ($18).

Regular flatbreads include a personal favorite that is topped with homemade maple-fennel sausage and sun-dried tomatoes, caramelized onions, organic mushrooms, cheeses, and herbs ($16, or a half order for $8.75). Or compose your own from the free-form list. We have brought many slices home over the years and found that unlike other leftover pizza, this pizza was always eaten up with appreciation the next day. The Punctuated Equilibrium flatbread is made with kalamata olives, rosemary, red onions, red peppers, goat cheese, mozzarella, garlic, and herbs ($15.25).

The regular dessert, a brownie sundae ($5.50), consists of a rich brownie that gets heated up in the oven a moment before the ice cream and chocolate sauce are piled on. The hot dense cake makes the cold ice cream delicious, or is it the other way around? Often a fruit crisp on the specials board demonstrates the same magic with cooked fruit.

Gilbert's Chowder House (207-871-5636), 92 Commercial Street.

Open every day 11–11. Cheap, fine fried seafood is served in a plain room and on a wood deck on the wharf in warm weather. There are old ship models and a few old catches mounted on the walls, plain linoleum on the floor, and Formica tables. It's a perfect place for kids, because most of them go for the style of flour-thickened chowder served here in Styrofoam bowls ($4.50 for a small). Adults can enjoy a pint of local Geary's or something from the full bar, and the fried whole-belly Maine clams or oysters, or a broiled or fried haddock filet ($11.25 for lunch, with french fries and coleslaw), or a Maine crabmeat roll ($12.95). There's news on the TV over the bar if you need a fix after the long whale-watch delivers you back on shore just down the street. Maine microbrews are on tap.

The Good Egg at the Pepperclub (207-772-0531; www.pepperclub restaurant.com), 78 Middle Street.

Open Tuesday through Friday 7–11, Saturday and Sunday 8–1. The highest-quality ingredients are at work in the breakfast here, where co-owner Mary Paine has revived The Good Egg, a Portland institution from the 1980s and 90s. Its homemade corned beef hash ($6.75 with two eggs and toast) is a primo recipe with corned beef, potato, onion, carrot, and parsley. The Eggs from Hell ($5) are my own favorite, with chipotle hot sauce in a cup to stint or slather according to preference on two eggs cooked as you like, tender black beans, and tomato salsa. The sticky buns are a mesmerizing swirl of buttery tender sweet bread and chopped nuts. Even the multigrain and the wheat English muffins are made here, toothsome and fresh.

Granny's Burritos (207-761-0751), 420 Fore Street.

Open Sunday through Thursday 11–10, Friday and Saturday 11–midnight. This business started around the corner in a small shop, with a few stools and chairs, for takeout only. Pretty soon everyone knew this was where to go when on a strict budget and in need of always fresh ingredients in your large and satisfying burrito. All the burritos are plump handfuls of folded, fresh tortillas—six kinds offered—filled with a choice of black beans, pinto beans, or both, and cheese, rice, salsa, tomatoes, lettuce, sour cream, and guacamole ($6.50 for the veggie), or sweet potato ($5.50), or chicken with mango salsa ($6.75), or chorizo sausage ($6.25), among many others. Nachos ($5.50 for veggie) or guacamole ($1.75) are on the appetizer list and could go along with a beer upstairs, where there is table service every night and all day Friday through Sunday. The menu offers many vegan and vegetarian choices.

Norm's East End Grill (207-253-1700), 47 Middle Street, open daily 11–10, Sunday 4–9; and Norm's Bar and Grill (207-828-9944), 617 Congress Street, open daily 11:30–10.

Friends of mine go to Norm's East End for takeout every Friday night; their barbecued ribs are famous, and the corn bread and fixings rate high. Another friend calls this one of his favorite restaurants. Casual atmosphere and attractive decor are part of Norm's popularity, but the fact is that all of the food is served in enormous portions and it's fairly good. There is only the slightest invention going on, but since most meals are classic favorites, there's little to criticize. At an earlier location you could sit at the bar and watch the meat spatter close-up, but now you'll have to wait to feast your eyes until the server brings it to the table. Salads at the Bar and Grill, like a steak salad special ($10.95), with spinach, blue cheese, corn, and a sweet balsamic vinaigrette, sang a chorus in my head as I debated ordering it or, say, the fish-and-chips or the Greek salad with fried calamari ($9.95). Deciding on the steak, I was delighted when it arrived in a big-rim soup bowl with six slices of rosy rare steak; it quieted the inner ogre within a minute or two. Chocolate cake with espresso frosting made by Doug, famous locally for this one thing, is $4.50. Some items can be found at both Norm's, but the heroic platters of ribs are all at the East End, which is crowded on weekend nights. The establishment's sweet potato fries ($4) with a lemony sauce, and its onion rings ($4.50), make eating fools of us all.

Portland Lobster Company (207-775-2112; www.portlandlobster company.com), 180 Commercial Street.

A busy establishment on the dock in the heart of Portland's tourist district, this is a reliable place to get good, fresh fried seafood, steamers, and boiled lobster. The clam chowder comes garnished with crispy bacon and chives ($5.99), and the fried calamari is accompanied by hot chili pepper sauce ($6.99).

For a Maine main course, the fried Maine shrimp are perfect little bites of seafood ($13.49 with fries and coleslaw), and the fried clams (market price) are fresh.

A Downeast Feast starts with steamers and includes the boiled lobster of your summer dreams, corn on the cob, coleslaw, and fries. But a crab salad with avocado, a Maine shrimp salad, or a lobster salad can be enjoyed outside on this dock without requiring any hard work to get at the tender meat. Same goes for the lobster roll, with meat from a 1-pound lobster mixed with a little warm butter, served in a toasted roll, with mayonnaise and lemon on the side. Local beers, a few wines, and whoopie pies complete the deal.

Sophia's (207-879-1869), 81 Market Street.

Open for breakfast and lunch Thursday through Saturday 10–5, dinner Friday through Sunday 5:30–9, Sunday brunch 10–4. This business also belongs below, among the bakeries. The campagnolo, a dense, pungent bread made from several grains, comes already sliced and basted with olive oil, with a thick slice of aged, tawny Asiago, for a baker's lunch offered in summer ($2.50, $3.50 with anchovies), or it can be bought by the quarter loaf. Stirato, a free-form baguette, and Luna, soft, floured half-moons of chewy white bread, are sold on Sunday only. Fruit breads are made according to season. Pastries like *torta di limone* and pistachio bars are phenomenally good. Large pizzas include one with fresh tomatoes, basil, and fresh mozzarella, sold by the slice for dinner.

There have been so many changes here that I recommend a call about new ones. The dinner hours had just begun as this book went to press, with a simple, but no doubt thoroughly virtuous, menu of pasta and *minestra di pollo,* a giant bowl of chicken soup ($14). Owner Stephen Lanzalotta is a

Sophia owner Stephen Lanzalotta makes some of the best bread in Portland, as well as his good meals.

cook, an artist, a musician, and lately an author of *The Diet Code: Revolutionary Weight Loss Secrets from Da Vinci and the Golden Ratio.* His meals are based on his ideas, and it really doesn't matter if you agree with them, since the integrity of the bread and food here is so high.

Simple food, soups, lots of caponata, dried salami and fine cheese, beans, and dishes like Penne Parmigiano ($8), are all priced low and reasonably portioned. The meals are served on paper plates. At Sunday brunch, *pane alla brace* ($8.50) is an almond-crusted thick French toast with blueberry-Marsala syrup.

Takeout, Bakeries, and Markets

Portland is blessed with wonderful bread.

In the early 1980s, the now-gone Port Bakehouse was a lone bakery on Fore Street. Bars and clubs have taken over that address, but not far away in the Old Port, several wonderful bakeries, each with its own ambitious excellence, are growing, and the old ones continue to surpass themselves. Maybe someday all the cotton-wool bread factories will shut down.

Big Sky Bread Company has two locations in Portland: one at **536 Deering Avenue (207-761-5623),** open Monday through Friday 7–6, Saturday 7–5, and Sunday 8–2; and a new base at **Market House on Monument Square, Congress Street,** open Monday through Friday 8–7, Saturday 9–7, and Sunday 5–9.

Big Sky granola is the best on planet Earth. Deeply toasted and stuck together in crunchy clumps (if all granola eaters ate stuff this crunchy, they'd deserve their epithet), a mass of almonds, sesame seeds, and oats, this stuff solved the mystery of why anyone would ever consume granola in the first place.

The bakery is a little on the crunchy side, culture-wise. Its big quarters out on Deering Avenue, with tables and newspapers and coffee, are child-friendly, with a wad of dough usually available for rolling out and messing around with on a little table. Not for eating, of course. Both locations sell big loaves of honey whole wheat, oatmeal, pumpernickel, and English muffin bread, and scones and cookies. Both also now sell sandwiches, like roast turkey and mozzarella, herbed chicken salad, and peanut butter and preserves on white.

Borealis Breads brought its delicious breads right into the **Hannaford at 295 Forest Avenue,** where it has installed a wood-burning oven. You can buy absolutely fresh ciabatta, chewy little loaves that make delicious hamburger buns that were getting snatched up for cookouts one July 4th weekend. Their rye, multigrain, and cinnamon-raisin breads are dense and full of character.

The Full Belly Deli (207-772-1227, fax 207-773-3067), Pine Tree Shopping Center, Brighton Avenue.

Open Monday through Friday 7–7, Saturday 7–4. "All corned beef is not created equal," the ads announce. David Rosen makes corned beef sandwiches with a choice of light, dark, or marble rye bread or a bulky roll, with half a sour pickle spear. It's a real New York deli. Why not become fully initiated? Try the George Bress sandwich, filled with corned beef, chopped liver, tongue, and Swiss cheese.

The Market House, 28 Monument Square, Congress Street, is the new location of several vendors from the now-defunct Portland Public Market. **Maine Beer and Beverage (207-228-2024)** sells all the best Maine microbrews, along with a large variety of wines, and milk and juice. **K. Horton Specialty Foods (207-228-2056),** run by Kris Horton, stocks fine cheeses with a special emphasis on the best in Maine. Here is a good spot to find Sunset Acres Farm "granite," aged goat cheese molded in little pyramids, and anything for which Maine is known, as well as French and Spanish cheeses, and olives from the Mediterranean. Good smoked salmon, including wild salmon products, and also local organic produce from Laughing Stock Farm. **Big Sky Bread Company (207-228-2040;** see description above) has an outpost here, with its fine whole wheat bread made with wheat grown in Maine's Aroostook County, and sandwiches and soups for lunch. **A Country Bouquet (207-228-2030)** sells beautiful flowers.

Oh No Café (207-774-0773), 87 Brackett Street (corner of Gray and Brackett).

Open Tuesday through Friday 6:30 AM–9 PM, Saturday 8–8, Sunday 8–6, closed Monday. This small neighborhood café and store opened up in summer 2004. Breakfast sandwiches are made with bagels, croissants, and English muffins; you can mix and match eggs with bacon, sausage, ham, smoked turkey, prosciutto, cheddar, and Gouda. Specials, like a hummus sandwich with red onion, tomato, and lettuce with a side salad of baby spinach with balsamic vinaigrette, are delicious. The menu could feature two great salads, one made with grilled shrimp and the other with spinach and flank steak. The Baja Chicken Taco with guacamole, *pico de gallo* (a tangy sauce of tomato, jalapeño, onion, and lime),

At K. Horton Specialty Foods, one of the businesses in The Market House, Kris Horton sells fine cheeses, smoked fish, and olives, among other things.

and plantains is $6.95. You can get some food ready to heat up from a take-out cooler, along with wine, beer, chips, and a small selection of groceries.

Rosemont Market and Bakery (207-774-8129), 559 Brighton Avenue.

Open Monday through Saturday 8–6, Sunday 9–4. John Naylor and Scott Anderson run this fabulous market, opened in January 2005. Anderson's work stocks the bakery, its bread cupboard shelves filled with high-quality breads, like the whole wheat scala, a tender crumb loaf with a nutty flavor, perfect as toast; the rustic torpedo, a chewier, crustier loaf with some whole wheat, makes wonderful sandwiches. All-butter croissants and *pain au chocolate* are flaky and tender. Semolina rolls, pizza, and focaccia are a few more of the breads, in addition to pies and cookies, baked by assistant Erin Lynch. She takes advantage of the seasonal produce appearing in the front of the market, making not only blueberry pies, but also strawberry-rhubarb pie in summer, and pumpkin, apple-cranberry, and pecan in fall. Her cookies, like the hermits and blondies, are another treasure.

But wine and produce, meat, cheese, and deli products, like white bean spread, guacamole, and pesto, make this place the only place anyone needs to shop—except the fish store.

The range of local cheeses, from Hahn's End creamy Blue Velvet to aged goat cheeses from Sunset Acres Farm to the fresh cheddar curd, butter, and crème fraîche from Silvery Moon Creamery, will inspire much gratitude for the pastures of Maine. See "Wines and Breweries" below for more information.

Standard Baking Company (207-773-2112), 75 Commercial Street.

Open Monday through Friday 7–6, Saturday and Sunday 7–5. This is the grand dame of them all, opening more than 25 years ago on Wharf Street and selling the best baguettes Mainers had ever seen. They are still the best. The signature morning bun, a sticky bun made with rich, flaky pastry and densely coated with walnuts or plain, has stood the test of time, remaining a popular item. In its present large quarters under Fore Street Restaurant there is a large assortment of breads painstakingly crafted according to the company's high standards, with long, slow rising times and premium flours and spices. I've moved on from the superior baguette to the fabulous rustica, a chewy loaf in various shapes; the dense whole rye; seeded whole wheat; and the amazing fig anise.

Pastries are delectable, from a bittersweet, rich brownie to apricot-walnut scones to the excellent gingerbread.

Two Fat Cats (207-347-5144; www.twofatcatsbakery.com),
47 India Street.
Open daily Monday through Friday 9–6, Saturday 9–5, Sunday 10–4 (closed
on Sunday in deep winter). Classic American bakery, with seasonal fruit pies
and special occasion cakes; whoopie pies are filled with marshmallow buttercream (no shortening in this one). Coffee cake has fruit and nuts or changing
ingredients.

   Chicken potpie makes a good dinner; order in advance if you want to make
sure of picking one up.

West End Grocery (207-874-6426), **133 Spring Street.**
Open daily 8 AM–9 PM. The best sandwiches, wraps, and salads in town are all
made in the small back kitchen of this modest grocery store on the corner of
Spring and Park. Daily specials are listed on a piece of paper posted to the right
of the ordering counter in the back, and always include a vegetarian choice.
Classics include the smoked salmon with capers, cucumbers, and red onion on
a baguette; Caesar salad roll-up with chicken (crammed with savory romaine);
and a hummus, cucumber, and sprout roll-up. The grilled chicken wrap makes
one member of this family's day. On any lunch hour you'll find the back of the
store full of locals waiting with patient anticipation for their delicious lunch to
go. Fruit, wine, brownies, and prepared meals (in the cooler) are also available.

Farmer's Markets

Portland has two chances for lucky consumers to buy the best from local harvests. Saturday from 7 AM to noon farmers line up along a street in **Deering
Oaks Park,** off Deering Avenue, selling seedlings from late April and everything that ripens through the summer and fall until the end of October.

   Wednesday from 7 to 2 some of the same farmers park on **Monument
Square** around the Civil War statue, *Our Lady of Victories,* in the middle of
the city on Congress Street, to sell bouquets, jars of honey, and produce.

Coffeehouses

Acoustic Coffee (207-774-0404), **32 Danforth Street.**
Open 8 AM–10 PM Monday through Wednesday, until 11 Thursday and Friday, 9 AM–11 PM Saturday, closed Sunday. Just up from the statue of Henry Ford

that directs traffic, a few slouchy upholstered chairs, a lot of wooden ones, and occasional music from local talent are all offered. Poets read their work here too on Tuesday—"Spoken Word" night. Good chai and fine coffee, of course.

My favorite coffeehouse is **Arabica (207-879-0792), 16 Free Street.**
Open Monday through Saturday 7–5, Sunday 8–1. The cappuccino is delicious and comes to your table, after you order at the counter, with beautiful patterns drawn in the milky foam on top, a signature of barista skillfulness that has always been standard at this long-lived coffeehouse. Chocolate cake with espresso icing, blueberry pie, and great cinnamon toast are served to the fortunate customers.

Breaking New Grounds (207-761-5637), 13 Exchange Street.

Open daily 7:30 AM–10 PM except Saturday and Sunday 8 AM–10 PM. A busy place on a summer night, or a winter one, and a good place to get homework done, or brood, or get a good cookie to do homework and brood while drinking tea or good coffee. Orange and lemon tea breads, rich pound-cake-like treats, and cookies and pastries also are sold here.

Coffee By Design (207-772-5533), 620 Congress Street.

Open Monday through Thursday, 6:30 AM–8 PM, Friday and Saturday 6:30 AM–9 PM, Sunday 7 AM–8 PM. A sister business at **67 India Street** closes one hour earlier on each of those days; Monday through Thursday, 6:30 AM–7 PM, Friday and Saturday 6:30 AM–8 PM, Sunday 7–7.

Very good coffee, and the changing art exhibits are usually startling or beautiful, or both.

Java Net Café (207-773-2469), 39 Exchange Street.

Open in summer, Monday through Friday 7 AM–10 PM, Saturday 8 AM–10 PM, Sunday 8–8; in the off-season, open Monday through Friday 7 AM–9 PM, Saturday 8 AM–9 PM, Sunday 8–8. A few computers are available to use while you drink a huge cup of tea or a reasonably sized cappuccino. Bagels, coffee cake, scones, and doughnuts are sold; in colder months you can get soups and sandwiches too.

And there is, of course, the ever-reliable **Starbucks, 176 Middle Street in the Old Port (207-761-2797)** and **594 Congress Street, next to the Portland Museum of Art (207-761-0334).**

Open Monday through Thursday 5:30 AM–10 PM, Friday and Saturday 6:30 AM–10:30 PM, Sunday 6:30 AM–8 PM. Winter hours may be a little shorter.

The Udder Place (207-780-6666), 428 Brighton Avenue.

Open 6 AM–5 PM Monday through Saturday, 7 AM–2 PM Sunday. A friend considers their cappuccino the best around. Vegan scones, bagels with many cream cheese spreads, muffins, cookies, and croissants.

Fish Markets

Browne Trading Company (207-775-7560, 1-800-944-7848; www.browne-trading.com), 262 Commercial Street at Merrill's Wharf.

Open Monday through Saturday 10–6:30. This place provides fish to the stars of the restaurant world. New York City restaurateur Daniel Boulud is quoted on the Web site, saying he relies on owner "Rod Mitchell's consistently superior products." You can see Boulud giving a spoonful of caviar the once over. If you visit the store on Commercial Street, you can get a freshly filleted piece of their extremely fresh fish for yourself, or some of the salmon smoked and packed here, another product sold in high-end markets in New York City. Or you can order fish, oysters, and other fresh foods for overnight delivery from the Web site. The retail store sells great cheese and wine too (see below) and has the advantage of being open a little later than some of the other places on Commercial Street.

Harbor Fish Market (207-775-0251, 207-772-6557, 1-800-370-1790; www.harborfish.com), 9 Custom House Wharf (across from the Custom House).

Open Monday through Saturday 8:30–5:30. More than 30 years in the business of selling fish and shellfish, this place is the picturesque storefront photographed in a favorite Portland postcard, and the destination of many, many holiday shoppers. An employee directs traffic as Christmas approaches, to keep the customers from arguing in the limited area off Commercial Street where you can park. Visitors can usually get a lobster displayed and can always buy as many as they want. In winter the eel tank draws in the curious. The crabmeat is fresh, the fish fabulous, and the employees courteous, even at the height of busy days.

Portland Lobster Pound and Fish Market (207-699-2400) Hobson's Wharf (behind Becky's Diner).
Open Monday through Saturday 9–6, Sunday 10–4. Lobster, clams, fish, and more.

Wine and Breweries

Allagash Brewing Company (207-878-5385, 1-800-330-5385; www.allagash.com), 100 Industrial Way.
Open Monday through Friday 10–4; tours are given Monday through Friday at 3. Brewing Belgian-style and experimental ales that will amaze your mouth, this brewery is raking in awards and praise for ales that have a creamy bubble. Some grow more wonderful over time. The reserve line uses *méthode champenoise,* with two fermentations, the second in the corked bottle. But the original Allagash White, a wheat beer with orange peel, coriander, and other spices giving it an uplifting aroma, is adored throughout Maine. Some brews are released only in the store. In spring 2007, for example, Allagash will begin selling Victor Ale, brewed with grapes, but only from the store at first. One new, yet-unnamed beer made with all-Maine hops also will be released in spring 2007.

Browne Trading Company (see above) stocks extraordinary wines from around the world. Collector wines, rare vintages, glorious burgundies and bordeaux can be found here, as can a wonderful bottle of 20-year-old port, and a couple of glasses to go with it, for a Christmas present. Tastings are held the last Thursday of every month.

The Clown (207-756-7399; www.the-clown.com), 123 Middle Street, with branches in Belfast and Stonington.
Open Monday through Wednesday 10–6, Thursday through Saturday 10–7. The Clown has a cellarful of good wine, with an emphasis on Italy, where the owners have a villa and bottle their own vintages. The knowledgeable clerks can guide you in the selection of a new wine, or help you understand the names, for instance, of the Portuguese possibilities. Glassware from Riedel, some of the best stemmed glasses for wine, is sold here. Upstairs is a gallery and collection of European ceramics and kitchenware. Wine tastings are held the first Thursday of every month.

D.L. Geary Brewing Company (207-878-2337; www.gearybrewing .com), 38 Evergreen Drive.

A small store is open 8–4 Monday through Friday. Tours are offered by appointment; call for a reservation. The 20th anniversary of this brewery was December 12, 2006. Special brews released for this event may reappear bottled, in the store or at the local pub, in the future. Hampshire Ale, with a flavor full of hops and toasted malt, is a perennial favorite.

Gritty McDuff's Brewing Company (207-772-BREW), 396 Fore Street.

The first brewpub opened in Maine since prohibition—the Web site proclaims—and still a vibrant center of conversation, raucous, gentle, and in between. The copper-top bar is a beloved spot for an ale after work and on weekends. The Gritty's ales fermenting in the copper-domed brew kettle, visible from Wharf Street, are their five standards, including Black Fly Stout. Bar food, chili, sandwiches, and roll-ups are on the menu.

Rosemont Market and Bakery (207-774-8129), 559 Brighton Avenue.

Open Monday through Saturday 8–6, Sunday 9–4. This is my favorite wine store. Wine tastings are held on one Friday of each month and are often real parties, with the market's terrific focaccia to munch on for free, or someone else's handmade chocolates; call for times. Co-owner John Naylor prides himself on his well-priced wines. The big cupboard facing the front of the store is filled with inexpensive and delicious choices—"good value wine buys," Naylor calls them, mostly under $10 and often from France and Italy. Other shelves around the back walls hold niches of Portuguese and South African wines, as well as German, Austrian, Argentinean, and American wines, all well worth trying. If it's sold in Maine, it tastes good, and doesn't cost the moon, you can bet on encountering it here, often for a dollar or two less than elsewhere.

Shipyard Brewing (1-800-273-9253), 80 Newbury Street.

The store is at 86 Newbury Street. Tours Monday through Saturday beginning at 12, every hour until 4. Store hours Monday through Saturday 10–5, Sunday 12–5. Check for different tour hours in the summer. Among 13 varieties of ales, Maine's biggest brewery makes deservedly popular Shipyard Export Ale. It got its start in 1994 at Federal Jack's in Kennebunk. The Old Thumper Ale is a good bitter; Shipyard Pumpkinhead, brewed at Halloween, won third place for fruit beer at California's Brewers Festival in 2006.

Specialty Items, Chocolate, Jams, and Ice Cream

Beals Gourmet Ice Cream (207-883-1160; www.bealsicecream.com). Two Portland locations: 12 Moulton Street, in the Old Port, and 18 Veranda Street, just off Washington Avenue.

Banana Cream Pie and Cappuccino Crunch are just two of the dozens of flavors from which to choose. The Old Port location is a great spot for people-watching in summer, with a few picnic tables; air-conditioning inside makes it a refuge in the hot weather.

Fuller's Gourmet Chocolates and Ice Cream (207-253-8010), 43 Wharf Street.

In summer open weekdays 11–10, weekends 11–11; in the off-season open weekdays 11–6, weekends 11–8. Fuller's ice cream is made with Hood milk; it has 16 percent butterfat and comes in Mud Pie Slide, Coconut, Cherry Chip, Ginger, Rum Raisin, and Black Raspberry, to name a few. In summer, Susan Fuller makes 32 flavors, and you can enjoy them at tables outside. She also makes all the chocolate, and that includes truffles, turtles, caramels, and clusters. The large truffles, especially the Baileys Irish Cream, Grand Marnier, and Kahlúa, are favorites.

Maine's Pantry (207-228-2028, 1-877-228-2028; www.maines pantry.com), 111 Commercial Street.

This is the best source for the finest Maine products. Guzman's Cranapple Salsa, Stanchfield Farms Strawberry Jam, and pancake mixes and blueberry syrup from Stonewall Kitchen are a few possibilities. The Key lime garlic tartar sauce from Maine Chefs can't be beat, and their Wasabi Cocktail Blaze would be unbeatable with boiled shrimp. Don't bother with the tacky souvenirs when a jar of Swan's Wild Blueberry Creamed Honey, for instance, will please the folks back home so much more. Baskets are put together creatively, and can be shipped anywhere.

Saco

Lily Moon Café
(207) 284-2233
17 Pepperell Square, just off Main Street (Route 1)
Hospitality—Very helpful, attentive, and eager to please
Open for breakfast and lunch Tuesday through Sunday, dinner Wednesday through Saturday
Entrées $17 to $22
BYO wine

 A quiet little place with charm and good meals

The friendly space here is filled with white-painted wooden chairs at wood tables set on black and white squares of linoleum, with a few upholstered booths. Spanish guitar music pleases the ears; bring a bottle of wine from the outside (the café will provide you with glasses). This charming place was built with the help of a whole community after the first Lily Moon burned down on Mother's Day, 2003. Despite more trouble from an absconding accountant, it looks like the community, in the form of repeat customers, won't let them down.

We chose a couple of dishes served on angel-hair pasta on the cold night of our visit. Shrimp scampi ($17.95), with a light sauce of cream, tomato, and red peppers, came in a large bowl with a side of sautéed vegetables and a small slice of cantaloupe. The sauce was indeed light, as described on the menu, and the snow of grated Parmesan made a salty, flavorful crust on the fresh shrimp.

The chicken primavera, with marinara and Parmesan, was delicious, with tender slices of chicken breast made savory with the cheese and the tomato sauce ($16.95).

Other entrées included a caramelized salmon filet ($17.95), a blackened Jack Daniels rib eye ($19.95), and Tournedos McCallum ($22), filet mignon served on baguette croutons with cabernet demi-glace and grilled shrimp.

A creamy cheesecake is topped with fresh strawberries or blueberries ($4.95 for all desserts), and a chocolate dessert is made with layers of cake and mousse. Lemon meringue pie is always on the dessert list.

Coffeehouses and Desserts

Milliken House (207-283-9691; www.millikenhouse.com), 65 North Street.

Open Tuesday through Saturday 4 PM–10 PM in summer; closed Sunday and Monday from May to Labor Day. From Labor Day to mid-December, open Friday and Saturday 2 PM–10 PM. The couple who bought this house in 1998, Lisa and David Norburg, has restored its interiors from "1960s revival" to the Victorian splendor of its 1877 birthright. And 1877 is the year they want you to think you have returned to when you step inside for a dessert and a cup of tea or coffee. The servers are dressed like parlor maids and curtsy when they greet you. Lisa Norburg sometimes wears a gown based on a design by Charles Worth of Paris, haute couture of the period and perfect for Christmas teas.

Soup and bread make a small meal, but the real focus is on tea and dessert. The menu features Tower of Babel ($5.45), four layers of fudge cake with chocolate icing, and Gâteau Lemon, three layers of lemon cake with raspberry-peach filling ($4.50), and many other cakes and pastries, along with ice cream, coffee, and tea. The house silverware is ornate and heavy, the tables in the front parlors are set with linen, and the whole feeling here is formal, but with a sense of humor. The fellow in the foyer, Elias, will shake if he's plugged in, but apparently that freaked out too many people—he looks awfully real. A gift shop in the house contributes any profits to missions around the world.

Farmer's Market

You can buy glass-bottled milk, maple syrup, and, of course, corn, apples, and tomatoes in-season Tuesday and Saturday 7 AM–noon, mid-May until the end of October, at the **Saco Farmers Market (www.sacofarmersmarket.com)** in the Valley Shopping Center.

Scarborough

Black Point Inn
(207) 883-2500, 1-800-258-0003
510 Black Point Road
www.blackpointinn.com
Hospitality—Comfortable and formal
Open daily for dinner 6–9:30
Entrées $16 to $36

☛ *An old hotel with an uneven history in its dining rooms*

A cocktail on the long, wide porch overlooking one of Scarborough's best clam flats would be appropriate before dinner—if it's dark or raining, the small bar is fine; better yet are the upholstered couches of the lobby, in front of the big fireplace. In any event, along with the gin and tonic in its heavy glass you can drink in the old-world surroundings and catch up with your fellow guests.

Inside the large, carpeted dining room, tables are swathed in smooth white linen. The capable staff have gratified every inclination for food and drink on our visits over the years, but in 2006 the food was disappointing.

A change in management in the works in late 2006 makes it likely disappointment will end. Although no menus were available before this book went to press, the new management company's stellar work in other restaurants in Maine, like The Edge in Lincolnville (see page 187) and the dining room at inland Migis Lodge, augurs well for the folks in Scarborough. Check out the inn's Web site for up-to-date details.

The Downs Club Restaurant
(207) 883-4331
State Road, off Route 1
www.scarboroughdowns.com
Hospitality—Up or down, depending on your luck
Open for dinner at 6 PM April through September on race days; call about race times.
Entrées $16 to $23; Wednesday and Friday might still be two-for-one nights ($21).

☛ *A meal served while you gamble on your favorites and watch the races*

All right, this is not the best food in the world. In fact, some of it is downright awful. But most of it is reasonably edible, and you won't be paying much attention anyway, because your focus is on the race. Order your filet mignon ($20.99) with béarnaise sauce, but don't go for the seafood casserole ($20.99) unless your need for cream sauce renders you irrational. And then order another drink, because you've already swallowed the first too quickly in order to hop up the stairs—the tables are set along ascending rows, so everyone can see out the huge windows to the racetrack—to get your bet in on the first race. The daily double will be coming up, so you have another chance in a few minutes, and beginners have a strange knack of picking winners, even when they have no clue about how to read the arcane racing bill. You watch the odds changing on the sign across the track as the bets are placed and the system recalculates. It's so much fun to win an exotic wager, like the exacta for two horses winning first and second in the order you tell the bet taker at the top of those stairs; or the perfecta for first, second, and third; or the four finishers in the superfecta—fun because the odds are astronomical, sometimes as high as 100 to 1, and more, and less, and almost never achieved. The minimum bet is $2. Seasoned bettors do not try to win the superfecta, but you are not a seasoned bettor, so what the hell. Dinner slowly cools on the plate you're ignoring as the horses round the far turn. Is that your horse in the lead? The restaurant is spellbound, the groans rise from the tables, the tension flares, people shout out—and it's over, and you can't believe it; you won the daily double.

It happens all the time.

First and Last Tavern
(207) 883-8383
240 Pine Point Road
Hospitality—friendly, and on top of everything; the service here is great
Open nightly except Monday in summer, fewer days off-season; closed
January through April
Entrées $10 to $17
Handicapped accessible, reservations recommended

☛ *Wonderful pizza and Italian classics, fresh salads, and good wines make dinner here comfortable and delicious.*

This restaurant is a sibling to others of the same name in Connecticut, serving a popular selection of honed Italian meals, chewy and crusty fresh-baked bread from a recipe that has been perfected over years of fine tuning, terrific pizzas, and good desserts. The one in Avon, Connecticut, won a Zagat's "Top Italian Restaurant in America" vote. Since the owner of the one in Maine is using the recipes of her brother's place in Hartford, you can be sure the food is thought out and good.

Mike Iyer, the chef in Scarborough, is a scrupulous cleaner, a neatnik with an obsession for freshly prepared ingredients and high quality.

Eggplant marinara, mussels cooked with white wine and garlic or with red sauce, and fried calamari are a few of the appetizers. Fresh mozzarella and tomato salad is here in late summer, with ripe tomatoes.

Among the pizzas are the Neapolitan ($10 for a small, $16 for a large), with sliced tomatoes, basil, and mozzarella, and the artichoke and chicken pizza ($12, $19). Chris Iyer, one of the hosts at this family-owned restaurant, likes the spinach pizza best.

Calamari *fra diavolo* is tender squid cooked in a spicy marinara ($15.95) and served on linguine.

Shells with a meatball, a sausage, and a salad, all on the same plate ($11) is called The Original Special. Chris, who also bakes the bread and does some other baking, makes a delicious spinach pasta lasagna as a fresh pasta special, with béchamel and Bolognese.

Homemade gelato ($4.95) comes in vanilla, chocolate, and cappuccino, plus varying specialty flavors.

Ken's Place
(207) 883-6611
207 Pine Point Road (Route 9)
Hospitality—Fast counter service in an immaculate, simple dining room
Open daily for lunch and dinner April through the third week in October at 11 AM
Inexpensive

☛ *Squeaky clean, from the floors to the oil that fries the fish, with high-quality seafood classics*

Ken's Place, around since 1927 and owned by David Wilcox since 2000, gets plenty crowded in the height of summer; but you can count on Wilcox's crazy energy to keep the freshest, best-quality seafood coming and the place in order.

This is a classic seafood place, with windowed counters at which to order and big menus up on the wall to contemplate during the wait in line. The fried clams, with either crumbs or batter, were $16.95 (a pint is $14.50) when we visited; dug from nearby clam flats, they were the best we'd had in years. Fried onion rings ranked above the french fries, the chowder is a past prizewinner, and fish, boiled lobsters, and fried scallops and shrimp vie with the clams for first choice.

Some customers buy the clam cakes by the dozen. They put them in the toaster for breakfast, according to Wilcox.

A lobster roll is $10.99, with 3 ounces of lobster served on a buttered, toasted hot dog roll, and the meat is picked here; frozen processed lobster is not used. Haddock is cut right off the boat on the morning it arrives; "It's extremely fresh," Wilcox said.

Wilcox insists on the freshest seafood and noted that one supplier called to say he wouldn't bother to bring what was available, because it wasn't going to meet Wilcox's standards. "I've thrown out hundreds of dollars of seafood," Wilcox said.

He added that he rotates, filters, and recycles the oil in his six fry kettles daily, and that was clear from the taste of the food, which had no overtones of anything but the fresh clams of which it was made.

A raw bar and beer and wine are available in a corner of the dining room.

Wilcox has some rules—you can't come in without a shirt on, and we saw him usher a visitor out during our dinner. But tables are spread out the front and side lawns for warm nights and summer days, and customers who don't want to put on their shirts are welcome there.

The neatness in the dining room made the casual dining more pleasant than usual, but the high standards for the food itself will get us to come back, just as they do the regulars and summer repeats who make a line out the front door in July and August.

Specialty and Fish Markets

Bayley's Lobster Pound (207-883-4571), corner of Jones Creek Drive before the lobster co-op, Pine Point.

Open Sunday through Thursday 9–5; Friday and Saturday 9–6, until 5 in the off-season. Also a takeout, this place sells lobsters and cooks them free of charge. Selling both wholesale and retail, they also sell clams, haddock, and other fish. Lobster, shrimp, and crab rolls are sold inside.

The Cheese Iron (207-883-6917; www.thecheeseiron.com), 200 Route 1.

Opened in summer 2006, The Cheese Iron holds the area's first cheese cave, where cheeses from around the world slowly ripen to perfection. Vincent Manciaci delves into the wheels of Manchego and others with his slender cheese iron to test their maturity, replacing the sample if the cheese is not yet ready, or bringing the wheel out to the case if it is. Jill Dutton, his partner, also runs this lovely store, full of fine chocolates and good wine. For a wonderful treat, ask about cheese and wine pairings, and take home something worth lingering over. Sandwiches are made here with Italian meats like prosciutto, and you can also find olives and a delicious single estate coffee.

Pine Point Fishermen's Co-op (207-883-3588), 96 King Street, Pine Point.

Open in summer Monday through Sunday 10–7, off-season until 6. Although the retail store closes in the middle of winter, anyone can come and get a lobster year-round. This is the place the local clam diggers bring their clams, and the boats deliver their loads of lobsters. This is the place to get fresh seafood.

South Portland

One Fifty Ate
(207) 799-8998
158 Benjamin W. Pickett Street
Hospitality—Friendly counter service in an informal room and backyard
Open for breakfast and lunch Tuesday through Sunday 7–2
Lunch items $4.50 to $6.50

☞ *My absolute favorite lunch place, with great soup and fine sandwiches*

This place was my refuge from everything harsh and demanding one year when I ate lunch here two or three times every week. Although I might have started going because the soup's price was right, I ended up staying because the cooks were showing my palette all kinds of things it needed to know, like the splendor of big chunks of salty bacon in a thick black bean soup, or the taste of the best tomatoes when they first come off the vines this far north, sometime in August.

The bagels are renowned. Misshapen, big, and chewy, they wear poppy seeds, sesame seeds, and "everything," including fennel and sunflower seeds. People who want to buy a dozen or more are sent down the road to the branch

Come to One Fifty Ate for the best bagels in town, along with salads, good soups, and sandwiches.

bakery and deli in Willard Square, now called Scratch Baking Company (see page 112), because the café needs a selection to make the bagel and egg, bagel and egg and cheese, and bagel and egg and ham and cheese ($4.50) sandwiches that light up the breakfast hours. There's also Lefty's Granola Funk Express ($3.50). Come lunch, 11:30–2, soups are served with a big chunk of bread according to the lights in the kitchen, always right on.

Sandwiches include turkey with green goddess dressing, local greens, and sunflower seeds ($6.50), or salami, provolone, and tapenade ($6.25). I still hunger for the smoked turkey with pear chutney that showed up on the chalkboard one fall. A cold rice-noodle salad was on the seasonal menu in summer, with carrots, cabbage, and onions in a peanut dressing ($5.50). And the plain egg salad with a touch of mustard was great on that levain.

The coffee reigns supreme, even under the assault of ice, and could suck you into a slice of the cake sitting on the counter, or one of the other great pastries everyone else was snatching up as you watched anxiously during lunch.

Bakeries and Takeout

The Buttered Biscuit (207-799-5005), 347 Cottage Road.

Open Monday through Friday 10–7:30, Saturday 10–6. Strictly takeout, the Buttered Biscuit can provide you with every course of a great meal. Sesame noodle salad and other dishes show off in the cooler, and boxed chicken potpies sit in the refrigerator case every Wednesday. Other dishes vary; Hungarian mushroom soup gives way to tomato soup in late summer. The freezer holds artichoke dip, lasagna, and meat loaf; and the baked goods include date bars, brownies, and delectable almond moons. Everything is homemade, made from scratch, with a menu changing daily.

Scratch Baking Company (207-799-0668), 416 Preble Street.

Open Tuesday through Friday 6–6, Saturday 7–6, Sunday 7–12. This bakery and deli sells a variety of delectable cheeses and sausages. Its Molinari and Sons *sopressata,* air-cured and "so damn good," sells for $8.49 a pound. The cooler also had some Humboldt Fog, a fabulous California aged goat cheese covered with a layer of vegetable ash, and Vermont Butter & Cheese Company's cultured butter. On the counter stood lavender shortbread and individual lemon pound cakes with blueberries, along with breads and bagels. Tuesday you can find wheat levain and pumpernickel, Wednesday and Friday multigrain—among others.

The South Portland Farmer's Market is held on Friday noon–4 from early

May to late October in the Maine Mall parking lot off Philbrook Road, across from Romano's Macaroni Grill.

Yarmouth

Royal River Grill House
(207) 846-1226
106 Lafayette Street
www.royalrivergrillhouse.com
Hospitality—Well-trained and adept
Open for lunch Monday through Saturday 11:30–2:30, Sunday brunch
11:30–2:30, dinner daily 5–9
Entrées $18 to $39

☛ *A local favorite for an upscale lunch, and for making a dinner out of a couple of appetizers*

With a pretty setting on the Royal River along the waterfront in Yarmouth, this spacious restaurant keeps the meals inventive and fresh. A married couple I know likes to come here and make dinner out of a couple of appetizers, choosing from a changing list of items such as duck confit and apple and walnut salad ($10), and fresh mozzarella and heirloom tomato salad ($10), or sautéed Prince Edward Island mussels with garlic herb butter, tomatoes, and Vidalia onions ($12). The crabcakes with the roasted red pepper aioli are good, too ($12). Entrées also are enticing, like a West Coast cioppino ($19) with mussels, shrimp, calamari, and scallops in tomato broth over pasta, as well as many steaks. The wine list stretches the envelope with unusual bottles, many in the $20 range, and several up over $100. Either strawberry shortcake ($6) or Smiling Hill Farm Ice Cream ($4.50) would make a great dessert.

SeaGrass Bistro
(207) 846-3885
30 Forest Falls Drive
www.seagrassbistro.com
Open for dinner Tuesday through Saturday from 5:30
Entrées $22 to $28
Handicapped accessible, reservations recommended

☛ *The local farm's best produce and a local woman's best work combine for fabulous dinners.*

Stephanie Brown opened this sleek spot in 2005, and has been cooking heavenly vegetables, meats, and fish ever since. Some object to the space, because the noise can ricochet off the hard surfaces. But otherwise, with fine service and friendliness all 'round, how can you not have fun? A good wine list can get you started off right, with long, crisp thin cheese bread sticks to enjoy while you contemplate your order.

I fell for the grilled vegetables and goat cheese in a crisp phyllo crust ($22) with its sublime contrasting of charcoal notes and goat cheese's tart creaminess. A base of roasted kale and huge yellow butter beans in a butter sauce made this feel like a garden on a plate. Vegetables, often afterthoughts, play some of Brown's leading roles. Salads are fresh and inventive, and side vegetables are cooked precisely, neither too crisp nor overdone.

In winter it would be hard to resist pork ribs and hot Italian sausage braised with roasted tomatoes and red wine on angel-hair pasta ($24). The short ribs are smoked in-house with hickory, lashed with molasses and brown sugar, and set on pureed parsnips ($22).

And don't neglect the desserts, like butter pecan ice cream with hot fudge sauce ($5) or perhaps a lemon curd napoleon ($7). Lucky you!

Lunch, Markets, and Takeout

Day's Crabmeat and Lobster (207-846-3436, 207-846-5871), 1269 Route 1.

In summer the take-out window is open Monday through Saturday 11–8, the lobster pound Monday through Saturday 8–5 and Sunday 8–3; shorter hours for both off-season.

This is the place for fresh crabmeat, steamed lobster, and crab and lobster rolls for a picnic at a table behind the business or on your sailboat—ordered from the take-out window. The crabmeat is picked by hand on-site, and one person I know who is a stickler for fresh won't buy it anywhere else. Crabmeat rolls were $9.30 with tax in summer 2006, and a full menu of fried fish (and the inevitable hot dog for that unbeliever) filled the rest of a big board by the window. Ten picnic tables sit behind the building along a marsh and its tidal river, and a few more are under an awning on the side.

You can also buy fresh lobsters to take home and cook or ship out.

Haggerty's Cafe (207-846-0488), 189 Main Street.

Open Monday through Friday 7–6, Saturday 8–2. This business got off to a popular start in 2006 with its array of local products, like Maine goat cheese and Laughing Stock Farm greens. But since it puts those things to such good use in sandwiches, wraps, and soups, as well as prepared dinners, residents have been giving it good business year-round.

Roast lamb can be had in a salad and in a sandwich, and can also be taken home for dinner. Espresso and other coffee drinks are served here, along with croissants and scones. Wine, beer, and bottled juice, too.

The Rosemont Market and Bakery in Yarmouth (207-846-1234), 96 Main Street.

Open 8–6 Monday through Saturday. Like its mothership, Rosemont Market and Bakery in Portland (see page 97), this store stocks a wide selection of local produce, fresh-baked bread, fabulous wine at reasonable prices, and wonderful cheese. Olives, olive oil, cookies and pastries, chestnuts at Thanksgiving—all the good things in life are here.

CHAPTER 3

Brunswick and Bath

WITH THESE TWO LARGER TOWNS along Route 1, the Maine coast begins its unique, glacial topography of long peninsulas stretched south like fingers reaching into the sea. The persistent, unchanging, and unchangeable rural character of the coast develops from this geography, where it really is awkward to "get there from here."

If you miss a turn, for instance—and some of the turnoffs are so discreet they are very hard to see—or if you turn south on the wrong road, you can find yourself a long drive away from a destination that you can see close by, lying across a stretch of water.

But the roads to the Harpswells, and to Georgetown and Robinhood and Cundy's Harbor and Phippsburg, all scenic, all with fine Maine seafood places tucked into their harbors, are all well-marked. Be sure to study the map before driving through Bath, however.

If you can afford the greatest luxury of aimlessness on your vacation or your Sunday drive, going down any of the roads that lead to water south of Route 1 can be a pleasure. The landscape and the water are lovely. You will likely find one or more of Maine's charming seafood places; all seem like classics to the people with the good luck to be able to live near them. They vary in atmosphere from as plain as the deck of a wharf to full-service casual, but the best ones are still making their own desserts, picking their own lobster meat, and buying clams from somebody who digs them nearby.

For dinner at a more elegant destination, like the Robinhood Free Meetinghouse (see the Georgetown section), you will probably need a reservation; but it's worth a chance if you're nearby to stop and find out if there's a table. The chefs who succeed at drawing their customers off the main highway are proven talents, and Robinhood's Michael Gagne has been drawing us in for years. Down winding Route 144 you'll find an elegant old inn, the Squire Tarbox, serving good meals under ships' beams.

Several of the talents in Brunswick and Bath also have our allegiance. In Brunswick, graced with Bowdoin College's elegant campus and its art and arctic museums, Henry and Marty's and the Back Street Bistro both make such good dinners that they are worth a long drive.

In Bath, standing under the tall cranes of its largest employer, Bath Iron Works, the latest company to make this city one of the East Coast's important shipbuilding ports, MaryEllenz Caffé and Mae's Café have their ardent fans.

Bailey Island

Cook's Lobster House
(207) 833-2818
Route 24
www.cookslobster.com
Open daily for lunch and dinner 11:30–10, reduced hours off-season
Entrées $7 to $30
Handicapped accessible

☛ *A giant seafood restaurant with water all around, and excellent pies*

This place doesn't do only one shore dinner—it does four. The first and traditional shore dinner includes chowder or lobster stew, steamed clams or mussels, a boiled lobster, salad, and potato. From there you could opt for fried Maine shrimp or fried clams instead of steamed clams or mussels, or exchange the boiled lobster for a baked stuffed lobster, or choose both, fried clams or shrimp and the baked stuffed lobster, for somewhere north of $40.

The old interior is full of glossy golden pine tables and photos of fishermen, and the deck outside the bar has a great view.

From late June until Labor Day, Casco Bay Lines schedules a ferry from Portland that arrives here at noon, delivering people to eat lunch and taking other people away for an hour-long nature tour among the islands. If you are worried about arriving just as three busloads of tourists dock, call ahead and ask how lunch looks.

Clams are bought from local diggers who visit Look Out Cove, Merrymeeting Bay, and other nearby areas to dig the flats. The steamers are excellent ($10.95 for a small bowl). The fried clam dinner is $15.95 when you order from the "lighter side" of the menu, and plenty big enough for almost all of us. With a crunchy but light crumb coating and impeccable freshness, these clams rate as some of the best you can find on the coast. The chicken sandwiches, however, do not.

The raspberry pie and the blueberry pie were jammed with tart fruit inside flaky crust, worth every calorie. Desserts are made in-house, with strawberry shortcake, cheesecake, apple crisp, carrot cake, and ice cream also on the list.

With 40 tables, each of which can handle six people, this place can absorb several busloads. A wharf next door, where lobstermen deliver during the day, sells live lobsters that can be shipped.

Bath

Beale Street Barbeque and Grill

(207) 442-9514
215 Water Street
www.mainebbq.com
Open daily for lunch and dinner 11–9, Friday and Saturday until 10
Entrées $6 to $18

☛ *Casual barbecue in a laid-back atmosphere*

Mark, Michael, and Patrick Quigg started things here 1996, and now Michael and Patrick run this long-standing barbecue place that serves pulled pork, pulled chicken, beef brisket, and slabs of hickory-smoked ribs. You can choose a couple of sides, including coleslaw, barbecued beans, french fries, and rice, along with a bun or jalapeño corn bread. There is also a sampler platter that heaps up a choice of pulled pork, chicken, or beef brisket with a half slab of ribs, a quarter of a chicken, and smoked sausage. Jambalaya, fish of the day, shrimp Louisianne, and *penne al pesto* offer some respite from the barbecue. This 50-seat restaurant in an old building in downtown Bath has checkerboard floors, and booths and tables.

Desserts feature Key lime pie, and a chocolate special called The Terminator ($4.29) that features a cakelike, dense chocolate terrine.

Mae's Café

(207) 442-8577
160 Centre Street
www.maescafeandbakery.com
Open for breakfast, lunch, and dinner Tuesday through Saturday 8 AM–9 PM, Sunday 8 AM–2 PM; closed for one week after January 1
Dinner entrées $14 to $21

☛ *All three meals with a wide choice from a large menu, and excellent baked goods*

Mae's Café, formerly Kristina's, has been hopping since July 2004, when Katie and Andy Winglass began running things. The bakery staff that operate the ovens also bake the "world's best sticky buns," as Katie Winglass called them, along with the pies, scones, dinner rolls, and biscuits that come with every dinner entrée.

The restaurant serves an enormous breakfast, with big omelets, Belgian waffles, and cinnamon twist bread made especially for French toast, or just plain eggs and bacon. Wireless Internet access works well with the espresso in this big place that can seat 120, constructed from two old farmhouses joined together.

Lunch includes fresh calzones like The Carleton, with pesto, grilled vegetables, and provolone, and large salads.

Dinner should at least once in a while start with fresh oysters on the half shell, and could go on to grilled hanger steak with balsamic reduction and Gorgonzola. Roasted duck breast with blueberry and ginger pan sauce, or roasted vegetable ravioli, are among the dinner-menu highlights.

A *dacquoise* made with chocolate cake and toasted hazelnut meringue is layered with mocha buttercream and dark chocolate ganache—something to consider splitting indeed. Of course, the bakery makes many kinds of pie.

It sounds like the annual Bath Heritage Days Blueberry Pie Eating contest, which takes place around the Fourth of July, is a lot of fun here, with people signed up by friends and police officers doing their best to prevail. If you win you receive a free 9-inch pie of your choice.

MaryEllenz Caffé
(207) 442-0960
15 Vine Street
www.maryellenz.com
Open for lunch Monday through Friday 11:30–2:30, tapas until 5:30, and dinner Monday through Saturday 5:30–8:30 or closing
Entrées $8 to $25
Reservations recommended, especially on weekends

☛ *A casually elegant dinner place with an Italian bent*

A beautiful, big new space houses MaryEllenz Caffé, owned by Mary Ellen Hunt and Mary-Ellen Pecci. They opened in a smaller spot in 2000 with an emphasis on Italian from Hunt's close acquaintance with an Italian restaurant in Florida, and because Bath, as Hunt said, "could stand a different kind of restaurant." It's proved true.

With their new digs, they have also given Bath sophisticated tapas, and a martini bar with an upbeat, urban feeling. From 2:30 PM onward you can enjoy tapas like an Asian veggie pancake or spanikopita ($5), beef empanadas ($5), or lobster and artichoke bruschetta ($6). Chilled Manzanilla, a wonderful dry sherry, can be found here for a traditional pour.

Lunch offers a vegan sandwich with hummus, cucumber, tomato, and asparagus ($7); a BLT with Canadian bacon ($7); daily soups, like a cold raspberry-rhubarb soup in summer; and crabcakes. A small serving of the four-cheese lasagna that is a favorite at dinner is also on the list.

Chicken salad is highly thought of here, the meat cut in cubes, and combined with celery, sweet onion, pesto, and sun-dried tomatoes.

Four dinner classics are in charge. Spaghetti carbonara ($15) is made with cream, prosciutto, onion, and Fontina—the MaryEllenz version does not use raw egg. Shrimp scampi ($20) is served over pasta. White zuppa di pesce ($25) holds lobster, shrimp, haddock, calamari, and clams in a white wine, garlic, and tomato broth. And the chicken saltimbocca ($20) will leap into your mouth.

Prices for wine here are exceptionally modest. Pecci calls the inexpensive glasses and bottles "Good business," and who can disagree? The wine list offers wines from Australia, France, Italy, and California ($18–30 per bottle). Everything is available by the glass ($5–7).

Tiramisu, made to order; chocolate chocolate pie; and Swedish Cream (a *panna cotta* with a berry sauce) come at the end of the good meals.

Mateo's Hacienda, A Mexican Kitchen
(207) 443-3511
56 Centre Street
www.mateoshacienda.com
Open Monday through Saturday 11 AM-8 PM
No credit cards

☛ *Dishes unusual to Maine are fresh, always new, and made with authentic Mexican recipes*

With beef, pork, and chicken locally raised, and as much else from surrounding farms as he can find, chef Matthew Sanderson has made a fine resource for people on the coast who crave something with spicy, Mexican flavors. Burritos are stuffed with *rajas de poblana* ($5.25), strips of poblano chilies, onions, and tomatoes along with beans, rice, salsa, tomato, lettuce, and cheese, or with those same fixings and marinated steak ($5.75).

A special quesadilla came with squash blossom; from the regular menu, quesadillas are available with a choice of fillings from the same list as the burritos.

Salsas like Mango Fuego, "wicked hot," or chipotle, medium hot, vary the intensity.

The Carnitos Tacos ($2.25)—topped with cheese, raw onions, cilantro, and salsa verde—are what Sanderson calls "authentic street food."

Solo Bistro

(207) 443-3373
128 Front Street
www.solobistro.com
Hospitality—Perfectly accommodating
Open for dinner Monday through Saturday from 5 PM
Entrées $18 to $25

☛ *Upscale design and well-organized dishes create a sophisticated dinner spot.*

Of course there is hanger steak ($18), with horseradish mashed potatoes and grilled scallion butter adding unique touches, but some of the pleasure here is the atmosphere: sleek steel, glass, and colorful modern chairs. The owners' neighboring Danish design store supplied some of the restaurant's decor, like the Jorge Pensi orange, blue, and green "bikini chairs."

A wide selection of wines taste particularly good in large glasses. And even though we managed to break one of them, by accident, our waiter sustained his patience and consideration.

Elaborate salads, one with a large piece of French goat cheese and giant toasted pecans called Solo Greens ($9), made a memorable start. The crabcakes ($12) a special, were well-made too; and a wild salmon appetizer ($10) arranges smoked salmon on light creamy goat cheese on top of a crisp potato pancake.

COURTESY OF SOLO BISTRO

Solo Bistro, in Bath, has a hip, sunny interior

Crispy salmon ($24), organic fish from Canada, was nicely cooked and accompanied by haricots verts and Israeli couscous that, out of this kitchen, atypically tasted great in a savory sauce. Chicken mole ($24) on more of that couscous had been concocted with a sauce of peanut butter, cocoa, chicken stock, herbs, peppers, and cumin.

Desserts like crème caramel, and warm apple and frangipane galette ($8) wooed us all over again, with fresh flavor and richness. Off another menu, the chocolate bread pudding with ginger and buttermilk mango sherbet sounds like it would do the same.

Starlight Café
(207) 443-3005
15 Lambard Street
Open for breakfast and lunch Monday through Friday 7–2, Saturday 7–11
Lunch $3 to $9

☛ *A great place for breakfast and lunch*

Almost everything here is made from scratch, including the vegetable soup with its huge list of ingredients, curried squash soup, spicy black bean soup with smoked ham, and the spicy chili. A turkey is roasted in the oven every day, and green onion garlic rolls and others are baked every day as well. Those and Borealis Breads are used for the sandwiches. Desserts—bars and cakes and pies and brownies—are fresh, too. "Big as your head" cinnamon buns, just over a dollar, are baked every morning. "They're our thing… they're not really big as your head, but big as your fist," Angie Edgecomb, the owner, said proudly. She took over in May 2006 and now also does catering. She has added bread pudding, grapenut custard, and other old New England desserts to her popular menu.

Market, Farms, and Coffeehouse

Bath Natural Market (207-442-8012), 36 Centre Street.
Open Monday through Friday 9–6, Saturday 9–5, and Sunday 9–4. With value wines at $4.49 a bottle and a wide selection of others priced not a lot higher, this store's wine section is a find. Mark Schoninger has the largest selection of organic wine in Maine. You can find products from Borealis Breads, Black Crow Bread, and Tuva Bakery —winner of the Common Ground Fair's 2006 Best of Show award—Coffee By Design beans, and a big display of Oyster Creek dried mushrooms.

One fall Sunday, Schoninger listed farms providing produce here: Morning Dew Farm offers mesclun with flowers, baby kale, basil, garlic, and romaine; Sparrow Farm in Pittston stocks scallions, delicata squash, and cranberries. Squire Tarbox Farm in Westport provides arugula and intends to grow it year-round in a greenhouse. Blueberry Ledge Farm in East Pittston provides green beans, too, and there's Maine-ly Poultry chicken, Caldwell Farm beef, and Post Family Farm raw milk.

Café Crème (207-443-6454), 56 Front Street.

Open Monday through Saturday 7:30 AM–8:30 PM, 8:30 AM–4:30 PM on Sunday. Serving Maine's Coffee By Design coffee and espresso, and Smiling Hill Farm Ice Cream. Every morning the Hardcover Café at Brunswick's Bookland (see below) delivers cookies, muffins, cinnamon buns, stuffed croissants, brownies, date bars, and dream bars, and lasagna for lunch; Mr. Bagel delivers bagels. Lunches, from quiches and burritos to salads, take care of the crowd at this busy place. Sushi is served daily except Saturday and Sunday from Kiyo Kim in Brunswick. Whoopie pies and Needham Candies, made in Georgetown, are perfect treats.

The Bath Farmer's Market is held Thursday 8:30–2:30 and Saturday and Sunday 8–12, May through October, at Waterfront Park behind Main Street in Bath. **Goranson Farm** sells from their huge array of produce here, including a wide selection of winter squash and root vegetables, which can be purchased at their farm stand at **250 River Road in Dresden,** too, along with their fine maple syrup.

Brunswick

Back Street Bistro
(207) 725-4060
11 Town Hall Place (just off Maine Street)
Hospitality—A wonderful atmosphere prevails in this well-run place.
Open at 5 daily for dinner
Entrées $16 to $20
Handicapped accessible, reservations recommended

☞ *Snappy concoctions and seasonal ingredients make for good dinners.*

From the upstairs deck you might be able to watch the firefighters at the next door fire station play catch—and glancing up for a little admiration after a tricky catch.

Another attraction will be the chewy bread, fragrant olive oil, and a good glass of wine.

Salads won my heart here, with spinach and prosciutto, cantaloupe, and grapes under pink peppercorns and a serving of smooth chèvre ($8).

Seafood gumbo ($16), a large bowl full of shrimp, mussels, lobster, bay scallops, and escolar, held a thick spicy soup that earned its unctuousness with bits of dissolving okra. Its andouille might have been spicier, but everything else was perfect.

A pasta dish with *pappardelle* ($15), the slippery, broad flat noodles that seem to improve so much, was a rich arrangement of mascarpone, Parmesan, and herbs. It would have held asparagus if my friend had been a little more grown up and a little less anti-asparagus (kudos to the kitchen for accommodating her), but as it was, lots of roasted red pepper contributed a sweet vegetable flavor.

Steaks are a regular part of the menu; roasted quail with apple and bacon stuffing may again be on the fall or winter menus, which change regularly.

Check out Support Your Local Farmer, a ratatouille served during the fall harvest season at El Camino in Brunswick.

A chocolate torte with fresh berries ($5.75) came all gussied up in raspberry and custard sauce patterned like a cobweb; with a little less sugar, the cake would have been everything I dream up. I don't like sugar that much, but everybody else seems to.

The peach crème brûlée was beyond criticism.

El Camino
(207) 725-8228
15 Cushing Street
Hospitality—Friendly and irreverent
Open for dinner 5–9 Tuesday to Thursday, 5–10 Friday and Saturday; later hours in the bar
Entrées $12 to $15

☛ *Spicy and inventive Mexican with a devotion to fresh local ingredients*

The utterly fresh ingredients and reverence for seafood and meat without hormones or antibiotics show up in inventive, spicy dishes—plates of endlessly reimagined Mexican classics.

Salads and soups start these meals; the soups are always vegan or vegetarian. A black trumpet flan, or a watercress and pomegranate salad, comes in summer. In fall, all specials are made with local organic produce, like wild mushroom tacos with heirloom potatoes.

Hahn's End Queso Fresco ($12.50) is a find, here added to mixed greens, arugula, tatsoi, and kale cooked down with raisins and pine nuts and served with roasted heirloom tomato sauce.

"My whole philosophy is that good food should be available to everybody," said Eloise Humphrey, chef-owner with her twin sister Daphne Comaskey. The restaurant opened in 2004 in June. Humphrey cooked in high-end restaurants before she started this place, and keeps the prices as low as possible.

Support Your Local Farmer is a ratatouille with smoked cheddar. Everything on the fall menu is from Maine, except avocados and some of the beans. Meat is Sunset Acres Farm pork and beef, chicken is from Maine-ly Poultry, and seafood is from Harbor Fish in Portland. She reserves hundreds of pounds of winter squash from farmers for winter use.

Post Family Farm from St. Albans supplies the cream and milk, and some of that goes into the chocolate *pot de crème.* Other fall desserts are pumpkin flan with maple caramel and rice pudding with *cajeta,* goat's-milk caramel made with milk from Maine goats. Flower Power desserts are made by Maureen Faust, who also sells them at the Crystal Spring Farm farmer's market.

The Great Impasta
(207) 729-5858
42 Maine Street
www.thegreatimpasta.com
Open for lunch and dinner Monday through Saturday
Entrées $10 to $16

☞ *Well-loved Italian classics like melanzana Parmigiana and stuffed manicotti*

This place has won several awards over the years, including best Italian restaurant on the Maine midcoast for nine years and more. The friendly welcome makes that understandable, and the great Italian food makes popularity inevitable. Sometimes the waiting list grows long, but the restaurant puts you on the list if you call from home. Pollo Mediterranean ($14), a chicken breast baked with a pesto cream sauce, prosciutto, and tomatoes, is popular. Salmon poached in white wine and served in a Tuscan-seasoned reduction over fresh spinach ($15.50) is one of the restaurant's several fish entrées.

There is a good selection of vegetarian dishes here, too, like Foriana ($11), a sauce of pine nuts, walnuts, raisins, pesto, and olive oil served on linguine.

Desserts include Italian classics like cheesecake, tiramisu, and spumoni, along with an American special, like chocolate peanut-butter pie. "It's so loved that we have regular customers order it for birthday parties," said Alisa Coffin, the owner for 20 years.

Henry and Marty's
(207) 721-9141
61 Maine Street
Open for dinner Tuesday through Saturday 5–9, closed two weeks in January
Entrées $14 to $26
Handicapped accessible, reservations recommended

☞ *A hip place with ambitious dinners, growing to meet the demand*

Started by Henry D'Alessandris and Marty Perry, this restaurant has grown in reputation and popularity. It has also taken over the space next door and can seat more than 50, while including a small bar with four stools. Black and blue checked flooring and loops of burgundy fabric cast a colorful aura, and exuberant art gives the room a little urbanity.

The tiny bar is a good spot to wait for a table drinking the bartender's invention, a Bisous-Bisous ($8), "kiss-kiss" in French, made with Grey Goose vodka, triple sec, lime, and pomegranate juice.

The changing menu will most likely feature the incredibly fresh mussels ($9) in wine, garlic, and tomato broth I enjoyed here in 2006. After a summer of disappointing mussels, these were a revelation, and reaffirmation, of the pleasure of the lowly bivalve.

Morse's Lobster Shack
(207) 725-2886
18 Bath Road (Old Route 1 right by Bowdoin College)
Open for breakfast 5–11, lunch and dinner 11–8; may close for part of the winter, reopening in March
Entrées $5.55 to $17

☛ *A drive-in with all three meals*

Lobster stew, fish chowder, and clam chowder are served at this place with a big kitchen. Waitresses can serve customers in their cars, but for those who don't want to endanger their car upholstery with a messy burger, there are 30 seats inside. The place has been decorated with nautical paintings that the Morse family has collected over the years.

A 6-ounce cheeseburger can be enjoyed with bacon.

A brownie sundae, blueberry crisp, whoopie pies, and strawberry shortcake are on the dessert menu.

Richard's Restaurant
(207) 729-9673
115 Maine Street
Open Monday through Saturday for lunch from 11–2 and dinner 5–9, Friday and Saturday until 9:30
Entrées $11 to $21

☛ *German entrées interspersed with Black Angus steak and other favorites*

When you can get tournedos in three versions—the Wilhelm, with mustard and onions; the Karl, with asparagus and mushrooms with hollandaise; or the Erik, with béarnaise (all $19.95)—and German classics like Wiener schnitzel, jaeger schnitzel, zigeuner schnitzel, or paprika schnitzel, with a choice of *spätzle* (noodles), *klösse* (dumplings), *heisser kartoffelsalat* (hot potato salad)—and more— you have a way to encounter a culture that is our source for romantic music and great art without crossing the sea. *Rindsrouladen* ($11.95), thinly sliced beef rolled with onions, bacon, mustard, and pickles, is a Thursday-night special year-round.

A taste of the Sacher torte ($6) might transport your taste buds back a century to an elegant café in Vienna; something *mit schlag* (with whipped cream)?—order the strudel.

Scarlet Begonia's
(207) 721-0403
212B Maine Street
Open for lunch and dinner Monday through Saturday 11–8, Friday and Saturday until 9
Entrées $7 to $13

☛ *A Bowdoin College hangout with pizza, pasta, and sandwiches*

Scarlet's Harlot, linguine with a puttanesca sauce of garlic, olives, and capers goes for $11.95; and Stephen's Dilemma, penne with sausage, chicken, mushrooms, roasted garlic, and spinach in a marinara sauce, is $12.75. Crabcakes ($14.50 when the market price is high) with chipotle mayonnaise are specials only, with a little corn bread, for an appetizer. This casual place feeds its customers inexpensively on pizza too. The pie called Phoebe's Feast, with roasted garlic, red peppers, feta, kalamata olives, and cheese, is $11.25. The Florentine ($10.75) is a spinach pizza with roasted garlic and cheese. Salads at the top of the menu include Caesar, and a Cobb salad, with romaine, bacon, tomato, blue cheese, and chicken ($9.95).

Lunch, Takeout, Coffee, and Markets

The Bohemian Coffeehouse (207-725-9095), 4 Railroad Avenue, next to Hannaford.
Open Monday through Saturday 7–7, Sunday 8–2. Selling espresso and brewed coffee as well as beans, this coffee shop has free wireless Internet access and smoothies.

Hardcover Café at Bookland (207-725-7033), Cook's Corner Shopping Mall, Cook's Corner.

Open Monday through Saturday 9–8:45, Sunday 9–5:45. With the added attraction of Maine's largest independent bookstore (with its two branches, one here and one in Rockland) alongside, this place makes all its muffins, scones, cinnamon buns, and cookies from scratch. Soups, salads, and ethnic entrées, including lasagnas, burritos, and quiche are available. Dessert can be a pumpkin cake with a walnut topping, Heath Bar cake, Key lime pie, or strawberry or raspberry cakes. Espresso, of course. A new Hardcover Café has opened in Rockland at **Breakwater Bookland.**

The Humble Gourmet (207-721-8100), 103 Pleasant Street.

Open Monday through Friday 8–5, Saturday 8–3; closed Sunday. Six-grain, buttermilk-honey, and oatmeal are a few of the breads baked here. Turkey and cranberry, and the veggie Reuben with sauerkraut, roasted peppers, red onions, carrots, and tomatoes on rye, both make great lunches. So does the almond tarragon chicken salad ($5.95). Every Friday there's always a chowder, made with heavy cream, onions, and potatoes—sometimes haddock, corn, or clam. Other soups are also a source of pride. Desserts, morning pastries, coffee cake, and prepared food to go make this a great place to stop on the way up the coast.

Morning Glory Natural Foods (207-729-0546), 64 Maine Street.

Open Monday through Friday 9–7, Saturday until 6, Sunday 11–5. This grocery store sells some prepared foods from Wild Oats (see below). Muffins and scones come from Zoe's Market in Belfast, which makes good cookies too. Wine and organic groceries also are offered. Squire Tarbox Farm, Hatchet Cove Farm, Dandelion Spring, and Bondeson Farm all bring local produce here for sale. Betsy's of Maine Sweet Blueberry Butter, a creamy blueberry spread made by Elizabeth Gravalos, is a popular, locally made condiment perfect for entrées and alongside cheese, as well as on toast.

Tess's Market (207-729-9531), 54 Pleasant Street.

Open Monday through Saturday 8 AM–9 PM. This market is known for its wine. Montepulciano d'Abruzzo sells for around $8. Côte du Ventoux, a grenache syrah blend ($8.18), is a wine Anne Tessier Talbot, manager and daughter of the original owner, called a beautiful bottle, Rhône-style with medium body and well-balanced fruit, moderately dry. Wine tastings are offered once a month.

   A blend of provolone and mozzarella tops all the pizzas, made with fresh pizza dough from Sorella's in Portland. When this place started 52 years ago, with hot dogs, the next step was sub sandwiches; by the 1960s Tess's made its own pizza, but they recently outsourced the dough to Sorella's. Hot buttered crust—bare baked pizza dough—is offered with sugar and cinnamon, or garlic and oil. Homemade meatballs are used in the meatball subs, and a large variety of sandwiches is available. "I'm packing 35 sandwiches as we talk for the football team," said Tessier Talbot, one September afternoon.

Wild Oats Bakery and Café (207-725-6287), 149 Maine Street.
Open Monday through Saturday 7:30–5, Sunday 8–3. This family-owned business is not connected to the big grocery chain. Bread is baked fresh five days a week, and the café includes a deli with pasta and sandwiches, soup, cakes, and baked goods like muffins and scones. This favorite stop for everyone downtown has about 10 tables inside and a porch with umbrellas outside; a hall in the mall offers more places to sit. Changing soups might feature fish chowder; the turkey BLT ($5.95) is a favorite. But everyone makes their own sandwich combinations from the posted list of ingredients. One clerk's favorite cake is carrot, plain and without raisin; but even better are the fresh salads like the chicken salad, edamame salad, and sunshine salad full of red vegetables like beets, red peppers, and carrots.

Brunswick Farmer's Market is held on Tuesday and Friday 8–3 at the Brunswick Mall and Saturday 8:30–12:30 at Crystal Springs Farm from May to the end of November.

Georgetown

Five Island's Lobster Company
(207) 371-2990
1447 Five Islands Road
www.fiveislandslobster.com
Open daily 11:30–8 Memorial Day through Labor Day, weekends for lunch and dinner 11:30–7 from Mother's Day to Memorial Day and Labor Day to Columbus Day
Entrées $12 to $17

☛ *Picturesque, of course, with fresh lobster off the boats and fried seafood*

The main things here are the lobster, the locally dug soft-shell clams, the fresh corn, and the farm-raised mussels. But the **Love Nest Grill** also serves fried clams, fried salmon, and a grilled haddock sandwich that can be ordered with inventive sauces, like a tartar sauce with fresh dill or a cilantro mayonnaise dressing. The crabcakes are touted to be without crumb filler, and the serving of homemade onion rings, made fresh, is generous. Hot dogs, steak-and-cheese sandwiches, and even a veggie burger take care of the rest of us.

The Osprey Restaurant
(207) 371-2530
Robinhood Marina, at 340 Robinhood Road
www.robinhoodmarina.com
Open May through October, with a shorter schedule in fall and spring
Entrées $15 to $22

☛ *A restaurant with good chowder, at a marina where you can dock your boat*

The osprey nest on a piling outside the windows has been here since long before our friends called for a rescue after the engine on their sailboat failed, and we drove to get them and revive ourselves with lobster stew in this pleasant dining room. Now with a tavern open for drinks, the Osprey serves boiled lobsters and fried clams.

The Robinhood Free Meetinghouse
(207) 371-2188
210 Robinhood Road
www.robinhood-meetinghouse.com
Hospitality—You are served with exquisite attention and care here.
Open mid-May through mid-October for dinner daily 5:30–9; and off-season
Thursday through Saturday 5:30–8
Entrées $18 to $25
Reservations appreciated

☛ *High-quality, unique, and inventive food in a lovely old building*

Robinhood Free Meetinghouse is a magnet on the coast, attracting people from far away for a special dinner on its dark and lonely peninsula, because the chef has been sending so many home with fond memories for so many years. Michael A. Gagne makes such good dinners that nowadays his restaurant is packed on holidays like Valentine's Day, Mother's Day, and Thanksgiving. You will definitely want to make a reservation if you choose a popular night.

The building looms up out of the trees as you finally make the last turn in the road that brings you here. Resplendent and tall, this Greek Revival white-clapboard building housed prayers and services by both Methodists and Congregationalists beginning in 1855. It underwent a renovation after some years as a high school and as a library in 1995, and now is one of the classiest restaurants you can find. Drinking a large glass of wine in a pew upstairs can be startling, but soon the conversation at the tables up on the altar area and behind the pews puts you at ease. Or is it the great wine? The long list will please the most demanding customer, as I know from having accompanied him here.

Four mushrooms in puff pastry ($10), with button, shiitake, portobello, and oyster mushrooms lending their strong presence to cream, make a fine way to begin. But Gagne's signature wide range fills the appetizer list, which leans toward Greece with *kreatopitas* ($8), phyllo pastry with ground lamb, feta, and onion, and veers south with grilled shrimp adobo on homemade tortillas with banana salsa ($10).

Entrées shift the globe-trotting into high gear. Beef Stroganoff ($26), and Szechuan tuna ($28) with a crust of green, black, and white peppercorns, stare out from the top of the list on a menu that changes in a few items every day but remains for the most part the same year-round. Tournedos with two sauces, béarnaise and roasted garlic, brought all the pleasure of that classic to my lips; and the beef attained a sublime tenderness. My friend submitted to being pleased by the pecan-encrusted haddock with a beurre blanc after sending back the bottle of bordeaux. He found a cabernet sauvignon that pleased us both. Valentine's Day, always a prime time for a fight, slipped away without conflict, although we had to decline all the glorious chocolate desserts, devil's food cake, and chocolate mousse with Grand Marnier, and even the profiteroles ($8–8.50).

Markets

Five islands Farm (207-371-9383; www.fiveislandsfarm.com), 1375 Five Islands Road (end of Route 127 South).
Open mid-May through December. You can find all of Maine's starring artisan cheeses here, from Appleton Creamery to Liberty Fields Farm. Local fresh eggs, organic beef, Maine-ly Poultry chicken, wine, and Borealis Breads are sold in this charming store.

Harpswell

Dolphin Marina & Restaurant

(207) 833-6000
515 Basin Point Road, South Harpswell
www.dolphinchowderhouse.com
Hospitality—Friendly and outgoing
Open daily for breakfast, lunch, and dinner 11–8 from May 1 to late October
Entrées $5 to $22

☛ *Well-loved for its lobster stew and fish chowder; you can moor your boat here*

Both the chowder and the lobster stew here are accompanied by a blueberry muffin. A bowl of the rich milk-and-cream-based lobster stew was $15.95 in 2006, market price; and many people make the journey here just for this. A bowl of fish chowder ($10.95) and a fried haddock sandwich are two of this well-known restaurant's other favorites. A haddock dinner, with the fish fried or broiled, is $18.95. Burgers, grilled cheese, and chicken dishes are on the menu too. Specials include crabcakes with zesty cilantro sauce, seafood au gratin, and lasagna. Desserts always feature pies. The selection changes with the season; apple and pumpkin were up on the board in fall, for $4.25 a slice with a scoop of vanilla ice cream. When blackberries are ripe you might find a blackberry napoleon. Beer and wine are served.

Estes Lobster House

(207) 833-6340
1906 Harpswell Neck Road
Hospitality—Counter service with servers who bring out the meals and clean up
Open daily for lunch and dinner 11:30–8:30 Mother's Day through mid-October, changing hours after Labor Day and before Memorial Day
Entrées $8 to $30

☛ *A huge place that can seat 300 people inside, with more room on the deck*

Most people who come here love fried clams or the lobster dinner, with a 1½-pound lobster. Clams are bought from a local digger, haddock and scallops from Canada, and shrimp from the Gulf of Mexico.

A menu for seniors over 60 is served from 11 to 4 and features broiled scallops with eight different additions, like a beverage and sides. Small portions are perfect and very popular for the folks who come here after church on Sunday.

Blueberry and apple crisp, strawberry shortcake, and a brownie sundae are all made here. The popular blueberry crisp is served hot with vanilla ice cream.

A Lazy Lobster—four claws and two tails, accompanied by corn on the cob and coleslaw—can make dinner easy. A lobster pie with 4 to 5 ounces of lobster meat in its seafood stuffing, and lobster salad on romaine, are also on the menu.

"We never have a wait," said Amber Crooker, the manager and daughter of owner Larry Crooker, who has worked here off and on since she was a kid. Over the years things have changed. Full service is no longer offered; after placing an order at the counter, customers get their meal from servers who find them by looking for a table flag. Everything is served on paper and plastic. Leftover lobster shells, especially from jumbo lobsters, go into Crustacean Creations, lobstermen sculptures built by Larry Crooker.

Holbrook's Wharf and Snack Bar
(207) 729-0848
984 Cundy's Harbor Road
Open end of May through mid-September for lunch and dinner daily 11:30–8
Entrées $9 to $15
No credit cards, BYOB

☛ *Relaxed atmosphere and a great location for good chowders and seafood*

With a middle section that has lights and heat and carpet, this simple seaside restaurant has turned into more of a lunch and dinner place. But you can't beat the outdoor seating for 120 people, with a great view of Cundy's Harbor, and tuna fishermen unloading their big catch close to your table. Tie up in your own boat if you want, and enjoy homemade lemonade.

This place sells seafood fried and baked, a vegetarian sandwich, and BLTs and chicken sandwiches and organic burgers for those opposed to or overwhelmed by seafood. The fish comes from a nearby supplier. There are no clams, but you can dine on haddock, scallops, and shrimp, all from Maine—there's nothing from Canada here. The lobster stew and fish chowder, with creamy broth, please the customers. And the kitchen makes the desserts—homemade cookies, brownies, and a crisp of the season, with a rhubarb crisp starting in early summer, changing to blueberry, and to peach. It might be sold out, though, if it has been a busy day. **Lexie's Ice Cream Shop** serves Gifford's Ice Cream.

Morse's Lobster
(207) 833-2399
Off Route 123, Harpswell Neck
Open, weather permitting, for lunch and dinner 11–8, July 1 through Labor Day
Entrées $1.50 for a hot dog to about $13.50 for a 1½-pound lobster
BYOB

☛ *The epitome of a summer seafood place, with no frills*

Simplicity, simplicity, simplicity. The season is strictly allied to the good weather here, because meals are enjoyed outside at picnic tables on a wharf. The small place is just down a hill to an open deck with about 20 tables covered by green umbrellas that do not keep off the rain. If it's raining, the restaurant is closed.

A cooked lobster was $8.95 a pound in 2006. Locals love this place with reasonable prices. Lobster cookers are simmering most of the day, but at lunch lobster rolls ($13.95), with close to 5 ounces of lobster meat, are the favorite. Fried clams, a haddock dinner, a haddock sandwich, a Caesar salad with lobster salad, crab salad, chicken, and hamburgers are all available. For dessert, the biggest sellers are whoopie pies. Sometimes there's strawberry shortcake, and 75 percent of the time there's a blueberry or apple crisp.

Wine and Markets

Black Sheep Wine Shop (207-725-9284; www.blacksheepwine.com), 105 Mountain Road.
Open May through December Monday through Saturday 10–6, closed Sunday; open January through April Monday through Friday 12–6, Saturday 10–6. A great selection of more than 600 fine wines, imported beer, and good chocolate, cheese, and other specialty foods. Wine tastings are held; call for schedule.

Moe's Country Store (207-833-5383), 1220 Harpswell Neck Road.
Open daily, usually 6 AM–8 PM, Sunday 7–8. The only store out here with gas; you can also get pizza, hamburgers, and subs. Breakfast sandwiches, bagels, and French toast run the gamut for breakfast. Raspberry and apple turnovers are made at the store. Coffee is made with Green Mountain Coffee beans.

Phippsburg

Anna's Water's Edge Restaurant

(207) 389-1803
75 Black's Landing Road (take Route 209 to 217)
www.thewatersedgerestaurant.com
Open daily 11–9 for lunch and dinner May through September
Entrées $11 to $29

☛ *A fresh seafood place in an old clam depuration shed on the water*

Now offering fried local seafood, Anna's Water's Edge Restaurant still serves Maine shrimp scampi, with butter, garlic, and herbs on pasta, and its reliable Today's Fresh Fish specials, like baked cod with crabmeat stuffing in a Parmesan cream sauce. Some like the grilled kielbasa appetizer, and the industrious can opt for lobster legs ("the little ones") served with butter. Crabmeat dip and steamed clams (1 pound with butter and broth) are made with creatures that grew up nearby. Salads, sandwiches, and, of course, boiled lobster can be matched with beer and wine.

North Creek Farm

(207) 389-1341
24 Sebasco Road (Route 217)
Open year-round: summer 9–6, meals 11–3:30 daily; off-season 10–6 with same meal hours
Sandwiches $6.50

☛ *An idyllic setting for summer picnics, but winter lunches are perfect too because perfectly made, as much as possible, from Maine produce and fruits from the garden*

"We're the only thing down here in the winter," Suzy Verrier, the owner, said. But watch out for inaccurate MapQuest directions; rely on a DeLorme *Maine Atlas & Gazetteer* if you can.

After 10 years in a plant nursery business, Verrier started a smaller nursery and then began serving food in 2001. First selling gardening goods, cut flowers, and produce, she added cheese, wine, and meals. Summer visitors love to eat outside, where they can admire 3 acres of display gardens. But indoor dining with three tables accommodate people in bad weather.

Homemade and homegrown everything can be found here on frosty winter days, when the soups are as welcome as summer's tomatoes used to be.

"We cook like we're cooking for ourselves," she said. She serves mostly soups with homemade stocks, chowders, and sandwiches, using seasonal ingredients. Sandwiches are usually panini-grilled—like the popular tuna in olive oil with artichoke hearts ($6.50), a little bit of oregano, tapenade, and Gruyère on rosemary bread from Borealis Breads.

Homemade pies, like gooseberry pie with berries that were in abundance in summer 2006, are customers' favorites. When the apple pie run exceeded her own trees' apples, she bought local fruit to supplement it. Her focus is on what Maine does best, when it does it. Soups are stocked in the freezer.

Spinney's Restaurant and Guesthouse
(207) 389-2052
987 Popham Road
Hospitality—Enthusiastic service
Open daily mid-June through mid-October, 8 AM–8:30 PM; also open in May, but call for hours
Entrées $9 to $27

☛ *A classic restaurant for quality seafood in a lovely, informal setting*

Dinner here in this classic seaside restaurant features something called the Wood Island Wreck: 3 jumbo shrimp, 5 scallops, 4 hand-cut sirloin tips grilled "on the barbey, and wicked good," according to Glen Theall, who has owned Spinney's with his wife, Diane, since 1998. The restaurant started serving seafood dinners in the late 1930s, here next to one of Maine's most beautiful beaches, and Theall has tried to jack up the quality while keeping the theme fresh seafood and good beef. "Good coast of Maine home cooking," he called it. "We grind our own hamburger. We serve the freshest possible ingredients we can get our hands on."

The large fisherman's platter, with four different seafoods and all the other fried food, is made with 100 percent vegetable oil that's changed frequently. "There's no scrimping there," Theall said.

Lobsters come from the waters in front of the restaurant, and the clam flats where the clams are dug are visible from the restaurant—they're some of the best flats in the midcoast, Theall claimed. Homemade biscuits are fresh every day, and the kitchen serves up three meals a day, seven days a week, except after Columbus Day and in May, when breakfast, with its home fries and roast beef hash, is made on weekends only.

Brownie sundaes and wild Maine blueberry shortcake are made in the kitchen here, not bought frozen off a truck. Theall doesn't think much of the majority of Route 1 area restaurants, which rely wholeheartedly on the freezer and the Frialator. Although he does use frozen french fries, he gets the best he can find, he said; and the onion rings are cut and made fresh every day.

Westport Island

The Squire Tarbox Inn
(207) 882-7693, 1-800-818-0626
1181 Main Road (on Route 144, off Route 1 just south of Wiscasset)
www.squiretarboxinn.com
Hospitality—Servers have been well-instructed in taking care of their tables.
Open daily for dinner 6–8:30 PM June through October; open Thursday
through Saturday in April, May, November, and December (when Swiss Nights
offer raclette and cheese fondue)
Prix fixe $33.50 to $38.50 for five courses
Dinner is by reservation only

☛ *Dinner in a handsome old house in a quiet green landscape, with good food and wine*

After we drove around the twists and turns of Route 144, the inn appeared like a refuge. We arrived when fall was just starting to nip at our toes, reminding us of the end of summer. The inn's dining room, with dark, bare beams pulled from a ship's belly, copper saucepans, and a range of cowbells from tiny to enormous hanging from a rafter, gave me the feeling of an old cloak pulled up around my shoulders. The glass of Renwood Zinfandel added to the pleasant sensation, while my friend enjoyed her Castello d'Albola Pinot Grigio. We read the menu and ate crackers with goat cheese and olives from a tray set out for inn guests and diners.

My friend started off with a rich onion soup, served in a small bowl with the right amount of melted Gruyère and Appenzeller cheese. My own soup of pureed mushrooms had a rich strong flavor of its own, and preceded a tender filet mignon with Damariscotta morels in a delectable sauce. Asked from where the mushrooms came, innkeeper Mario De Pietro brought out his collection from a mushroom seller at the Damariscotta farmer's market, a big hunk of orange hen-of-the-woods and a fine bowl full of little oyster mushrooms.

My friend found the large serving of haddock, crusted by a potato pancake, moist and good.

Both entrées came with a slew of thin strips of squash, sautéed and crisp, with a baked tomato full of summer sunlight, topped with crumbs. Vegetables and salads were grown in the inn's own organic gardens. Frozen Grand Marnier soufflé made a delicate dessert. My Pavlova, a simple pleasure, set meringues under a crown of whipped cream and strawberries.

Our meals cost $35.50 for the beef and $34.50 for the fish, which included the soup and dessert, and to which a 15 percent tip was already added. "Don't you want more than that?" I asked our pleasant waitress, who smiled and shrugged, and surely didn't mind when I tacked on another 5 percent.

CHAPTER 4

Wiscasset to Damariscotta

I N THIS SECTION OF THE MAINE COAST lies a town that has been a tourist destination for generations. Boothbay Harbor, crammed with shops and restaurants, fills up with crowds in the hot summer months. Sited in a lovely stretch of harbors and islands, it's a good place to start, but a great place to leave—for a drive southwest to Southport Island, either for dinner at an old inn like the Lawnmere, over the swing bridge on Townsend Gut, or for lobster on a deck at Robinson's Wharf, overlooking an uncrowded harbor.

Or drive east and south to Ocean Point, another classic inn with simpler meals; there's a place for tea on the way.

Just around the harbor itself, down at the end of Atlantic Avenue, you can enjoy the most elegant meals in the area at the Spruce Point Inn.

But Boothbay, while many people's destination, shouldn't keep a visitor long. A drive farther up the coast leads to more charming stretches of windswept, granite peninsulas, ending at Pemaquid Point and its lovely lighthouse. Or wind around Round Pond, with its artists in residence and lobster served on a wharf. The peaceful loneliness of this landscape paradoxically draws those crowds, but a taste of the forests are at hand for anyone who cares to walk down the many land trust and park trails.

Wiscasset and Damariscotta, the former right smack on Route 1, to many of its inhabitant's dismay, and the latter smugly just off, on Business Route 1, are delights to visit, with good antiques shops, bookstores, and clothing stores, along with several fine places for good meals.

Wiscasset also is the site of a friendly rivalry that mirrors the coast-long competition to serve and sell seafood, in particular the best lobster rolls.

A while ago a place in Damariscotta, Larson's, now closed, sold the biggest lobster rolls, with perhaps 6 ounces of lobster meat in each roll.

Now the little toasted and buttered hot dog rolls with 4 ounces are considered the gold standard, and two businesses face off at the bottom of the hill in Wiscasset, by the bridge on Route 1. Sprague's Lobster and Red's Eats both claim to serve that fully adequate amount. It's easier to buy one from Sprague's, at least so far, because there is not usually a line.

Boothbay Harbor

88 Grandview and Bogie's Hideaway
Spruce Point Inn
(207) 633-4152
88 Grandview Avenue, P.O. Box 237
www.sprucepointinn.com
Hospitality—Well-trained, accommodating staff
Open daily for dinner mid-May through late October
Entrées $24 to $30

☛ *Elegance and fine dining in a beautiful location at 88 Grandview;
high-quality casual food in a stylish lounge at Bogie's Hideaway*

The long, pale cream dining room of 88 Grandview, the formal room in this resort, can fill with light reflected off the water just down the slope outside. Brown plaid curtains and room-dividing swags of brown linen keep the large space from seeming huge. We came in early summer, were ushered in by a friendly hostess, and were soon supplied with a glass of Wild Horse Cabernet. Then our server brought us an *amuse bouche,* free from the chef: a fried pork spring roll with a strong meaty flavor.

The next course I ordered myself, a napoleon of grilled portobello, Bermuda onion, tomato, roasted pepper, and fresh mozzarella ($8). Lovely to behold, it worked in the mouth too, the thick slice of onion sweet and fresh. A lobster napoleon with fried heirloom tomatoes and cayenne beurre blanc, and a lobster spring roll, are appetizers from another menu.

The roasted sea bass entrée, with miso butter sauce and served on a bed of wasabi potato with four teeny bok choy that had a sweet hot bite to them, held great moist white flakes of the fish in its large portion, tender and well-contrasted by the brown sauce.

A scaloppine of pork tenderloin with sage prosciutto and smoked mozzarella in a mushroom Madeira sauce also argued for complication.

The crème brûlée, with tender custard, did not meet the density and richness required by my in-house crème brûlée expert, who nonetheless polished off every scrap. The Chocolate Oblivion Torte formed a mass of solid chocolate, relieved only by the crème anglaise and some zigzags of raspberry coulis, and was perhaps too much. I could have had the four-berry pie instead, though no doubt the butterscotch and hot fudge sundaes would have been much of a sameness. Dense and rich were the themes of our fine meal.

Bogie's Hideaway serves more casual, less expensive food. It's where families dine, with hamburgers for the kids and more inventive food for the adults.

The Lobster Dock
(207) 633-7120
At the east end of the Boothbay Harbor footbridge
www.thelobsterdock.com
Open for lunch and dinner 11:30–8:30 early June through early October
Entrées $12 to $25

☛ *Famous for doing lobster rolls hot with butter and cold with mayo*

Sometimes when you mess with a classic it works out. This place has won attention and praise for messing with the lobster rolls, serving them warm with melted butter or cold with mayonnaise, and their customers love both. The lobster stew is made with all the knuckle and claw meat left from the busy business in lobster rolls. You can be assured there's no frozen lobster meat here. A seafood *fra diavolo*—scallops, shrimp, mussels, and a whole lobster cooked in a spicy tomato sauce full of herbs, garlic, and bay leaf, served on linguine ($24.95)—made one customer exclaim it was the best he'd had.

But seafood lovers can explain to their reluctant children and spouses who can't stand shellfish that there's a nice strip steak here, or some crunchy garlic lemon-butter artichoke hearts ($5.95).

93 Townsend
(207) 633-0777
93 Townsend
www.93townsend.com
Open daily for lunch and dinner 12–9 or later, depending on the crowd
Entrées $16 to $22

☛ *A touch of originality is so welcome on this menu, also full of familiar dishes.*

Bill Clifford, chef and owner, has won awards for his inventions like lobster "risotto" with orzo pasta. With braised lamb shanks, he is willing to dance around the mainstays of Maine menus and come up with a surprise.

Something to perk you up on the appetizer list, and another award-winner, is french fried asparagus, which customers like; but there is still a question mark about the sauce, cabernet ketchup ($10.93), which seemed too fruity on one tasting. Seared chicken liver salad ($9.93) with collard greens, bacon, and corn bread is right up my alley, and a welcome sight on a menu that isn't from Fore Street in Portland.

Crab and shrimp nachos ($13.93) sounds like a crowd-pleaser.

For dinner, there are seared scallops in carrot broth with fried parsnips ($18.93), grilled sausage platter with peach mustard ($16.93), and shrimp scampi on bowties ($19.93).

Ports of Italy
(207) 633-1011
47 Commercial Street
Hospitality—Eager service
Open for dinner 5–9:30 Monday through Saturday April through mid-October, closed Sunday
Entrées $20 to $28
Reservations suggested

☛ *An adept hand in the kitchen makes great classy Italian food, with everything by the season.*

One of the best meals of my life was a risotto *alla pescatore,* eaten alfresco at a Roman restaurant. So when I saw the same dish offered in a place in the middle of Boothbay Harbor, I had to try it. It evoked all that memorable pleasure, its Arborio rice cooked to a creamy, chewy consistency, expertly combined with tender scallops, shrimp, and squid. Salty, with bits of tomato and a spike of rosemary, the big dish more than satisfied my hunger for both the recollected meal and the new one.

Christa and David Rossi (David is from Milan) opened this bright place in 2004 and managed to collect customers quickly, filling its bright yellow, second-floor room. Reservations are a good idea, especially on weekends.

Astici della Maine, Maine shrimp, could have been ordered in three ways on the day of our visit, with cherry tomatoes, celery, and red onions in a citrus vinaigrette; with julienned carrots and fennel with lemon dressing; or with baby arugula, potatoes, and pomegranates in citronette. A good simple dish of penne with a bright, flavorful tomato sauce and mozzarella made another good meal, but next time we want to try the gnocchi, or the spaghetti *alla vongole,* with cherrystone clams, garlic, and wine. And we'll be sure to place another order for the great sabayon, made with egg yolks and Marsala and served with toasted slivered almonds over seasonal fruit. One foodie in Boothbay is having her 60th birthday party here, and calls this restaurant wonderful.

Casual Meals, Wine, Takeout, and Treats

Blue Moon Café (207-633-2349), 54 Commercial Street.
Open Monday through Saturday 7:30 AM–2:30 PM, Sunday 8–1, from April to mid-October. Best to hit this popular spot after the height of lunch hour. Order the good crabcakes ($8.95) at the counter, or the splendid chicken quesadilla with melted Boursin, tomatoes, and big chunks of chicken ($8.95). Lots of wraps and grilled sandwiches, clam chowder, and high-quality deli sandwiches and salads. If you're lucky you'll snag a table on the deck over the water.

Boothbay Region Lobsterman's Co-op (207-633-4900; www.booth baylobsterwharf.com), Atlantic Avenue.
Open from 11:30 AM mid-May through mid-October. A retail business selling lobsters, clams, and mussels is open year-round; they can cook the seafood to go during summer. In-season, this is the place of choice for discerning visitors interested in an annual lobster dinner. The picnic tables inside and out are informal and comfortable, and you won't need to worry about the liquid squirting out of the lobster claw you just cracked open. Crabmeat rolls, corn on the cob, and a few seafood alternatives make the menu work for families.

Daffy Taffy and Fudge Factory (207-633-5178), the By-Way.
No credit cards. Open daily 10–9 in-season, making candy almost every day. The taffy is pulled, and cut and wrapped, and fills up the little skiff inside the store for the passing children to bail out.

Down East Ice Cream and Yogurt Factory (207-633-3016), the By-Way.
Open 11–10:30 in the height of summer. Make your own sundae here with hot fudge and other toppings, and homemade hard ice cream.

Ebb Tide (207-633-5692), 43 Commercial Street.
Open 6:30 AM–9 PM daily, closing at 9:30 on Friday and Saturday, closing one hour earlier all days off-season. Fresh peach shortcake and a scallop stir-fry were the specials on our visit, when these pine walls and booths were filled up with happy tourists. Homemade pies, Grapenut pudding, and a hot fudge

brownie sundae vied with the chocolate, vanilla, strawberry, and coffee frappes for our allegiance, after the fried clams and fish entrées.

88 Baker's Way (207-633-1119), 89 Townsend Avenue.

Open daily 6 AM–9 PM; Vietnamese menu available from 11 AM. Many people never get farther than the baked goods ranged in the glass cabinet in front, and the standard menu of ham and cheese or breakfast eggs. But lemongrass stir-fries, ginger stir-fries, and beef and shrimp curries are on the "other menu," just as ably prepared by the Vietnamese owners as the doughnuts and apple dumplings Boothbay teenagers scarf up by the dozen.

We enjoyed a wonderfully tender dish of stir-fried squid ($8.25). Scored in a crisscross, this local seafood came richly flavored with lemongrass and garlic in a spicy sauce that turned chunks of celery, strips of carrot, and pieces of broccoli into exotic foreign vegetables. The vermicelli rice noodles with thin-cut pork, crumbled bacon, shredded lettuce, onion, and bean sprouts, topped with chopped peanuts and hot chili sauce, was another delight unanticipated in Boothbay Harbor. We enjoyed both in the simple back garden, surrounded by small maple, dogwood, and magnolia trees. And our waitress was wonderful.

MacNab's Premium Teas & Tea Room (207-633-7222, 1-800-884-7222), 5 Yu Yu Tea Lane (off Back River Road).

Open Tuesday through Saturday 10–5 in July and August, 10–4 from September to June. Pots of tea come in a variety of patterns, and the cozies are phenomenal, the knitting creativity of a resident genius. Our Darjeeling, steeped before it was brought to the table, tasted like the best tea I make for myself. And the cookie medley, with an apricot bar, was delightful in the midafternoon, as it's meant to be. Cock-a-leekie soup ($5 a bowl), scone sandwiches, and highland pie, with ground beef in an oat-and-onion crust ($10.95), cover some of the savories. Sweets of cake and blueberry scones with lemon curd cover some of the rest. Tea paraphernalia, and tea itself, are for sale in this charming little house in the country.

Oak Street Provisions (207-633-3622), 43 Oak Street.

Open 7–7 daily in summer, Memorial Day through Columbus Day. Wine and fresh seafood, produce, sandwiches, and Vie de France breads.

The Whale's Tale (207-633-6644), 125 Atlantic Avenue.

Open 11–3 for lunch 5–9 from April to sometime before Christmas—but call in case it's staying open later in the year. With a lovely view over the water at Boothbay Harbor, the 40 patio seats are particularly fine.

Steamers and mussels are on the appetizer list. Seafood chowder, with lobster, clams, and shrimp, "is a real meal," said Jack Cogswell, owner since 2002. He was the owner of the Upper Deck in town for 10 years before that.

Coconut sea scallops are on the dinner menu, along with sirloins, and prime rib is served every day. Rack of lamb might be a special; the Downeast T-bone, a 14-ounce steak with lobster sauce with lobster meat is $18.95. Twin lobster specials, all 1½-pound lobsters, and haddock, salmon, swordfish, and tuna are some of the seafood on the menu.

According to Cogswell, the large paella can feed a whole family with its array of seafood and meat in seasoned rice. Seafood scampi is made with shrimp, scallops, and lobster. The lobster rolls are made with lobster picked in the kitchen, using a whole 1½-pound lobster each, which has about 4 ounces of meat. They're served on a grilled hoagie roll with lettuce, with a side of mayonnaise and of drawn butter.

The Boothbay Harbor Farmer's Market is held on Thursday 9 AM–noon at the Town Commons on Route 27 from mid-May to early October.

amariscotta

Andrews' Pine View Restaurant
(207) 563-2899
769 Main Street (by the intersection of Business Route 1 and Route 1 at the north end of Damariscotta)
Open daily for lunch and dinner 11:30–8, call for hours off-season
Entrées $5 to $20

☛ *A casual family place serving both lunch and dinner anytime*

The menu for lunch and dinner is the same, and all items can be ordered at any time. Pasta Alfredo with marinated grilled chicken ($14.98) comes with a salad and homemade bread. Haddock Lester ($9.99 small, $15.99 large; most entrées are available in two sizes), baked haddock with crumb topping with Parmesan, lemon, and garlic, is the most popular choice on the dinner menu. Honey buttered scallops ($11.99 small, $17.99 large) have scallops baked under honey and butter.

Craig Andrews had his own restaurant in Boothbay Harbor, Andrews' Harborside, for 17 years before he moved out to Route 1. With a degree from the Culinary Institute of America, Andrews presides over steaks, fried seafood, and salads. A children's menu makes this a fine stop for families.

Homemade desserts include blueberry cobbler, apple crisp, lemon cake pudding with raspberry sauce, brownie hot fudge sundae, Grapenut pudding, and chess pie ($2.75–4.50).

Backstreet Restaurant
(207) 563-5666
Elm Street Plaza, 17 Back Elm Street
Open in summer Sunday through Thursday 11:30–8:30, Friday and Saturday
until 9; call for winter hours
Entrées $13 to $20
Handicapped accessible

☛ *Casual dining and good food with a water view*

Look for this place off Main Street, in the Elm Street Plaza. It's right on the river, with views of the water from many of the approximately 100 seats in the dining room, with deep red walls.

Grilled asparagus with portobello pine nut ragout and chèvre ($8) was a complicated success. Salads are well-made, with mesclun and house-made creamy light blue cheese dressing. The hamburger is big and accompanied by perfect french fries, both tasting especially fine with a glass of malbec from the wine list. Fried fish keeps lunches simpler and absolutely dependable.

An encounter with a seafood stew that was less than stellar was one glitch. A steak with lobster claws in hollandaise was okay. Surf and turf with pork tenderloin and shrimp ($21), with black sticky rice and well-dressed greens, was a winner.

Desserts are all made here and change every week. I can recommend the vanilla bread pudding ($4.75) glazed with caramel and accompanied by vanilla ice cream.

Damariscotta River Grill
(207) 563-2992
155 Main Street
Open daily 11–9:30 (closing at 8:30 in winter), Sunday brunch 9–2:30
Entrées $14 to $22

☛ *Well-made meals that cater to everyone who likes good food and reasonable prices*

This hopping place with exposed brick and two floors offers pan-seared scallops with a balsamic reduction, spinach, and roasted tomatoes; a risotto and a roast of the night; and prime rib every Friday on a menu that changes seasonally. Favorites are the lobster cakes with hand-picked lobster, and oysters on the half-shell or baked oysters topped with bacon, spinach, and Pernod cream sauce. Three sauces accompany the raw Pemaquid oysters, brought up from the water less than 10 miles away, and they are always popular.

Morning Dew Farm in Newcastle provides much of the fresh produce in the growing season.

Owned by the same family as the Anchor Inn at Round Pond (see page 160), this place in the middle of town offers a lot of fresh seafood and grilled meat. An upstairs bar and dining room handle summer crowds.

Italian Seafood Stew ($16.53) combined mussels, Maine shrimp, and fish in a savory, garlic-flavored broth. But a roast pork risotto sampled here was bland. A menu favorite that might be a better choice could be the seared scallops ($16.22) with roasted tomato, spinach, and balsamic reduction.

A baker makes all of the homemade desserts and bread. Eight to 12 desserts are offered every night and include crème brûlée, a variety of cheesecakes, and bread pudding flavored with Amaretto that tasted wonderful one night (desserts all about $4).

King Eider's Pub
(207) 563-6008
2 Elm Street
www.kingeiderspub.com
Hospitality—Bustling staff usually handle the busy meals well
Open daily 11:30–11
Entrées $9 to $19

☛ *Longer hours make this the place to go early and late for seafood, soup, and desserts.*

"We're the home of New England's finest crabcakes," Todd Maurer, one of the owners, told me, a claim under local, not to mention statewide, dispute, and one with which I cannot agree. He also said the crabcakes are made following a secret recipe, and with the freshest local ingredients.

But everyone agrees Damariscotta oysters are some of the best in the country, and they are served here on the half shell, shucked to order (six for $10.99), so enjoy.

Downstairs is a cozy pub, outside are tables for warm-weather dining, and upstairs is a restaurant.

Breads, including baguettes and rye and corn bread, are made by the restaurant, come with the meals, and are used in the sandwiches served at lunch.

Dinner could be a spicy cioppino ($24), a seafood stew with a tomato base and fresh herbs. Another easy way to enjoy seafood would be the seafood pot-pie ($20), with lobster, haddock, salmon, and scallops. Bangers and mash are ready to succor the seafood-sick.

"Molly's famous homemade desserts" are another of Maurer's selling points. They could include a bread pudding with Irish whiskey sauce, toffee apple pie, or

Fresh oysters and lots of seafood are on the menu at King Eider's Pub in Damariscotta.

Guinness chocolate cake. The locals like this place, and we loved its clam chowder late one cold night, when everyone else had shown up and the place was like a warm bright hearth sheltered from the night.

Salt Bay Café
(207) 563-3302
88 Main Street
Hospitality—Friendly, fast service
Open for breakfast 7:30–10:30, lunch 11–4, dinner 4 to closing
Entrées $7 to $22

☛ *A big vegetarian menu, and many good meat and seafood dishes, with low prices*

Consistency has made this place successful; almost everything is made on the premises, said Peter Everett, owner for eight years.

You can find breakfast, lunch, and dinner at family-friendly Salt Bay Café in Damariscotta.

Everett offers crabcakes, fresh seafood, steaks, and seafood pastas, with a full vegetarian menu of 20 to 25 items making this a favorite establishment for vegetarians. Roast duck, chicken Florentine, and many other dishes make up the four-page menu. Fried oysters would be a good choice, or try the Gaelic Steak, an 8-ounce tenderloin with Irish whiskey and hot heavy cream. A lobster dinner, the classic, is $17.95.

74 Maine Bistro
(207) 563-7444
74 Main Street
www.74maine.com
Open for dinner 11:30–9 Monday, Wednesday, and Thursday; 11:30–10 Friday and Saturday; closed Tuesday
Entrées $12 to $25

☞ *Welcomed with open arms by grateful area food lovers, 74 Maine Bistro makes fine food.*

Since opening day on August 16, 2006, the dining room has been busy.

Lunch is sandwiches, burgers, and big salads, a Greek or a Caesar, or the 74 Bistro ($8) with blue cheese, roasted peppers, and balsamic vinaigrette.

Chef James Metzger has cooked all over the East Coast. He returned to a contemporary house on Meetinghouse Road that his late father designed and built, and said to himself, "I'm not working for anyone else." One part of his space, inspired by his father's architectural work, has a blue floor with a big wine rack set in the middle; wines include Saintsbury Chardonnay and Canyon Road Merlot. The Mad Housewife Cabernet ($5 a glass, $18 a bottle) sounds just about right.

Metzger likes to put together fresh fish and fresh salsas and relishes, like shiitake mushrooms and poblano chutney, or blue cheese merlot sauce. A calamari appetizer is sautéed in olive oil and garlic and served with greens, kalamata olives, and tomatoes. Salmon ($14) is grilled with a miso-honey marinade and served on mixed greens. A simple pasta dinner here is *pappardelle* with mixed wild mushrooms, olive oil, basil, and Parmesan.

Breakfast, Lunch, Groceries, Farm Stand, and Ice Cream

The Breakfast Place (207-563-5434), Main Street.
Open 7–1 for breakfast only in summer, and for lunch as well in winter. Anything customers want they can have at this accommodating place, or they can choose from a menu that lists a Toad in a Hole, among many other things. The wide selection of baked goods, all made fresh each morning, included muffins (blueberry, raspberry, blackberry, banana-nut, corn), cinnamon buns, cheddar biscuits, English muffins, and white, wheat, oatmeal, cinnamon-raisin, anadama, rye, pumpernickel, and cheddar breads on the day I visited. Homemade crabmeat and cream cheese omelets are often ordered, as is a popular shrimp Creole omelet made with Maine shrimp.

Clark's Farm Stand (207-563-6866), 380 Main Street.
You'll have to get off Route 1 and drive into town to find this farm stand, where the blueberries are extraordinary and the rest of the produce beautiful.

Rising Tide Natural Foods Co-op (207-563-5556), 15 Coastal Marketplace Drive.
Open daily 8–7. Rising Tide sells Rosario Vitanza's Italian Bread, Tuva and Black Crow breads, and Café Miranda dips and sauces. Mobo, a partnership between Café Miranda and Borealis Breads, makes terrific little pizzas. Organic local produce in-season, local organic eggs, Straws Farm raw whole milk from

Newcastle, and Wicked Joe roasted coffee are also available. There's a café offering sandwiches, muffins, cookies, and soups made here every day, with all-organic ingredients.

Round Top Ice Cream (207-563-5307), Business Route 1.

Open from the first weekend in April to Columbus Day from 11:30 to 10 in summer, until 8 off-season. This Round Top provides many coastal businesses with their ice cream and makes the stuff year-round. Brenda and Gary Woodcock have owned this business for 18 years, but worked at it for 34. The business has been established since 1924 and started at the nearby Round Top Farm. With 15 percent butterfat, the product is properly called a super-premium ice cream. More than 60 flavors are made, as well as sorbets, sherbets, and frozen yogurts. Fall flavors include pumpkin, Indian pudding, ginger, cinnamon, and apple cinnamon; all are made with cream from Maine's three biggest dairies. Different creams goes into different flavors, because the cooks here are very alert to the creams' tastes. In the summer, try the red raspberry swirl.

The Uptown Café (207-563-7000), 212 Main Street.

Open for breakfast and lunch Monday through Saturday 8–5, Sunday 8–2 for brunch. Enjoy your morning in the flowered-cushion window seat while you check your e-mail with the wireless Internet.

For brunch the café serves frittatas, huevos rancheros, and buttermilk pancakes, two kinds of hash, one of them roast beef and the other veggie, homemade granola, and seven or eight breakfast pastries, like croissants and cream puffs. Beanstalk Coffee Roasters from Wellfleet, Massachusetts, roasts the coffee, using organic Fair Trade beans. "We don't have shortening in this café," said Ruth Jones, the barista, who added that the wedding cakes made here are a big part of the business. There are only 15 seats inside; you can get lunch to go too. When summer comes, drink the fresh lemonade, and enjoy homemade ice cream, like blackberry.

Weatherbird Café (207-563-8993), 72 Courtyard (just off Main Street).

A small café with good lunches, including panini with prosciutto, and a wide range of ingredients. Soups, such as asparagus with wild rice, often sell out. Fresh-baked scones might include mascarpone-filled and ham-filled, or ginger-pear and raspberry. Pecan brioche are also available, and coffee comes from Rock City Coffee Roasters. Linzer tortes are from a local baker, and lavender-lemon

The highest-quality cream goes into fine Round Top Ice Cream.

and rosemary-lemon pound cakes and great gingerbread with crystallized ginger also are available. Gelati from New Hampshire are featured too.

Produce, local and imported cheeses, eggs, great wines, and prepared foods to go are sold. Outdoor seating is available in summer.

The Damariscotta Farmer's Market is held Monday 9–noon from late June to late August at the Damariscotta River Association Preserve, just off Route 1 on Belvedere Road; and Friday 9–noon mid-May through late October at the same location.

Newcastle

Lupines Restaurant
(207) 563-5685, 1-800-832-8669
At the Newcastle Inn, River Road
www.newcastleinn.com
Open for dinner Tuesday through Saturday at 6 Columbus Day through May,
Friday and Saturday only; closed January
Prix fixe dinner, $55, as well as à la carte

☛ *Elegant meals with ingredients culled from surrounding sources*

The prix fixe dinners that are well-known here are now not the only way you can order a meal; à la carte dinners started in fall 2006.

Dale Swartzentruber, who worked with Sam Hayward at Fore Street, is the chef here. Using fresh local produce, he makes a fine wild mushroom consommé from locally foraged and market mushrooms.

Nine wines can be bought by the glass. A long wine list is constantly expanding, and the wines are sometimes chosen to particularly complement the menu.

Start with local favorites: Damariscotta River oysters served with lemongrass mignonette, or Swango Farm asparagus, or scallop chowder with bacon and lovage. Dinner entrées could be smoked duck breast with greens and grits; wild sockeye salmon with peas and carrots and semolina pudding; or a

Local cheeses and many other Maine specialties are served at Lupines at the Newcastle Inn.

stew of foraged mushrooms, leeks, and green garlic with potato dumplings.

A cheese course might feature Scarborough Faire, Appleton Creamery's herb-crusted ewe's-milk cheese.

Chocolate torte ($8) varies often, with different kinds of chocolate and toppings according to the seasons and the chef's whim.

New Harbor

Bradley Inn
(207) 677-2105, 1-800-942-5560
3063 Bristol Road
www.bradleyinn.com
Open daily except Wednesday from the end of May through October, Thursday through Sunday off-season
Entrées $23 to $28

☛ *A pleasant ambience with candlelight, and elegant food to match*

At the tip of the Pemaquid peninsula, this old sea captain's home has weathered more storms than any of us and wraps itself around diners with a congenial atmosphere. Meals could include a pecan-crusted lamb loin or sea scallops with pasta in a cognac beurre blanc.

Cupboard Café
(207) 677-3911
137 Huddle Road
Hospitality—Order at the counter and your food will be brought to your table.
Open Tuesday through Saturday 8–3, Sunday 8–12 for breakfast only (table service); closed Monday; call for hours off-season
Lunch $5.25 to $9.25

Everything is made here, from scratch, from the salad dressings to the roast meat and chicken in the sandwiches. The breads, cinnamon buns, and muffins are baked in the daylight basement kitchen and, like everything else, come upstairs on a dumbwaiter before being served. Tables fill the homey building, and a few more are on the small deck.

A rich chowder or homemade soup could be Texas Stew with beef, sausage, and chicken with a barbecue flavor; tomato, mushroom, and peas; or curried carrot for vegetarians. Haddock chowder is made daily (soups are $2.95 cup, $4.95 bowl; chowder each $1 more). I can vouch for the haddock chowder, a milk-broth version that is light and savory. Wednesday is chicken potpie day; take one home in a little aluminum foil casserole ($9.95; feeds two).

A popular sandwich might be the Reuben, with corned beef and fresh rye. Fred's Favorite is a sandwich with turkey, dressing, and cranberry sauce ($6.25). The salads are perfectly fresh.

Sandwiches and good soups precede the tempting desserts at the Cupboard Café in New Harbor.

Apple dumplings ($4.50) show up in the case in fall, served warm with fresh whipped cream, or try the cream puffs filled with French pastry cream with ganache on top. Mary Dee Grant and her parents, Fred and Claudia Hatch, own the business together, started August 2004; Grant works upstairs getting orders and delivering them, while her parents cook below. Everyone is glad they are here because this is now the best place for breakfast and lunch in the area.

Shaw's Fish & Lobster Wharf
(207) 677-2200
129 State Road (Route 32)
www.shawsfishandlobster.com
Open daily 11–9 in summer; Sunday through Thursday 11–8 in fall; Friday and Saturday 11–9 off-season, from the Thursday before Mother's Day until the Sunday after Columbus Day
Entrées $10 to $30

☛ *One of the great, huge seafood restaurants on the coast*

A triple lobster can be more than $30 when lobster prices are high, other times around $25, but most people go for the twin special at this huge seafood restaurant. One woman from down south of here extolled its true Maine flavor, downscale and straightforward.

With counter service and paper and plastic, the kitchen serves customers their orders when their numbers are called. Three hundred people, 100 inside and 200 out, can make this a crowded spot; Lloyd Mendelson, one of the two owners, estimated he serves 100,000 people in a summer. I've known it to look decidedly weary after a busy night. It's set where the Hardy Boat Cruises depart to take folks out for a glimpse of the repopulated puffins, and is therefore perfect for a casual meal before or after a cruise. In the busy season, you may have to walk down from a parking lot set up the road.

The place has a raw bar underneath the deck, right by where the boats dock. Pemaquid ale made in North Whitefield, Maine, by Sheepscot River Brewery is the most popular ale, and goes well with the revered Damariscotta oysters with lemon and cocktail sauce. Fried clams, shrimp, scallops, and haddock, all from Maine, are the most popular items on the menu, but broiled halibut and swordfish ($14.95) can be enjoyed here too. Homemade chowders and stews are well-loved. Full bar available.

Homemade strawberry and blueberry pies, among others, range from $2.75 to $3.75.

Pemaquid Harbor

Pemaquid Fisherman's Co-op's
Harbor View Restaurant

(207) 677-2642, (207) 677-2801
Co-op Road off Pemaquid Harbor Road
www.pemaquidlobsterco-op.com
Open daily 11–8 from Memorial Day weekend to Columbus Day
Entrées $7 to $21

☞ *Picnic-style dining indoors or out, in a spot that looks out on the Pemaquid River*

Fifty to 100 lobsters are picked each day at this ultimate Maine spot, where the lobster rolls hold almost a half pound of meat, 8 full ounces, and were selling for $14.95 in 2006.

But put such a feast together with one of the most peaceful, expansive views of the water, and you have a paradise indeed.

Picnic benches with plastic tablecloths flap in the breeze, both inside and outside the simple building. Every one affords a wide view of an endless green lawn and the four-square roof of a classic Maine house sitting just up from the endless blue water.

The serene ocean on a calm summer day can't be topped here at Pemaquid Fisherman's Co-op's Harbor View Restaurant.

An occasional special, the crabmeat roll ($8.95) competes with the regular menu of fried haddock, clams, shrimp, or scallops. A shore dinner with a 1¼-pound lobster, steamed clams, corn on the cob, coleslaw, and a roll was $20.95 in 2006.

The lobster, of course, tastes great here, at the oldest continuously operated fisherman's cooperative in the United States. Bring a bottle of wine and a salad, as many locals and summer residents do, and settle in for a beautiful evening.

Round Pond (in Bristol)

Anchor Inn
(207) 529-5584
Anchor Inn Road
Open daily in summer for lunch and dinner; closed some days off-season, Mother's Day through Columbus Day
Entrées $13 to $22

☛ *High standards set this casual seaside restaurant up on a level with its lovely harbor view.*

Run for 17 years by the same family and the same chef-owners, this restaurant set on beautiful Round Pond Harbor serves great crabcakes and seafood. Fresh boiled and baked stuffed lobsters are popular, and the chowder makes everyone happy. Steak and chicken are on the list that also includes five dinner specials, two of them fresh-fish entrées. One pleased customer enjoyed a crab melt, and recommended the Italian seafood stew and seared scallops with red and yellow tomatoes. The restaurant seats 100, with room at the bar for a dozen more, and has a wine selection with a few unusual white varietals, modestly priced.

Desserts are homemade, and may include Baileys Irish Cream Cheesecake or Kyle's Killer Chocolate Cake, with white chocolate ganache filling and dark chocolate ganache on the outside. There's a large variety of fruit and mixed-fruit pies, and an innovation—Swedish almond cream with fresh berries.

Southport

Lawnmere Inn

(207) 633-2544, 1-800-633-7645
65 Hendricks Road, P.O. Box 29
www.lawnmereinn.com
Hospitality—Our server went out of her way to make our meal good.
Open daily for dinner Memorial Day weekend through mid-October
Entrées $15 to $37 (for the baked stuffed lobster)

☛ *Old-fashioned comfortable seaside hotel with wonderful, up-to-date food*

The glassy water of the inlet reflected the stroking wings of the gulls moving across, close to the surface. We were looking at a cove off Townsend Gut from our chairs in the Lawnmere's knotty-pine dining room. A lawn sloped down to the water from the inn, and children ran across the grass while a couple paddled to shore in a kayak.

The lobby also looks out on the water at this comfortable, old-fashioned inn, and white and navy blue tablecloths and napkins keep the tables in the dining room spiffy.

A new chef, Pete Murphy, started working here in 2006. He graduated from Johnson and Wales in Rhode Island. Innkeeper Donna Phelps said the revamped menu includes comfort food and veers away from anything too fussy, with fried fish in one section, and a dish like tuna steak with crushed pepper, leeks, and potato gnocchi ($23) in another.

A salad and lobster or corn chowder might begin a fine dinner here. Steaks and Lobster Bellgion ($32), with the shelled meat of a lobster served with a cracked-pepper cream sauce, vegetable, and potato, are possible entrées.

Six wines can be ordered by the glass, some from Clos du Bois ($6); 15 reds and 15 whites, plus champagne, can be ordered by the bottle.

Chocolate torte, crème brûlée, and a nightly soufflé—chocolate or Grand Marnier—and cheesecake are for dessert.

You can enjoy breakfast here, too, whether you spend the night at Lawnmere or elsewhere. Try the homemade corned beef hash or blueberry pancakes. It would be a pleasure to stay the night at this nicely renovated inn that is keeping its old charm.

Robinson's Wharf

(207) 633-3830
Route 27 (just across the swinging bridge over Townsend Gut)
www.livelobstersfrommaine.com
Open daily for lunch and dinner 11:30 to close mid-June through Labor Day
Entrées $2 to $20

☛ *Away from Boothbay Harbor crowds, on the peaceful coast, with good seafood*

Lobster dinners, fried seafood plates, and seafood rolls are the highlights at this classic lobster shack, where the lobstermen make deliveries and the restaurant fills what was once the island's bowling alley. Outdoor dining in good weather puts you right on the water.

Clambakes for 20 to 25 people can be arranged in the main dining room.

You can buy live lobsters and clams here year-round; a small fish market sells wholesale and retail lobsters and other seafood year-round (open 8–3 daily off-season).

Wiscasset

Le Garage

(207) 882-5409
15 Water Street (at the town dock, one block south of Route 1)
Open daily in summer for lunch and dinner, closed Monday from Labor Day to June
Entrées $9 to $25

☛ *Casual down and more elegant up, with a view of Wiscasset Harbor; well-made entrées*

Light suppers are offered at this popular restaurant, like a charbroiled lamb and vegetable kabob ($14.95) served with a fresh vegetable, coleslaw, and potato or rice. Stuffed filet of sole ($12.95) and finnan haddie ($10.95) are other examples from the light supper list.

A regular dinner might be walnut-crusted fillet of haddock ($17.45) with vegetable, baked or mashed potato, or rice; bistro steak; New York strip sirloin; or grilled lamb steak ($21.95). The wine list is long, and several wines are offered by the glass.

Lunch brings fans of the sandwiches and salads, and a big assortment of omelets, like ham and cheese.

Rolls are made here, as are the desserts—cobblers, crisps, and crêpes.

Red's Eats

(207) 882-6128
Water Street (Route 1 just south of the bridge)
Open April through September 11 AM–2 AM Friday and Saturday,
until 11 PM Monday through Thursday, and noon–6 on Sunday
Lobster rolls about $14.95

☛ *The famous place with a line serves big lobster rolls with melted butter, and hot dogs.*

People stand in long lines to order the food at this little roadside stand. In the hot sun such behavior seems downright pathological, but it certainly ranks as one of the sights to see—a line alongside Route 1 all summer long—when you are driving through Wiscasset. There is a reputation here, an allure, and much buzz about the best lobster rolls, and that accounts for the patient waiting. You can get the lobster roll with just melted butter, and a big bunch of lobster meat, about 4 ounces, comes on the toasted bun ($14.95 in 2006). The lobster is processed elsewhere, as it is at many of the places on the Maine Coast that sell lobster rolls. Also, there are hot dogs.

Sarah's Café

(207) 882-7504
45 Water Street (corner of Main and Water)
www.sarahscafe.com
Open Monday through Friday 11–9, open at 7 AM Saturday and Sunday, until 8 in winter
Entrées $10 to $18

☛ *A good place for a meal on the road, with hot soup and fresh baked goods*

Sarah Hennessey, owner of Sarah's Café for 26 years, uses all her own recipes. She started a restaurant in Robinhood when she was 15, making pies, burgers, and fries, and hasn't stopped since. In 1981, her vocation was a home-delivery business in Boothbay Harbor; she moved to her present location in 1987. She bought and renovated the present restaurant in 1997, and added the pub.

All along Hennessey has been serving meals made from scratch. Home-made soups and chowders are made from a list of 578 soups developed over the years, and accompanied by homemade bread. The owner's little brother, Howard, is the lobsterman; Swango Farm in Woolwich is the biggest supplier of vegetables; and herbs come from Sarah's own garden in Georgetown.

Lobster cooked 12 different ways, including the Whaleboat, with spinach, tomatoes, and two cheeses in a dough turnover, are some of the favorites on the menu. There are always lots of specials, with seafood, salads, many vegetar-ian items, and Mexican dishes—the tostados are "smothered with beans and cheese"—filling the list.

The two outside decks have an engaging view of the water and the traffic on the bridge.

Sea Basket
(207) 882-6581
Route 1
Hospitality—Counter service in an immaculate, cheerful dining room
Open Tuesday through Saturday 11–8 from March to mid-December, closed mid-December through most of February
Entrées $5.95 to $15.95

☛ *A local favorite for lobster stew, fabulous scallops, and well-made fried fish*

Following the white arrows painted on the pavement makes walking into this bright, cheerful restaurant as easy as pie; and the perfectly trimmed shrubs and window boxes are signs in themselves of the well-organized, tranquil efficiency reigning inside. Blue molded wood benches fill the floor, and murals of green fields along the sea fill the walls with color.

The menu over the counter offers the classic favorites—chowders ($6.99 for a bowl of fish chowder), dinner baskets, and jumbo platters of fried fish. Sin-gle servings are thoughtfully available, without fries, rolls, or coleslaw ($6.50 for fried Maine shrimp); and all the offerings also come in sandwiches or rolls, like a big haddock filet sandwich ($6.99).

A kid's menu, with penne pasta with Parmesan ($3.99) and peanut butter and jelly sandwiches ($3.99, with fries), makes this place work for any family.

Scott Belanger works here now, a part-owner along with his mother and father; the Belanger family started the business in 1980.

Although many places along the coast stick to the trans-fat-filled oils, called

Everything is neat and trim at the well-run Sea Basket in Wiscasset.

partially hydrogenated, for their frying, Belanger said his choice to use high-quality canola oil and a convection-style fryer have been valued by every customer who understands the difference. His well-established business had a banner year in 2006, which he attributes to the high quality of his seafood.

Angela Emerson comes in at 6 AM every day to wash the place clean, from the ceiling to the floors, and trim those perfect bushes. "She saves me," Belanger said. The business is closed for only a short spell in winter because, Scott said, they want to keep the staff who run the restaurant so well, and they have a loyal local clientele who pop in to keep things going even in dreary March.

The restaurant is well-known for its lobster stew, which can be purchased frozen and brought back home, and for its great scallops, bought from the same boats every year.

Among several options for dessert, the rainbow of big whoopie pies stands out, from raspberry cream to peanut butter to classic chocolate (all $1.99 each). This place is a favorite, and many Mainers know just where it sits—on the inland side of Route 1 south of the village of Wiscasset. The extensive parking lots are ready to accommodate everyone. You can also bring your own beer or wine to enjoy with your meal—the restaurant does not have a liquor license.

Sprague's Lobster
(207) 882-1236
Route 1 (on the wharf at the western end of the Wiscasset bridge)
Open daily 11–8 mid-June through the weekend after Columbus Day
Entrées $3 to $15

☛ *Takeout, inexpensive shore dinners with fresh boiled lobster, and big crab and lobster rolls*

Lobster rolls, with 4 ounces of lobster meat, cost $13.95 in 2006; a haddock sandwich $5.95, a fish-and-chips basket $7.95; and one with homemade clam fritters, crabcakes, or clam cakes cost the same. There is a shorter wait, less expense, and a better view here than just up the road at Red's Eats.

Lobster bakes and clambakes are offered by this operation whenever and just about wherever a customer wants to have them—including Virginia. But most are held here in Maine. For their take-out business, owners Frank and Linda Sprague are hoping to add more room on their corner of the Creamery Pier, a town dock, with a few more picnic tables. Frank Sprague makes clam fritters fresh from chopped clams without the bellies but emphasizes that this is his

Steamed lobsters are just one possibility at Sprague's Lobster in Wiscasset.

Shop for lunch, hors d'oeuvres, and dinner at Treats in Wiscasset, and break for breakfast.

business's 18th year and that the centerpieces of his meals are the cooked lobsters. They each have their own timer when they go into the pot for your dinner.

Lunch and Takeout

Treats (207-882-6192; www.treatsofmaine.com), 80 Main Street.

Open Monday through Saturday 10–6, Sunday 12–3. This gorgeous food store makes Wiscasset a lucky place, but knowledgeable travelers can visit it easily. The interior, with its old butcher-block table, stone counters, and array of appealing food will rouse an appetite as you contemplate what to buy.

Customers sit at a long table in the rear of the store to drink the strong coffee and eat blueberry muffins in the morning, or to enjoy the sandwiches for lunch. The store makes different sandwiches every day, rearranging its turkey, roast beef, salami, and ham with various cheeses on bread from Black Crow and Borealis, delivered fresh in the morning.

Teas, jams, maple syrup, chocolate, and a fetching tower of homemade cookies beckon along the way through the store. In a neighboring area, another glass display case is stocked with cheese, including Hudson Valley Camembert. Along the walls filled with wine from $6 to $200, you can find a $44 Nickel & Nickel Russian River Valley Syrah. Value-priced reds are displayed in a basket, ready for dinner. Wine tastings are held every month.

I can't imagine not stopping here on the way through town, to get the last details of a picnic or a fabulous house present; it's on the right when you drive north, two blocks before the bridge out of town.

CHAPTER 5

Western Penobscot Bay

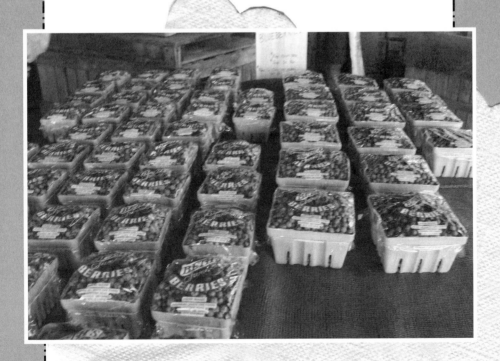

THRIVING TOWNS LINE UP in this wonderfully mixed section of the coast, the site of what some call the state's best restaurant: Primo, in Rockland. Here Route 1 gets to hug the water, turning north in Rockland, and crawls through the crowded streets of Camden. Camden has been an upscale tourist stop for a long time, but Rockland seems to be the place on the move now, with several good restaurants, bakeries, and cafés. This blue-collar town is vital year-round; Camden seems more livable after the summer season is done.

Belfast sustains its energetic mix of high and low, with Chase's Daily overflowing with the most beautiful produce you've ever seen in the summer and an elephant trumpeting from the roof of the Colonial Theater.

Of course there are always changes going on in the restaurant scene. With the growing tourist business here, some places are able to succeed and thrive. Francine Bistro, a small and completely admirable restaurant in Camden, makes the most sophisticated happy year-round. Jesse Henry, co-owner of The Edge at Inn at Ocean's Edge, plans to open a grill pub, the Knox Grill Company, in one of the Knox Mill buildings on Mechanic Street. Around the corner there will be a greengrocer selling fine products from farms in the area and offering the kind of marketing that is on the upswing on the coast, connecting customers with the land and to what is fresh. Soon what's for dinner will be what's growing that week, all over the state of Maine.

Belfast

Chase's Daily
(207) 338-0555
96 Main Street
Hospitality—Busy, but the service is up to speed and accommodating
Open Tuesday through Saturday 7–10:30 for breakfast, 11:30–3 for lunch (2:30 off-season), dinner Friday 5:30–8:30, brunch Sunday 8–1
Entrées $14 to $16
Reservations almost always necessary for Friday-night dinners

☛ *A beautiful vegetarian paradise (especially during harvest season) with great soups, salads, and lunch and breakfast, and Friday dinner feasts*

The Chase Farm in Freedom stocks the back room of this high-ceilinged space. On my visit in August, the crates of tomatoes, baby artichokes, French filet beans, and long, snaky pale purple Japanese eggplants filled that space with their glamorous shapes and colors.

Make a pilgrimage to Chase's Daily in Belfast during harvest season, when you can dine on, and purchase, wonderful fresh produce.

Those vegetables were on the menu in front, in the roasted eggplant sandwich ($8) with peppers, fresh greens, and walnut sauce on grilled white sourdough bread, and in the heirloom tomato salad ($9), worth every penny. The roasted escarole omelet with feta held slightly caramelized greens and liquefying tart cheese in buttery eggs. It was one of the best breakfasts I have had in years.

Some people have been known to complain about not being able to get bacon with their breakfast here. But when you can order a Swiss chard and feta omelet ($6.75) with potatoes and toast, or buttermilk pancakes with fresh blueberries ($6.25), you can postpone bacon, if not forever at least for a day.

The room is packed on Friday night for dinners of enchiladas and Middle Eastern specialties, or vegetarian tarts and baked dishes. One late summer item was an heirloom tomato tart ($16) with savory custard, Gruyère, and thyme, served with salad greens in a thyme vinaigrette.

Imagine for dessert the chocolate cake ($5) with raspberry filling and chocolate buttercream icing.

The bakery makes anadama bread, rye walnut loaves, and semolina bread, and bakes fresh ginger-cream scones and pear-almond muffins. Cheeses like Manchego from Spain and Great Hill Blue from Marion, Massachusetts, are available at the counter.

This is a place to seek out, especially in late summer and fall, and enjoy. One couple we encountered there had driven up from Portland just for lunch.

Darby's Restaurant and Pub
(207) 338-2339
155 High Street
Hospitality—Friendly and helpful
Open daily for lunch 11:30–3:30, Sunday 12–3:30, dinner from 5
Entrées $8 to $21

☞ *An old-fashioned space with a wide-ranging menu, burgers to pad Thai to fish-and-chips*

There are so many different things to eat here, under the tin ceiling or alongside the old bar, both of which have been restored and preserved since this place opened in 1865. Seafood à la Greque comes with a small salad and makes eating this supreme comfort food a little more respectable. The portobello sandwich is served on the restaurant's own bread, with sautéed onions, roasted garlic mayonnaise, and fresh mozzarella; hand-cut french fries are included. Big salads, pad

Thai, enchiladas, and sweet potato raviolis give a glimpse of the range here, and I shouldn't omit the potato latkes with sour cream and applesauce.

Seng Thai
(207) 338-0010
160 Searsport Avenue (Route 1)
Hospitality—Quick, attentive, and perfect
Open Tuesday through Sunday from 11:30 for lunch and dinner
Entrées $9 to $14

☞ *A great Thai place with spicy dishes and fresh ingredients*

I had the Japanese eggplant special ($9.95) for lunch; it came with red and green peppers, shrimp, and chicken all in a black bean sauce. Given a scale from 1 to 5, I asked for the spice level of 2. Brown rice was another $2, and white an extra $1. My friend ordered the pad Thai, which arrived with a carved white radish rose, lots of green scallions and bean sprouts, and a good, clear flavor not unduly adulterated with sugar.

My eggplant was one of the same pale purple, curved, slender beauties I would later encounter in the produce section at Chase's Daily (see page 171). Decorated with a beet rose, the plate gave off an enticing aroma of garlic, and I enjoyed every bit. I'd been warned the spiciness levels were serious. Level 2 was perfect, giving me just the slightest heat and mildest perspiration.

A couple of beautifully arranged platters of spring rolls were ready for an incoming customer who was throwing a party. You could call ahead and bring one to the house to which you've been invited some summer weekend.

The Twilight Café
(207) 338-0937
39 Main Street
Hospitality—Willing to go out of their way to accommodate you
Open for dinner at 5:30 Monday through Saturday in summer
Entrées $16 to $25
Reservations recommended

☞ *Somewhat upscale fish and beef dishes in a friendly, casual atmosphere*

With a short wine list that nevertheless spans the globe, the Twilight Café sets out to do a little more than its neighbors, while at the same time keeping its food to a fairly narrow path. Appetizers include mussels steamed with white wine, with a little cream and Dijon mustard; Ducktrap smoked salmon; and a plain classic, shrimp cocktail. Pecan-crusted lobster cakes with pumpkin-ginger crème fraîche headed up the entrées, and beef tenderloin with port wine mushroom sauce followed. The large room with a storefront window on the street has a good local base and does more business, of course, in summer.

Young's Lobster Pound
(207) 338-1160
Mitchell Avenue
Hospitality—The efficient counter service dispenses hundreds of lobsters to customers.
Open 7–7 in summer; open in winter for takeout only, closing at 5:30
Entrées $10 to $17 and up for lobsters

☛ *A big lobster pound and take-out place with views of Penobscot Bay*

This place keeps thousands of lobsters in its tanks—and as many as 500 people can find a place to sit and eat them, either upstairs or outside at a picnic table. Good weather is everything, because there is no heat in the big inside dining room. After the warm weather goes, the place is open for takeout only.

But when the weather is warm, this is one of the area's best spots for a lobster dinner. The picnic tables along the river have a wide-open view of downtown Belfast across the water, and the boat traffic on Passagassawakeag River.

The lobsters steamed at Young's Lobster Pound in Belfast are right off the boat.

You can always buy lobsters, clams, mussels, and crabs here, either fresh or cooked to go. An 8-ounce cup of lobster stew is $6.50, a lobster roll is $12.95, and a crab roll costs $9.95.

Sautéed lobster can be enjoyed for $20.95 (varies with the market price), served with potato salad, coleslaw, and chips. A lobster salad for the same price has the same trimmings. Oysters on the half shell are sometimes offered. In 2006 the Shore Dinner, with a 1½-pound lobster, steamers, a cup of clam chowder or lobster stew, corn or coleslaw, chips, and melted butter cost $28.95.

Lunch, Takeout, Coffee, and Ice Cream

Bay Wrap (207-338-9757; www.baywrap.com), 20 Beaver Street.

Open Monday through Friday 11–7, Saturday until 4; closes earlier in winter. Walk through Belfast Music to find this spot from Main Street, or come in by its street entrance. Try the daily soups, including turkey, black bean, and vegetable all stars (no meat). Or enjoy the popular wraps—maybe the Wraptor ($6.90), with roast turkey and garlic aioli, greens, tomatoes, onions, sprouts, and cucumbers in a flour tortilla. A list of eight vegetarian choices includes Delhi Delight ($6.90), with curried cauliflower, carrots, lentils, jasmine rice, Asian slaw, garlic yogurt sauce, and mango salsa in a tortilla. All were available in a small size for one dollar less.

The Belfast Co-op Café (207-338-2532), 123 High Street.

The store is open daily 7:30 AM–8 PM; grilled sandwiches and lunch specials available 11:30–7. Order from the chalkboard menu in this big health-food store. Roast beef and honey ham sandwiches were $5.95, and veggie and cheese $4.95. Flatbread pizza made with Mobo crust (see page 192) are baked here with spinach and feta or wild creations like baked tempeh, kalamata olives, and vegetables. White Orchard Dairy provides milk and cream. A vegan chef salad and a chef's salad (both $6.95) could be eaten in the café, with its blond wood, golden walls, and green railings and cornice. Quiche and spanikopita, as well as sticky buns and chocolate chip cookies, are from Zoe's; cakes are from Cedar Street Bakers. The curried cashews are wonderful.

Bell the Cat (207-338-2084), 1E Belmont Avenue, Reny's Plaza, Route 3.

This place has a very laid-back atmosphere and serves as a reading corner for the biggest paperback store in the state, which also sells music. The long list of sandwiches sticks to the tried and true, from BLTs to German bologna. They use good bread from Borealis Breads, and you can get a sandwich with hummus, roasted red peppers, and melted provolone cheese (hold the sprouts) ($5.95).

Alaskan salmon is great on a salad ($7.99) with greens, carrots, cucumbers, green peppers, sprouts, tomatoes, and honey Dijon dressing.

Or get a pecan bar, a lemon-raspberry cream cheese bar ($1.75 each), or a cookie from a range of glass jars (55¢ each, or three for $1.50) to go with a cappuccino. Sundaes and milk shakes too.

Scoops (207-338-3350), 35 Lower Main Street.

Open Monday through Saturday 12–10 in summer, Thursday through Sunday 1–10 in winter. Round Top Dairy in Damariscotta makes the ice cream, which is outstanding, and sundaes and other specialties can be enjoyed in the big comfortable room at tile tables with wooden chairs. The back wall is covered with owner Karen Rak's brother's caricatures. Chuck Rak has depicted folks like the renovation crew, regular customers, the mayor of Belfast, and others, and might be able to do an amusing drawing of you for about $20 if you see him; he may, however, be at the Grand Canyon. In any case you can always order Karen Ireland's Cure, ginger ice cream with hot fudge sauce ($3.95 for a small portion).

Crêpes with fruit; crêpe pizza with tomato sauce and cheese, and toppings from pepperoni to anchovy; and a taco *crepino*—these are light meals served with salad. "It's my excuse to stay open in the winter," said Rak. Look for piano music on Thursday night; Friday night is game night, with board games, chess, and cards, probably in winter only. The games are always available; there are tons of them in the cabinet.

Three Tides (207-338-1707; www.3tides.com), 2 Pinchy Lane.

Open Tuesday through Saturday 4 to late closing (bar hours) and Sunday 1–8, from Father's Day to the end of September; off-season, open 4 to close from Tuesday to Saturday. A place for a good drink. Also a fun place to hang out and eat good bar food, perhaps at the serpentine polished concrete bar, or in tan vinyl booths, or in warm weather on an outdoor deck overlooking the river. Small plates include crabmeat-stuffed mushrooms ($6.50), little pizzas ($8.50), and Cobb salad ($11). Pemaquid oysters from Damariscotta ($12 for six, $22 for a dozen) are extremely—and justifiably—popular, and get delivered to the door by the people who farm them every week.

Daily specials follow the local shellfish season; one September special was a lobster and garlic shrimp quesadilla ($11.95).

Wasses Hot Dogs, in Reny's Plaza on Belmont Avenue (Route 3).

Open Monday through Saturday 11:30–4, Friday until 5, closed Sunday. A kraut dog is about $2, and so is a bacon dog, and a cheese dog, at this small white building on the side of the Reny's Plaza parking lot.

Food and Wine

The Clown (207-338-4344), 74 Main Street.

A branch of the Portland store. The manager here said, "The people who run the store in Belfast cater to the Belfast customers," ordering wines especially for the town. Wine tastings held the third Thursday of every month.

Perry's Nut House (207-338-1630, 1-800-6PERRYS; www.perrysnut house.com), Route 1 just north of the Belfast Bridge.

Open Monday through Saturday 9–6, Sunday 9–5 in summer; Monday through Saturday 10–5 off-season; closed January through March. This business, opened in 1927, was once the biggest and best tourist trap on the coast, with a collection of nuts from all over the world that has since gone to the Smithsonian, and a big collection of animals and creatures on display after a taxidermist preserved them. George and Ellen Darling want to bring back some of the old attractions, and have plans for a second-floor display near the 1947 wall mural of Africa. An albatross with an 11-foot wingspan will be there, as well as an 1893 wild boar, and a lion and a cheetah. But the man-eating clam from the Philippines cannot be found. This was the Belfast Cigar Factory before it became a nut house, and it started in 1850 as a ship captain's house. Its roof ridge is built like the keel of a ship.

Nowadays there's an array of candy, dried blueberries, maple syrup, and honey for sale. A rare find is the chokecherry jelly from Colleen's in Searsport.

The Belfast Farmer's Market is held Tuesday, Friday, and Saturday 9–1, from early May to late October at Reny's Plaza parking lot at the junction of Route 1 and Route 3.

A second Belfast Farmer's Market is held Friday 9–1 on Main Street near the waterfront. Look for the marinated goat cheese from wonderful Appleton Creamery (www.appletoncreamery.com) at this farmer's market—and in Camden, Damariscotta, and Bath. The chèvre wrapped in a brandied grape leaf was a 2004 American Cheese Society award-winner; cheese also comes rolled in black pepper or herbs. In July and August you can probably find their chèvre buttons in olive oil with rosemary, juniper berries, and hot peppers. A slightly aged goat cheese is called Sennebec and is rolled in *herbes de Provence.* Great feta. Crofter's, in 5-pound waxed wheels, is a washed curd cheese that is semisoft and will melt when used in cooking.

Camden

Atlantica

(207) 236-6011, 1-888-507-8514
1 Bay View Landing
www.atlanticarestaurant.com
Hospitality—Long waits have been an issue here.
Open daily for dinner except Tuesday, reduced hours late fall; may close from New Year's Day to mid-April
Entrées $24 to $29
Handicapped accessible, reservations advised

☛ *An attractive bar and dining room, with a waterfront deck and satisfying dinners*

Chef-owners Ken and Del Paquin run this upscale place on the water, serving a rich version of seafood chowder that was so welcome on a cold night, good roasted fish with sides like asparagus and mushroom risotto ($29 for halibut), and filet mignon ($28) with smooth potato puree and cipollini onions.

The sophisticated decor of Atlantica in Camden pairs with a waterside deck.

Del Paquin looks out for the best stuff she can find in Maine to serve for dinner, like Maine-ly Poultry chicken, fish from Jess's Market in Rockland, and Pemaquid oysters from Damariscotta. She also updates her wine list with bottles you might not have tried yet.

Caramelized fig and Fourme d'Ambert cheese salad ($9), with red romaine and strawberries, sounds like a find. My only quibble with what I enjoyed here on a rainy night, when the heated deck was cocooned by vinyl windows and walls, was that a few sauces seemed to have lost their purpose, or taste, on their way to adding beauty to the plate.

Cappy's Chowder House
(207) 236-2254
1 Main Street
www.cappyschowder.com
Open for lunch and dinner daily in summer, closed Wednesday in winter
Entrées $9 to $17

☛ *A big place dedicated to inexpensive seafood*

Seafood pasta and specials, like fresh swordfish, are the top-priced items on the menu, at around $16.95. But the mainstays are chowder and fried fish. The hard-working staff serve as many as 1,000 meals a day at this spot that's good for lunch entirely without a view. You can take home cans of chowder from the store and pastries from the bakeshop.

Francine Bistro
(207) 230-0083
55 Chestnut Street
www.francinebistro.com
Hospitality—Great service from servers proud to work here
Open for dinner Tuesday through Saturday 5:30–10
Entrées $22 to $25
Reservations recommended

☛ *A fabulous place to eat*

After being told over and over to try Francine, I could only imagine it must be good. When I dug into my redfish with foraged mushrooms, crab, and green tomato chutney, with potatoes dyed green by parsley, I understood that word-of-mouth spoke the truth; the food is a wonder.

A corn soup with scallops and a circle of basil oil also pleased the whole table, though we could have done with a cup instead of the big bowl we were served. Beside us the chef's parents were enjoying an anniversary dinner, and his mother, sounding bemused, said, "That's the best soup I've ever had." On another evening, another soup would have been white corn with chorizo ($7).

Another entrée, roast pork loin with apple-rosemary puree, pistachio slaw, and beets, was also built too large, making the desire to consume it all a painful conflict between discomfort and greed. It looked great, with a ring of parsley cream so green it was psychedelic. Maybe it's not the chef's problem if his food is so good you eat too much of it. The combination of flavors in every dish made the best gustatory sense, persuading us all that we were getting to know a place to which we'd want to return. Steak *frites* ($23); braised short ribs ($24) with apple, horseradish, watercress, and chèvre gratin; and seared halibut ($26) with foraged mushrooms have appeared on the fall menu.

A lemon cake with lemon icing jumped onto our taste buds with singing lemon, and the roasted figs with butterscotch pudding ice cream that our friends had decided not to order—imagining they could restrain themselves—suffered repeated attack from every spoon at the table.

Chef-owner Brian Hill and his partner, Lindsey, who took Francine over after working here for a year, have made their bistro a place worth driving to reach. Their chewy, dense homemade bread makes it all obvious from the first bite.

Hartstone Inn
(207) 236-4259, 1-800-788-4823
41 Elm Street (Route 1)
www.hartstoneinn.com
Hospitality—A family-run room, with your host/server and your chef the married couple who own the inn
Open for dinner Wednesday through Sunday July through October, Thursday through Sunday in the off-season
Prix fixe $45
Reservations recommended

☞ *The small menu gives few choices, but what is made here is highly praised.*

Mary Jo Salmon, who owns the inn with her chef-husband Michael, takes care of up to 20 people at nine tables. Michael was awarded a medal for being the best chef in the Caribbean in 1996 before he came to Camden. Since it's rare that a table can be had at the last minute, especially in summer, reservations are usually made in advance; the inn is often booked two weeks ahead.

Every evening they prepare just a couple of choices, but many diners don't mind the small number of options because the food is done so well.

The five-course menu, changing every day, might start with Maine crab and shrimp cakes with corn relish and Caribbean rémoulade, then greens with snow peas and crisp rice noodles, then a peach sorbet. For a main course, try pan-seared duck breast with scallion mashed potatoes, ending with blueberry-hazelnut soufflé with toasted-hazelnut crème anglaise. Nine wines can be had by the glass, and the list of bottles is long—don't forget that Maine law allows you to take what's left in the bottle home with you. Good Mark West Pinot Noir is $28, and at the top of that list is a half bottle of Etude Pinot Noir from Carneros for the same price.

Natalie's at the Mill
(207) 236-7008
43 Mechanic Street
Open for dinner Tuesday through Saturday 5:30–9
Entrées $25 to $31

☞ *Overlooking the falls, Natalie's serves sophisticated dinners in an elegant space.*

If the weather is lovely a martini on the deck would be a tranquilizing way to begin an evening here, the rush of the water from the falls soothing away the frenzy of the workday. After all, think of what you have in prospect. The seasonal menu might hold an appetizer of seared foie gras ($16) with lobster, ginger, and red onion marmalade and huckleberries, or, somewhat less extravagantly, an arugula salad ($10) with mango and artichokes.

For dinner the crabcake ($29) with foie gras butter and charred tomatillos sustains the theme. Soybean, asparagus, and Maine feta raviolis ($25) with carrot-daikon slaw in miso broth sounds both healthy and delightful; but halibut ($27) with oxtail ragout, morels, and asparagus salad does, too.

A fall dessert was cinnamon-apple tart ($8.50) with apple-currant strudel and vanilla bean gelato.

In the summertime you can enjoy the bar menu both on the deck and in the bar, with meals of clam chowder, roasted Pemaquid oysters with foie gras butter, and a changing burger that was served in the fall with portobello mushrooms,

Gruyère, and fries that have been twice fried in peanut oil and garnished with fresh shallots and garlic.

The cocktail menu is tailored to pair with the menu, with drinks like mulled cider or a cranberry *mojito* in the fall.

The Waterfront
(207) 236-3747
Bayview Street on Camden Harbor
www.waterfrontcamden.com
Open year-round for lunch and dinner
Entrées $11 to $25

☛ *A great view, and good food with a low-key, casual atmosphere*

This place is our New York friends' favorite. They ate lunch here every day during a Camden stay, content with the salads and sandwiches and happy that their little girl felt just as at home as they did. You can get a steamed lobster for lunch or dinner, but the lobster roll, crabcakes, and haddock fish-and-chips ($14.95) compete with the fried haddock sandwich ($8.95) and a big hamburger ($7.95) for the most attention.

Panini are on the lunch menu; roast beef with sharp cheddar ($8.95) is served on black bread and comes with a horseradish dipping sauce.

Dinner gets a little more elaborate, with oysters, steamers, and mussels on the appetizer list, and entrées like aioli-crusted haddock ($16.95) and pork tenderloin saltimbocca with sherried figs ($15.95). Wild mushroom and spinach lasagna with an Italian salad ($11.95) is served in a smaller portion as a kindness for those of us with smaller appetites.

Seventeen wines were offered by the glass, and more than 20 beers and ales. Some of the items on the bigger menus are served between lunch and dinner and after hours, like grilled panini sandwiches, a hamburger, an herbed salmon burger ($8.50) with caper-basil aioli, and the lobster or crab roll.

White Hall Inn
(207) 236-3391
52 High Street (Route 1)
www.whitehall-inn.com
Hospitality—This inn makes sure to take care of everyone well.
Open for dinner Thursday through Sunday 6–9 mid-June through mid-October, breakfast daily 7–10, Sunday until 12
Entrées $18 to $28

☛ *An old-fashioned inn moving slowly but surely into updated dining*

After a change of owners and a renovation, you will find Frette butterscotch and white linen tablecloths on the tables, with gray-blue and beige checked napkins. These elegant accessories decorate **Vincent's** (named after Edna St. Vincent Millay), a large dining room bordered on one side by windows overlooking the back of the inn and its leafy woods.

Greg and Sue Marquise bought the inn before the 2006 season, installing a brand-new kitchen, dining room, and bar, and remodeling one-third of the rooms.

A menu from Vincent's begins dinner with old friends, like mussels and fried calamari ($8) with roasted garlic and shallots, and a novelty, vegetarian napoleon made with eggplant, zucchini, summer squash, and hen of the woods mushrooms, layered with ricotta.

For dinner roast chicken ($17) is served with fruit, like peaches; wild king salmon ($23) is grilled and baked in phyllo with beurre blanc. A vegetarian entrée is angel-hair *limone* ($18), slender pasta tossed with olive oil, lemon zest and juice, tomatoes, and garlic, with a choice of Parmesan or feta.

Fried ravioli is served with Marsala and wilted spinach, and grilled swordfish ($27) comes topped with mango, peach, and pineapple salsa.

The bar is called Gossip, in honor of the book *Peyton Place,* and is paneled with cherry. A *Peyton Place* movie scene was filmed at the White Hall Inn; the owners intend to put memorabilia from the movie on display, in honor of the 50th anniversary of the movie in 2007.

Fresh-squeezed orange juice at breakfast consumed 17,000 oranges in summer 2006; and pastries like sticky buns were classic favorites. A Dutch couple called it the best breakfast in the United States, having enjoyed the eggs Benedict, blueberry pancakes, and Crêpes Susanna.

Takeout, Ice Cream, Breakfast, and Bakeries

The Camden Bagel Café (207-236-2661), 25 Mechanic Street.

Open Monday through Saturday 6:30 AM–2 PM, Sunday 7:30–2. How pleased we were to arrive here after a long trip farther Downeast—far, far from any good bread and even farther from a decent bagel. These will set you up. Chewy and freshly made here, you can order them toasted with butter or cream cheese, or in sandwiches with a big range of fillings. But it's the bagel itself that makes it all worthwhile. The space is plain, with white shutters keeping out the sun, but the hummus is spicy. No credit cards.

Camden Cone (207-236-6448), 33 Bayview Street.

Ice cream in a wide range of flavors.

The Cedar Crest Restaurant (207-236-7722), 115 Elm Street (Route 1).

Open daily for breakfast, lunch, and dinner 7 AM–9 PM; closed Sunday evening. A local favorite for breakfast, with thermos urns of coffee left obligingly on the tables. Homemade breads make the toast a good thing. Lunches include wraps and sandwiches. The service is excellent.

Meetingbrook Bookshop and Café (207-236-6808, 1-800-510-MEET; www.meetingbrook.org), 50 Bayview Street.

Open Tuesday through Saturday 10:30–7, Sunday 11–4:30. This small bookshop serves delicious Austrian desserts, like *pflaumen kuchen* (plum cake). There are brownies, *pain au chocolat,* and much else. With Gregorian chant singing out of the speakers, wafts of chocolate and fruit from the baking, the tapping of the border collie's claws on the floor, and the welcome fire in the fireplace on a winter night, this is a refuge for all. It also hosts wide-ranging conversation on stories in the books and the state of the soul.

Scott's Place (207-236-8751), Elm Street, in the shopping center off Route 1, south of downtown Camden.

Open daily 10–4 in summer, 10–3 in January, February, and March. This is a little place in a parking lot that's stayed in business more than 30 years by selling inexpensive hot dogs and one person's nominee for the best lobster rolls in Maine ($8.99), with 4 ounces of lobster from Young's Shellfish (mixed with mayonnaise there) in a toasted, buttered hot dog roll. The little hamburgers are great.

The Camden Farmer's Market is held on Wednesday from 4:30 to 6:30 mid-June through September on Colcord Street, and on Saturday from 9 to noon mid-May through the end of October, at the same place.

Islesboro

Dark Harbor House
(207) 734-6669
Main Road, P.O. Box 185
www.darkharborhouse.com
Hospitality—Our waitress, an island woman, took wonderful care of us.
Open daily for dinner 5:30–8:30, May through October
Entrées $18 to $22
Reservations required

☛ *A ferry ride to this Georgian Revival mansion and a great meal make the evening memorable.*

You really have to spend the night here—or possibly at one of the two bed & breakfasts, or at your Islesboro friend's house—to eat a meal here. Our room had a balcony overlooking the lawn and distant water, and the next morning osprey wheeled overhead, calling between fishing trips.

The inn is full of the innkeepers' odd collections: mounted, tiny European antelope antlers hang in the library; masks from around the world overlook the beautiful double stairs. That ambience of eccentricity promised well for our dinner, and there was no disappointment. The kitchen uses a lot of local produce from a farm on the island and made a salad of greens ($5) that were impeccably fresh. We could also have started that night with a caramelized onion, Swiss chard, Gorgonzola, pine nuts, and olive tart ($6.50).

The house wine is Excelsior Chardonnay ($6) from South Africa.

The perfect piece of king salmon I ordered ($20) was poached, with a rare interior; the fresh fish lay in a rim soup bowl in a savory broth, surrounded by new green peas and semolina gnocchi.

The barbecued duck breast that my friend chose seemed on the sweet side, her preference but not necessarily mine. Its fragrant sauce gave off hints of cardamom, coriander, cumin, and cinnamon. A flatiron steak au poivre, and a vegetarian platter with stuffed eggplant, grilled portobellos, and tomatoes with Taleggio, were also on the menu.

Distant steel-gray water glimmered through the wisteria vine next to our window, where birds were feasting at a feeder. They didn't have our luck with dessert, though. We ordered a *dacquoise* with orange and Grand Marnier buttercream. The nutty texture of the hazelnut meringue and the tangy buttercream introduced us to this classic dessert, and made converts of us all. The homemade mango sorbet tasted of the fresh fruit.

Lincolnville

Chez Michel
(207) 789-5600
Route 1, Lincolnville Beach
Open April through mid-November for dinner Tuesday through Sunday, lunch and dinner Sunday
Entrées $12 to $28
Reservations advised

☞ *Popular for its mussels* mariniere *and lamb shanks; classy dishes from France*

This restaurant serves a duck au poivre ($19.95) and a steak au poivre ($21.95) (12 ounces of either rib eye or sirloin) that is served on a green-flowered Walker china dish and makes a superb French meal.

The rabbit pâté and fisherman's stew are also well-loved.

One local fan asked the chef to make up 18 orders of the lamb shanks, cooked with herbs from the chef's garden and from local farms, to be frozen and heated up during the long winter while Chez Michel is closed.

And people consistently praise the raspberry-glazed pie made every summer as the raspberries ripen, topped with a glaze made from the raspberries and Chambord. Some people reserve a slice of this pie when they call and make their reservation. The crème brûlée has made another good impression. The classic version ($5.50) is sometimes layered with a chocolate–Grand Marnier crème brûlée to make what they call a Tuxedo ($5.50).

The Edge Oceanfront Dining
(207) 236-4430
Inn at Ocean's Edge
24 Stonecoast Road (off Route 1)
www.innatoceansedge.com
Hospitality—Well-trained and unobtrusive
Open for dinner daily from 5:30 in summer; closed after New Year's Eve until late April. Open Wednesday through Saturday for dinner until July 4 and in the fall. Year-round, Sunday night is pizza night.
Entrées $28 to $34, four-course prix fixe $55
Handicapped accessible with golf cart service or valet, reservations recommended

☛ *In a sleek renovated space on the water, this upscale spot makes appetizing, fashionable food.*

A summer evening here on the screened porch, looking out at Penobscot Bay and Islesboro, will no doubt be full of culinary pleasures, whether it's Sunday's pizza night, when the wood-fired oven turns out dozens of simple and complicated pies, or the other nights of the week, when more complication is in charge of the small servings.

Fried quail on rhubarb and shallot compote was a lively match, savory complemented by tart, and each improved by textures from soft to crunchy. Roasted red bell pepper soup rang out its summery round flavor, augmented by a melting bit of lemon and sambuca *panna cotta.*

Little conceits, like a course called Teeny-Tiny Clambake—corn bread in a mini frying pan, six littleneck clams, and a few small carrots—seemed too cute, though they were perfectly good.

More serious dishes like the Truffle Mac-n-Cheese could not have been more rich; next up, three preparations of lamb ($34) worked well with a small seam of carrot-flavored grits. Barbecued short ribs, tender and fat, held the perfume of clove, allspice, coriander, cinnamon, and bay leaf that the young chef, Bryan Dame, has perfected. He is a Culinary Institute of America graduate with past work at the Inn at Little Washington in Virginia, and also at Hugo's in Portland and Vermont's Norwich Inn.

The Edge Oceanfront Dining in Lincolnville

Seven Ways to Eat Chocolate ($13) hits its high point in a small fried brownie-like ball of scented bitterness.

Menus promise continual change and close attention to what's ripe in the surrounding area.

Youngtown Inn and Restaurant

(207) 763-4290, 1-800-291-8438
Route 52
www.youngtowninn.com
Open for dinner daily in summer; call for hours off-season.
Entrées $22 to $27
Handicapped accessible, reservations recommended

☛ *Elegant dining based on classics that are made according to traditional methods*

The Youngtown Inn has its loyal fans, whose recommendations and enthusiasm have placed this restaurant in this book. Owner and chef Manuel Mercier is French, and so is the French onion soup, for example—onions sautéed with olive oil until translucent, and simmered with water and chicken stock for 20 minutes. Mercier describes this version as a typical French onion soup; "good and simple."

He said a popular dish is roasted rack of lamb—spring lamb from New Zealand, always the same high quality, which he marinates in olive oil, fresh rosemary, and garlic for just a couple of hours before it's cooked. Browned in a hot oven, then topped with herbed bread crumbs and roasted for 10 minutes, this rests for 5 to 10 minutes out of the oven. He likes it medium, "a point," but makes it to order. Alongside in winter Mercier serves *gratin dauphinois*—scalloped potatoes, with cream, Swiss cheese, salt and pepper, and nutmeg. Winter should always be so good.

One hundred and thirty people were coming for Thanksgiving in 2006 to dine on free-range turkey with sausage stuffing and homemade cranberry sauce (cranberries with maple syrup, orange juice, and cinnamon sticks, cooked down to a thick compote), with *gratin dauphinois* with sweet potatoes. Beaujolais Nouveau, just released, is served at this holiday meal. Mostly French and American wines, from a 1986 vintage wine for $270 to Perrin Côtes du Rhône ($24), are available on the wine list.

Winery

Cellardoor Winery and Vineyards (207-763-4478; www.mainewine .com), 367 Youngtown Road.

Open mid-May through October, 10–5. Stephanie and John Clapp have planted many acres with vines behind the barn that shelters the daily free wine tastings in the summer and fall; look back out on the rolling hill, and you'll feel transported to another place. This is the only vineyard in Maine that makes wine from its own grape harvest, but it makes wines from grapes and fruit it purchases as well.

Monhegan Island

The Monhegan House Dining Room
(207) 594-7983
www.monheganhouse.com
Open May through October for breakfast and dinner
Entrées $15 to $28
BYOB

☛ *A fine place for dinner on an island renowned for its artists*

The food at this faraway inn impressed our sources as the best on the island. With lobster spring rolls, tuna carpaccio, and lemon-basil shrimp risotto as possibilities on the changing menu, it's easy to see why. The meals use whatever ingredients from the sea and land are fresh and in-season. Also offered might be a Boursin-stuffed tenderloin of beef, boneless roasted chicken breast with pork and apple stuffing, or house-made beet pasta with artichokes, olives, kale, and sautéed onions in a cream sauce.

The inn has its own salad and vegetable garden. It does not serve wine—the island is dry and doesn't issue liquor licenses—but wine and beer can be bought at island stores and enjoyed here with the meals.

Behind the inn is **The Novelty,** a take-out shop for pizza, sandwiches, baked goods, and drinks. Ice-cream cones and sundaes, too.

Port Clyde

The Dip Net
(207) 372-6307
1 Cold Storage Road
www.dipnetrestaurant.com
Open in-season 11–9 Memorial Day through Columbus Day weekend
Entrées $9 to $21

☛ *Fine fresh seafood prepared with care (no trans fats here) and pizzazz; desserts by Mom*

This respected establishment makes a variety of items to eat indoors or on the wharf. There are seats for about 28 not including the bar, or for takeout.

The local draggers—"the second largest dragger fleet north of Gloucester"—bring owner Scott Yakovenko frequent supplies of gray sole, halibut, and haddock. He said monkfish is great sautéed with a fresh tomato sauce, and good also deep fried and served with a chipotle-lime aioli ($6.50).

Bouillabaisse ($21) is a typical special.

Crab and lobster rolls, and whole steamed lobster, are a favorites among summer visitors.

Come here for the healthy fried seafood. Yakovenko said he does all his frying with peanut oil; "Twice the price, and you're worth it," his motto goes. That makes the fried oysters doubly delectable, with a ginger shallot sauce ($6 for an appetizer; $14.50 in a basket with coleslaw and fries). For lighter fare, at least according to the menu, try the Port Clyde Poor Boy ($9), fried oysters with house tartar sauce in a roll.

Clams and mussels over linguine, with garlic, white wine, tomato, and pecorino Romano, is $15.50. Locally grown, hormone-free grilled strip steak ($19) and a summer vegetable plate with a tofu cutlet ($11.50) take care of everybody else.

"Desserts are by Mom; how often can you say that?" Her name is Sandy Yakovenko. She makes, among many things, gingerbread, served with vanilla ice cream, and blueberry pie with an all-butter crust. Herb tea and espresso are brewed here too.

Rockland

Amalfi Mediterranean Restaurant
(207) 596-0012
421 Main Street
Open for dinner Tuesday through Saturday 5–9
Entrées $15 to $26
Handicapped accessible, reservations recommended

☛ *The brilliant flavors of the Mediterranean in a warm, attractive space*

The inspiration here comes from Spain, Italy, France, Greece, and Morocco, but the BLT salad with Gorgonzola vinaigrette comes straight from the chef's imagination. David Cooke has a loyal following here, where customers sit in yellow-painted wood booths on plush blue and purple cushions, and the rosy glow is both from the light bouncing off the exposed brick and the good food and wine.

Don't fail to try the spicy, irresistible *kefta* ($6.95), oval meatballs made of lamb and beef that have been mixed with two hot chili pepper powders, cumin, pistachios, and two house-blend paprikas. Served in a savory sauce, this is a brilliant turn on ground meat, so much better at Amalfi's, in its spiced, Middle Eastern version, than any of the plain versions on the coast. Amalfi's fried calamari ($6.95) is a stellar example, too, crisp and tender. A special of hanger steak came with rich, pungent Gorgonzola sauce, on creamy mashed potatoes— an idea with less geographically precise origins. But the fish stew ($19.95) with a flavorful tomato broth did signal the sure sun of southern Mediterranean cooking, and the shrimp, mussels, scallops, and fish in the large bowl took to that broth perfectly.

Spinach manicotti with three cheeses and the signature paella show some of Cooke's range.

The paella is prepared in several ways, tailored to a customer's taste: with fish, shrimp, and mussels ($19.95); with chorizo, chicken, shrimp, and mussels ($17.95); and with vegetables only ($15.95). Each preparation accentuates the pleasures of saffron and short-grain rice.

The ricotta cheesecake ($6) is a good one, slightly grainy, not too sweet, with fresh ricotta and little else.

Café Miranda
(207) 594-2034
15 Oak Street
www.cafemiranda.com
Open for dinner daily at 5:30 in-season
Entrées $6.50 to $26
Handicapped accessible, reservations advised

☛ *The eclectic menu ranges world cuisines, and the kitchen delivers.*

The red neon sign looks fine on the gable-end of the clapboard house that is Café Miranda, on a side street in Rockland. A checkered linoleum floor and old Formica tables fit with the two flamingos in the windows. A side terrace with a parabolic tarp and black metal tables fills with patrons on warm nights.

Café Miranda is so successful that it is now selling its hummus and salsa at markets around Rockland; a new venture is Mobo, a partnership with Borealis Breads, for small frozen pizzas that tasted great when I sampled them at Maine Fare, a fall event promoting Maine food.

But come to the source for a chance to enjoy the full range here, from pierogi to Armenian lamb stuffed peppers to Thai pork to scallops and mussels with creamed leeks on fresh pasta.

The long menu is crammed on one side with 35 appetizers. Gnocchi with tomato-sage butter ($9.50) make the long winter endurable, and so does the Squash O'rama ($7.50), mashed butternut squash with farmer's cheese.

I wouldn't try the "Gnublu" if it remains on the list of entrées—too much blue cheese—but the fried artichoke hearts were a pleasure to eat, and the bacon, broccoli, and pecorino with hand-cut squares of pasta, called Cover Girl, was fabulous.

Enthusiasm is the besetting emotion, and it gets you intrigued with just about anything on the menu and the loquacious wine list. San Fabiano Chianti was one worth the fuss.

Contes
No phone
Harbor Park, Main Street
Hospitality: Gruff, occasionally stern, always capable
Open year-round
Entrées $17 to $19
No credit cards, no fried food

☛ *Ferocious integrity, with no menus and enormous portions*

Finding this place on the wharf, behind its very authentic nautical detritus, starts off the evening with a sense of adventure. Inside the door are the paper lists from which you order what's cooking that day.

Then you go to your butcher-paper-covered table, where salad and bread are already set out.

The salmon *pomodoro* one night was too plain, and the sauce too meager for the masses of spaghetti, even if it did turn into three meals, carted home in one of the Styrofoam containers pulled from the stack sitting behind the table.

But the ravioli with lobster in a Gorgonzola cream sauce was delectable, obviously rich as sin, and included whole lobster claws and lots of tail meat; though the mix of ravioli, tortellini, spaghetti, and linguine seemed a little odd. Gnocchi with sauce, and eggplant Parmesan with extra ricotta on top of the Parmesan, were good choices, too.

In Good Company
(207) 593-9110
415 Main Street
Hospitality—Fine service and no airs
Open for dinner Tuesday through Sunday 4:30 to close
Entrées $10 to $18

☛ *A fun place to drink wine, eat a little food, and nurture friendships*

The sign that hangs in front of the door says WINE. FOOD. FRIENDS. The friendliness of our welcome bore it out. This big, white room with a lovely, ornate plaster ceiling (with Hermes and an American Indian among the carvings) filled up with groups who said hello across the room to others and settled at the tables, the couch, and the bar. A glass of wine from the eight-page wine list, with around eight reds and eight whites available by the glass, comes with its own little carafe of extra wine, a happy touch that allows the lovely large glass to be filled to a low level twice. I loved the big, hem-stitched white cotton napkins.

Scallops with pancetta were perfectly cooked, and the thin watercress aioli made a great dipping sauce for the bread. Roasted green beans and pizza with smoked salmon, cream cheese, and caramelized onions (pizzas are $12–14) rounded out our little, delicious dinner. Angus beef tenderloin ($18) is also always available, with various sauces, like porcini butter.

White roses on the tables and crammed together in a big bouquet in the back room, where a large table accommodates a big party, imbued the scene with the same elegance as the pretty upholstery—coral and green fabrics, almost as pretty as the strawberries with cream in a wine glass that came for dessert.

The business is based on the idea of going to a good restaurant and eating an appetizer at the bar. Everyone seemed to be having a great time, so maybe this place is on to something.

Primo
(207) 596-0770
2 South Main Street (Route 73)
www.primorestaurant.com
Hospitality—Great, friendly service, with lots of napkin folding
Open for dinner Wednesday through Monday at 5:30; closed January, February, March, and part of April
Entrées $25 to $38
Reservations recommended

☛ *Exciting, inventive meals with very fresh ingredients have made a big impact, drawing in customers and inspiring accolades.*

The gardens are the first thing you might notice on a summer visit, laid out with charm and burgeoning with stuff for dinner. Primo has a big reputation these days for its fresh food, clarity of flavors, and delicious combinations—and pulling some of it out of the garden at the last minute has a lot to do with it. Up from the parking lot the pigs are rooting happily; they'll be contributing to dinner too, someday, as artisan sausage and other things.

We ate in the front parlor on our most recent visit, in a room on the second floor the time before; both rooms, filled with only a few tables, are good looking and comfortable. There is a view out to the bay in the front. But who's looking out there?

A Bellisima, with peach nectar and vodka, a Key lime *mojito,* and a blue martini with Gorgonzola-stuffed olives got us started well.

The $64 bottle of Chalone Vineyard Pinot Blanc, 2003, that was promised to "knock our socks off" and was something chef and part-owner Melissa Kelly had just found, flaunted dry, musky fruits and wood, perfect with a little freebie of crisp, oily bruschetta with tomato and salty tuna. We proceeded to up the salt with a shared appetizer of homemade *sopressata,* onions cooked in balsamic, smoked Manchego, and hot cherry tomatoes that did fireworks in our mouths.

You can dine here on a variety of pizzas: one with prosciutto, tomato, arugula, and Parmesan is $15, but the dinners are too good to forgo.

The wild striped sea bass Livornese came perfectly cooked, in a sauce of tomatoes, olives, and caper berries, with Swiss chard on Israeli couscous, the hot olives a joy to break with my teeth. A grilled duck breast with grilled Pluots, and grilled chicken breast with chanterelles, Swiss chard, and fava beans, were other pleasures among the entrées.

Our cannoli, crunchy and perfect, inspired one friend to say of pastry chef and part-owner Price Kushner, "I think he's improved the recipe."

Then we were served pecan shortbread and cocoa-covered truffles that bloomed in our mouths—really, the evening was full of this kind of moment, when the gorgeous taste of something took up all of our pleased attention. An earlier dessert menu included a caramelized banana cream tartlet ($9.50, as are all desserts), Calvados babas, and baked apple compote.

The Water Works
(207) 596-2753
7 Lindsey Street
Open daily at 11:30 for lunch and dinner, late pub menu until 9; closes Sunday at 8; closes earlier off-season
Entrées $9 to $24

☛ *Casual food, and fine beer and ale, in a place built for good times*

The atmosphere here is fun, and the meals casual and well-made, including a house sirloin ($14.95), lobster dinners in summer, and a shepherd's pie ($9.95) with layers of ground meat, corn, parsnips, and mashed potatoes with a cheese topping. You can also enjoy salads, including Caesar with chicken and steak, and a hot spinach salad also with steak or chicken.

But this place is best known for its in-house microbrews from Rocky Bay Brewing Company. All of the brewed beer and ale, seven taps, comes from the brewery. A light summer ale, an India pale ale called White Cap, and a blueberry wheat beer are made in summer. In fall there's an Oktoberfest lager, and in the winter Viking Plunder, a caramel beer with a toasty flavor. The winter brew goes best with any sort of meat dish, and some specials are tailored to make it sing.

Apple crisp and brownie sundaes ($4.95) are perennial favorites, and dessert specials are always offered.

Two Japanese Places

Oh! Bento (207-593-9216; www.ohbento.com), 10 Leland Street.
Open for lunch Tuesday through Friday 11–2, dinner Tuesday through Thursday 5–8, Friday and Saturday 5–8:30. From fried dumplings to seaweed salad, fresh sushi to tempura fried in canola oil, and with a welcome chocolate dessert at the end of the meal even if that's not exactly Japanese, Oh! Bento has been a favorite restaurant in Rockland for seven years.

Suzuki's Sushi Bar (207-596-7447), 419 Main Street.
Open Tuesday through Saturday 5–9, weekends until 9:30. This hot spot opened in 2006 to immediate popularity. A Maine Crab Roll; a dish with Maine bok choy based on the owner's childhood recipe; local sea urchin roe; and Maine shrimp and scallops offer fish lovers and vegetarians pristine examples of the goodness of Maine. Owner Keiko Suzuki Steinberger works with the freshest seafood she can find, shipping it up from Boston or gleaning it from the water.

Lunch, Casual Dinners, Fish, Bakeries, Coffee, and Provisions

Atlantic Baking Co. (207-596-0505; www.atlanticbakingco.com), 351 Main Street.
Open Monday through Saturday 7–6, in summer open Sunday 8–4. A great source of *ciabatta,* and whole-grain and rye breads, among others. Soups, sandwiches, salads, pastries, and cookies also are available. With several tables, and stools along the windows—all the better for you to enjoy a savory bacon, cheddar, and scallion scone, or a twice-baked croissant.

The Brown Bag (207-596-6372), 606 Main Street.

Open Monday through Saturday 6:30–4. The Brown Bag is packed at lunch because, as local chef Ellen Barnes says, it does what it sets out to do excellently. The great homemade breads, whole wheat, oat, rye, and sometimes Parmesan-basil and a seven-grain, make good sandwiches, and the soup and chowder are always top quality. Order at the counter, either breakfast or lunch, and carry it to a table or a picnic spot. A full breakfast and lots of baked goods; the Congo Squares with coconut, chocolate, and butterscotch fly out the door.

Hardcover Café at the Breakwater Bookland (207-593-9272; www.booklandcafe.com), 91 Camden Street, Suite 101.

Open Monday through Saturday 9–8:45, Sunday 9–5:45. A sister store to Brunswick's Bookland, this comfortable spot inside Maine's largest independent bookstore is prime relaxation territory. An espresso will keep you from falling into a doze, and so will the pages of an entrancing book.

Jess's Market (1-877-219-8653; www.jessmarket.com), 118 South Main Street.

Open year-round during business hours. Tanks of seawater are filled with lively lobsters at this great, family-owned seafood market. You can also buy clams, oysters, mussels, crabmeat, shrimp, scallops, and fresh fish. Everything can be shipped. Diver-harvested scallops are available from December to April.

The Pastry Garden (207-594-3663; www.pastry-garden.com), 313 Main Street.

Open 9–5 Monday through Saturday, 9–3 Sunday. This fine bakery makes excellent European-style pastries, specialty cakes, and cookies. They are especially well-known for their seasonal decorated cookies at Halloween, Christmas, and Easter, as well as croissants and artisan breads.

Rock City Books and Coffee (207-594-4123; www.rockcitycoffee.com), 328 Main Street.

Open Monday through Saturday 7–6, Sunday 8–6. This is the best place for a cup of coffee, made with beans roasted by **Rock City Coffee Roasters;** it can be served in a press pot, drip brewed, or as espresso. Tea and chai are available too, along with bagels, muffins, croissants, scones, and cookies. But stop reading that good book you just found in the stacks to savor these things, at least for a moment or two. Chocolate-dipped macaroons need total attention. One lunch favorite is the Thai chicken wrap ($6.25), heated on the grill, with chicken, red peppers, carrots, scallions, basmati rice, and a creamy peanut sauce. Sandwiches and wraps can be grilled or served cold; three breakfast wraps ($4.25) served until 11 include ham and Swiss, veggie, or the Santa Fe, with salsa and cheddar accenting the scrambled eggs in all three.

Rustica (207-594-0015), 315 Main Street.
Open Tuesday through Saturday for lunch 11–3, dinner 5–9. The popularity of basic Italian food, steaks, and fish was proven when Rustica opened in 2006. High-quality meals that are reasonable in price, with wine between $20 and $35 a bottle, work magic.

Fried artichoke salad ($6.50) stays on the list of appetizers, along with shrimp bruschetta, mussels, and roasted peppers stuffed with goat cheese.

Among the entrées is seafood scampi ($15) with local shrimp and mussels on linguine; the risotto is different every day. Another meal here is pan-roasted chicken breast over sun-dried tomato and roasted escarole risotto ($15).

For dessert there's tiramisu ($6, as are all desserts) and *boccanegra,* a flourless chocolate tort with cappuccino crème anglaise.

The Thorndike Creamery (207-594-4126), 385 Main Street.
Open daily 11–9 or 10. This ice cream parlor with marble tables and wire chairs sells Annabelle's Ice Cream from Portsmouth, New Hampshire; try the wild blueberry sundae with blueberry syrup and vanilla ice cream. Pizza is also served.

Wasses Hot Dogs, Route 1.
Keith Wass has become a legend, serving millions of hot dogs from his stands in Thomaston, Rockland, and Belfast since 1972.

The Wine Seller (207-594-2621), 15 Tillson Avenue.
Open Monday through Saturday 10–6, Sunday 11–5. This is the place to pair the meal you've bought with a good bottle of wine. Local wines are well-stocked.

The Rockland Farmer's Market is held on Thursday from 9 to 1 mid-May through late October at the Public Landing, downtown Rockland on the waterfront.

Rockport

The Gallery Café
(207) 230-0061
297 Commercial Street (Route 1)
www.prismglassgallery.com
Hospitality—Eager and attentive service
Open for lunch Wednesday through Saturday 11–3, for dinner 5–9, Sunday brunch 10–3, Sunday dinner 4-8
Entrées $17 to $35

☛ *Well-made meals in a handsome new space, with a bonus of glassblowing*

This restaurant opened to praise in summer 2004. When the air is warm and the back patio is open, the taste of the Macadamia nut crust Key lime pie seduces us into enjoyment.

A bar is now open in the lobby of the glass gallery; across from the gallery you can sometimes watch glass being blown in the studio.

Chef and part owner Lisa Sojka runs the kitchen, making a brunch that has featured smoked salmon eggs Benedict, crab omelets, and *caprese* salad. Lunch could consist of lobster macaroni and cheese, seafood cakes, or a steak sandwich.

Dinners work with Italian masterpieces like lasagna, linguine with clams, and Tuscan meatballs marinara, and fish entrées like swordfish puttanesca.

Bakeries, Markets, and Ice Cream

The Market Basket (207-236-4371), Route 1.
The Market Basket is a source for many house-made spreads, like smoked trout pâté and Boursin. Muffins and pastries are baked here daily; sandwiches are made with fresh breads; and a wide range of cheeses, including many from Maine, are sold. Wines, with a thoughtful basket of champagne splits, cover the vineyards of the world. Prepared meals are always available in the case. Coffee, and fresh hot chocolate, are also for sale.

State of Maine Cheese Company Store (1-800-762-8895; www.cheese-me.com), 461 Commercial Street (Route 1).

Open Monday through Friday 9–5:30, Saturday 9–5, Sunday 12–4. The largest cheese maker in Maine has a store filled with its own products and other fine things from Maine. The Katahdin cheddar and Aroostook Jack are as dependable as the sun. Almost a dozen varieties are made. A recent addition is a Welch cheese called Caerphilly, the Welch word for Castletown, the town where it was first made. Like cheddar, and made from cow's milk, it has a tang like feta. Samples are always available. When the cheese is being made, visitors can watch. Owner Cathe Morrill can give tours by appointment with a week's notice. Some goat cheese, and cheese spreads, are also sold here, along with pickles and jams and jellies; Maine-made potato chips, barbecue sauces, and maple syrup, and many other great Maine products.

Sweet Sensations (207-230-0955; www.mainesweets.com), 315 Commercial Street (Route 1).

Open daily 8–5:30, Sunday 10–5, but check for new hours when Sweet Sensations and the **Three Dogs Café** open in 2007. Construction began on a big new building in fall 2006 to house this growing business. It's mainstay is wedding cakes. But a casual visitor can indulge in an almond and coconut macaroon, plain or drizzled with chocolate, that tastes luscious with a cup of coffee or tea. Seasonal cookies, like a painted maple leaf, or a red lobster cookie, are crowd-pleasers. Fudge cake, lemon-lime tart, whiskey-pecan tart, and peach cream cake are all good reasons to volunteer to bring dessert.

Herb Garden

Avena Botanicals (207-594-0694; www.avenaherbs.com), 219 Mill Street.

Mill Street is a left turn just west of Tolman Pond on Route 90. Open May through October Monday through Thursday 9–5, Friday 9–1. Walks through the amazing 1-acre Avena Botanicals Organic Herb Garden will bring you knowledge about the uses of herbs, as you look at the more than 120 planted here. Herbs sold in the apothecary.

Searsport

The Rhumb Line
(207) 548-2600
200 East Main Street (Route 1)
www.therhumblinerestaurant.com
Open daily in summer, fewer days off-season
Entrées $21 to $28

☞ *Searsport's top-of-the-line, popular restaurant*

Entrées at this restaurant in a white house along Route 1 include orange-glazed roast duck ($25) with lentils and ginger-peach chutney, and curried Contessa shrimp ($23) with sweet potato ravioli with sweet olive chutney. The four ravioli on the plate are filled with sweet potatoes with spice, and occasional raisins and walnuts, which works with the curry; this dish has been on the menu for several years. Contessa is a brand of shrimp that has great flavor, consistently fresh, never with any odor, according to Diana Evans, who owns and runs the restaurant and cooks the meals with her husband, Charles. Both are trained "roundsmen" who take care of any part of the meal, and they serve as many as 45 to 50 people a night.

The chocolate–Grand Marnier mousse cake and lemon cream cake with fresh berries are homemade.

In its ninth year, the restaurant has several staffers that are original. Melinda is the head waitress, the only year-round original waitress, and is often asked for by grateful customers.

Lunch, Pastries, and Coffee

Abbracci (207-548-2010), 225 West Main Street (Route 1).
Open Wednesday through Saturday 7–5, Sunday 8–2. How often can you find a Greek Salad with watercress? The kitchen here uses what looks fresh and perfect. When it happened to be watercress, it made a great addition to the rest of the ingredients—tomato, cucumber, and feta.

Quiche, calzones, sandwiches, and soups provide a good lunch here, and when I asked, and no one objected, the TV was turned off. Coffee and baklava, cannoli, crumbcakes, or *sfogliatelle* are a just a few of the pastries you might choose to go with it.

The Craignair Inn overlooks Clark Island.

Coastal Coffee (207-548-2400; www.coastal-coffee.com), 25 Main Street (Route 1).

Open at 6 on weekdays, 7 on Saturday, 8 on Sunday; closes at 2. They serve coffee from Raven's Brew of Juno, Alaska, because owners Mike and Marsha Sloan spent many years in Alaska and met each other there. They moved to Maine in 2002 and bought the coffee shop in 2005. Breakfast sandwiches and baked goods are made here. Lunch includes chowders and deli sandwiches made with bread from Borealis Breads and Boar's Head meats and cheeses. Eggs are from Bowdoin Egg Farm's free-range chickens.

South Thomaston

Waterman Beach Lobsters
(207) 596-7819
359 Waterman Beach Road
Hospitality—Order at the kitchen window, and the server will bring your meal.
Open for lunch and dinner Thursday through Sunday 11–7 in summer
Entrées $2.25 to $25

☛ *Classic seaside dining, simple and beautiful, with no fried food, and homemade pie*

This traditional place has a big outside deck with picnic tables for enjoying the lobster dinners. A twin lobster special (no sharing) with chips, a roll, and butter, was $25.95. Big servings of steamers were $12.50 with melted butter and broth. Wine and beer are served along with lobster rolls ($11.95). The place is well thought of for the good homemade pies ($3.50 a slice, $4.25 with ice cream). Blueberry, raspberry, pecan, and other flavors. You could eat on the wide porch if it rained, but this is clearly a spot for a gorgeous day.

Spruce Head

Craignair Inn
(207) 594-7644, 1-800-320-9997
5 Third Street
www.craignairinn.com
Open May through October for dinner
Entrées $19 to $24

☛ *An old inn on a lovely point of land, with good dinners*

The inn's homey dining room is filled with wooden chairs and tables and has a fabulous view of Clark Island. The food on the plates is good looking, too. The crabcakes on which the restaurant prides itself ($9) are among the appetizers, as is roasted butternut squash and seared scallops with an Amaretto-lemon sauce ($9). Entrées might be a Maine seafood scampi on linguine ($21), haddock stuffed with shrimp, crab, and breadcrumbs ($20), or grilled 8-ounce beef tenderloin with a roasted shallot "demi," a lighter sauce than a demi-glace ($23).

Miller's Lobster Company
(207) 594-7406
38 Fuller Road, on Wheeler's Bay
Open for lunch and dinner June through September
Entrées $7 to $40 (for a 3-pound lobster)

☛ *A seaside shellfish restaurant*

Long, low red buildings stretch down to the open deck on the wharf at this simple, beautiful location, making fresh seafood all ways except fried. But sometimes they serve spectacular lobsters: A 3-pound lobster special on our visit was going for $39.99, a 2-pound creature cost $29.99, and a 1½-pounder was

$25.99. Lobster salad ($10.75), crab salad ($8.25), and shrimp salad ($7) were specials on the simple menu. Bring your own bottle of wine, or six-pack of beer. Homemade pie for dessert.

Stockton Springs

Just Barb's
(207) 567-3886
Route 1 (at the junction with Main Street)
Open April through October 6 AM–8 PM, October through April 6AM–7 PM
Entrées $5 to $9

☛ *Under new management and interested in getting the best local ingredients, especially the clams, this place has earned praise.*

Plain and simple, but with a growing enthusiasm for the local stuff growing in the area, Just Barb's serves chowder, fried clams, muffins, hash, and daily specials and desserts made from scratch.

The blueberries are from Wyman's; local tomatoes come from nearby; all of the meats come from W.A. Bean & Sons in Maine; and the potatoes come from Aroostook County. The clams come from Grant's Seafood in Stockton Springs, delivered fresh every day. Canola oil with no trans fats is used for frying. The oil is changed every other day, "so it's always clean and real good," said Doug Fraser, who started running Just Barb's in April 2005 and "increased business 300 percent." He grew up two houses down.

Farm Stand

Muskrat Farm Road Farm Stand.
Just off Route 1, in front of a beautiful and beautifully maintained 1850

This tiny farm stand sits at the end of Muskrat Farm Road on Route 1 in Stockton Springs.

Greek Revival farmhouse, is this small stand with honor-system sales of squash and other vegetables, and gladioli. Birdbaths also are sold, but you must find the owners to buy these.

Tenants Harbor

Cod End Cookhouse
(207) 372-6782
Commercial Street
www.codend.com
Open daily 11–8:30 Memorial Day through September (market open 7–7)
Entrées $9 to $22

☛ *A "cookhouse" that grew out of the present market to its own building serves fresh seafood and burgers at tables with great views.*

Fresh seafood specials, like broiled salmon, tuna, and halibut, come along with the regular fried seafood offerings here—clams, shrimp, and scallops, and steamed clams and mussels. Lobster dinners, lobster rolls, haddock rolls, and Mediterranean seafood stew, along with clam and fish chowder, are on the menu.

Desserts are pies, brownies, blueberry cake, and ice cream. All can be cooked and packed to go for a supreme seafood picnic at a cove of your own choice.

East Wind Inn
1-800-241-8439
21 Mechanic Street, P.O. Box 149 (bear left just past the post office on Route 131)
www.eastwindinn.com
Hospitality—Great service from an attentive Maine native
Open daily April through November for breakfast 7:30–9:30, for dinner 5:30–8:30
Entrées $16 to $26

☛ *Good basics and fabulous desserts*

The inn's porch makes a fine place for a glass of wine before dinner.

Once in the dining room with its sailing ships on the walls, we started with mussels steamed with sake, cilantro, coconut milk, and Thai red curry, but the spices didn't make themselves as obvious as we would have liked. The crabcakes, however, were filled with lots of fresh crabmeat, wonderfully satisfying with greens and dill and sherry aioli.

Lobster steamed in seawater was perfectly cooked. An order of the halibut special, served with a sesame sauce, pleased again with perfectly cooked fish, but the sweet sauce overwhelmed the subtle flavors of the fish, which came with a rice mold. A third entrée was scallops broiled in sun-dried tomato butter with Pernod and lemon.

But our good waitress, Judy, had forewarned us to save room for the homemade desserts, and her advice was a pleasure to follow. The bread pudding tasted good. Homemade blueberry buckle, with Maine blueberries, was fantastic if infamously rich; the fruit mixture exactly balanced the tart and the sweet. The apple crisp came warmed, with coconut, and was also delightful.

Sul Mare

(207) 372-9995
13 River Road
www.sulmarerestaurant.com
Open for dinner daily 5–10, Wednesday through Sunday in winter
Entrées $16 to $25

☛ *Grilled meat and fish, prime rib on weekends, with an Italian respect for straight flavor*

Kevin Kieley took a cement block building in St. George, north of the village of Tenants Harbor, and transformed it into an Italian trattoria complete with stuccoed walls. Kieley himself is, he said, 100 percent Irish, but a few years in school in Italy put a new face on food. He grills pork, lamb, and steak, serving dishes from a regional Italian menu and wines from a mostly Italian list.

Kieley was heading to Italy's Firenze and its Ristorante Oliviero for a month of work, and planning to stay at Selvapiana, a vineyard in Chianti, in spring 2007. Look for specials and inspiration when he reopens.

A new appetizer is lobster and corn fritters with maple and thyme vinaigrette ($12). Grilled chicken, caramelized onion, goat cheese, and arugula pizza ($16) will also be on the menu.

Biscotti-crusted halibut—the almond biscotti is ground up—comes with an orange and basil beurre blanc ($22). Kieley gets his halibut right off the boat in Port Clyde; "They make unbelievable stock." When it gets on the grill within 24 hours of being caught, the flesh is almost translucent, Kieley said, like the fresh scallops that are served during the winter, bought from the same fishermen's boats rerigged for winter. One scalloper saved big scallop shells for Sul Mare; in 2007 a lobster pie will be served in these gorgeous dishes.

Kieley also roasts prime rib on the weekends; that combined with Budweiser is the preferred meal for the lobstermen who are his guests. They've eaten enough fish, he said, and don't want to eat it for dinner when they go out—but their wives go for the lobster.

Desserts are always homemade, and might include tiramisu, chocolate cream pie, or individual bananas Foster tarts.

Kieley caught another tuna off Newburyport in summer 2006 (*Chow Maine*'s first edition described another one). He was by himself, and got lucky after catching live bait. The fish weighed 650 pounds and sold for $8,700, before flying away to Japan.

Thomaston

Thomaston Cafe and Bakery
(207) 354-8589
154 Main Street
www.thomastoncafe.com
Hospitality—Friendly, warm, quick service
Open for breakfast and lunch 7–2 Monday through Saturday, for dinner 5:30–8 Friday and Saturday, for Sunday brunch 8:30–1:30
Entrées $12 to $25
Reservations recommended for dinner

☛ *A favorite neighborhood place with a reputation for wonderful food*

The lobster ravioli with lobster cream sauce ($25) has been praised to the skies by many of the customers of this comfortable, casual restaurant. Although it fulfills its role as a neighborhood place to a 'T' and gives our friends who live a few blocks from the door something about which to feel quite smug, the quality of the meals makes it worth a trip from farther away.

One visitor from the southern end of the coastline extolled the diver's scallops. "The food was just unbelievable," she said. If the scallops aren't on the menu—and they will be there only if the restaurant has a fresh supply—there is plenty to tempt you, off the plainest piece of white paper, like the baked fresh haddock with crabmeat, crabcakes with rémoulade, fresh tuna with wasabi ($25), and broiled lamb chops ($22). All dinners come with a salad and two

A Lobster Primer

by David Corey

Here are a few rules about eating lobster that will make your visit to Maine a more enjoyable and tasty one.

☞ **Get your hands in it.** Make sure you remove all jewelry from your fingers and wrists; this includes watches. Lobster has a strong odor that might take a day or two to get out of your skin, so if you want to keep your jewelry clean, take it off. The same holds true for clothing. I've seen one or two Mainers actually turn their shirt inside out or remove it altogether. At least roll up your sleeves.

☞ **Get to know your lobster.** Menus may try to lure you into ordering a 2-pound or more lobster, but if you're looking for the most tender and sweet meat, order one between 1 and 1½ pounds; 1½ pounds is the ideal weight, and also the most common. There are two general types of lobster: hard shell and soft shell. Soft-shell lobsters—also known as shedders—are what most summer visitors will eat and are usually much sweeter and tastier than hard shells. (Lobsters molt. When they outgrow their shells, they shed them away, leaving only a soft membrane beneath. This membrane eventually firms back to a hard-shell form.) Despite the availability of nut crackers and picks to eat a lobster with, a good soft shell can usually be taken apart by hand, peeled like an orange.

☞ **Dig in!** The claws are the easiest "get." Stress the joint and twist. Then do the same with the remaining joints of the claw. Meat abounds. Remove the tail by bending it back toward the lobster's back while twisting your wrist. Then remove the tail fins (there are small flakes of meat in here too) and use your thumb to push the lobster meat out of the tail in one big piece.

Peel back a thin strip of meat along the length of the tail meat to reveal the intestinal tract. Pull this out and discard.

☞ **Finish the job.** First, peel the legs off one at a time. Place one in your mouth as far as you can, then clamp your teeth down. Slowly pull the leg from your mouth, keeping your teeth clenched, and work the meat out. As the juices trickle from the open end of the leg, suck the juice and meat into your mouth. They're wonderful, sweet little treats. Next, using the "stressed joints" method mentioned above, slide a thumb into the cavity at the base of the body where the tail once was. Pull the rounded red shell away from the spiderlike entrails. The first thing you'll notice is a greenish, soupy ooze called tomalley. It will look like nothing you would ever want to eat, but, again, keep an open mind. Using your pinkie finger, scoop up the tomalley and suck it off the tip of your finger. If you've gotten this far (many don't), and if you're pleasantly surprised (many are), repeat this process until the tomalley is gone. Next, take the spiderlike entrails in both hands and bend back the tops of the legs, exposing tiny pockets of meat. Using your fingertips, work the small bits of meat out and pop them into your mouth.

Once you're satisfied that all the meat is gone, lick all your fingers—one at a time—in a hedonistic manner, then let out a long groan and ask the person sitting next to you if he's going to finish his. After all, you're learning a process, and eating lobster takes practice.

sides. A vegetarian entrée, one night Israeli couscous with wild mushrooms and vegetables ($12), is part of the evening menu.

But dinner is served only Friday and Saturday. Breakfast, lunch, and Sunday brunch are made just as well, and could also be a destination meal. The cheese blintzes with berry sauce ($6.50)—I preferred the raspberry over the blueberry—are perfect wraps of eggy pancake and fluffy cheese.

For breakfast the orange juice is squeezed to order, the best way to serve it ($3.25 a glass and worth it). Haddock fish cakes, omelets, and pancakes all beckon. The Thomaston special is two eggs any style, choice of bacon, ham, or sausages with home fries and toast ($5.75). Bagels are good ones from the Camden Bagel Café (see page 184), and many other products come from local farms and waters.

Ice Cream and Fish

Dorman's Dairy Dream, Route 1.
Open mid-April until mid-October. Closed Sunday. Ginger is the best, some say; but with many flavors, and years of experience making ice cream, this locally loved ice cream stand has many "bests."

The Fish Truck.
Alvin Dennison's colorful truck is parked on Route 1 across from the cement plant and is the source of great fresh fish for many loyal customers.

Vinalhaven

The Haven Restaurant
(207) 863-4969
49 Main Street
Open Tuesday through Saturday with a 6 PM and an 8:15 PM seating in summer, closed January through May
Entrées $14 to $22

☛ *Relied on for its fresh ingredients and changing dishes; always good*

The Haven's always-changing menu is based on what's available, so diners can only be sure of encountering fish and meat. But you might find foie gras or crabcakes on lucky nights. Duck and shrimp gumbo, spiced scallops with bacon, sherry-vinaigrette-glazed chicken, and beef tenderloin with local wild mushroom butter were dishes on an early-October menu. Greens for the salads are from the Webster girls on Vinalhaven, who grow "beautiful, beautiful produce," said Tory Pratt. She has owned the Haven since 1991 and, she said, "I've been here forever."

"I love to cook desserts the most," said Pratt. The chocolate mousse, made with beaten egg whites and not cream, is really popular and "really chocolaty."

In the summer Pratt serves food in two dining rooms; one for reservations only looks out at the mouth of the harbor. In the second room she serves hamburgers and other casual food in summer, and a more elaborate menu in fall, when—because there's no heat waterside—the restaurant shrinks to this one room. The Haven has a wine list and a full bar.

The Starlight Cafe
(207) 863-2789
250 Main Street
Open 6:30–2 (2–5 for ice cream and coffee) Monday through Friday,
7:30–7:30 Saturday, 8–1 (1–7:30 for ice cream and coffee) for Sunday brunch
(till 7:30 for coffee and ice cream); closed Tuesday
Lunch entrées around $6 to $7

☛ *The place for good sandwiches, coffee, soup, and salads*

This new place on the island gets good supplies from the mainland, like Atlantic Baking Company bread and Rock City Coffee Roasters coffee. They bake their own muffins and cookies. Good burritos, and a Tacchino—a turkey panini with pesto, roasted red peppers, and provolone ($6.50). Annabelle's Ice Cream is sold.

Market, Casual Meals, and Wine

Downstreet Market (207-863-4500), Main Street.
A bakery, café, and whole foods store with espresso and baked goods in the morning, sandwiches and soup later.

The Harbor Gawker (207-863-9365), Main Street.
Open daily for lunch and dinner 11–8 in summer, closed Sunday. Counter service for chowders, fried seafood, lobster rolls, and blueberry pie. Wait for your number to be called after you decide on the seafood of the day, and enjoy the view of Carvers Pond. Finish up with ice cream from the dairy bar.

Island Spirits (207-863-2192), Carvers Harbor.
Open Monday through Saturday 11–6:30 in summer. Good wine, good cheese, beer, olives, and freshly ground coffee.

Waldoboro

Moody's Diner
(207) 832-7785
Route 1
www.moodysdiner.com
Hospitality—Swift and skilled in this busy, busy place
Open Monday through Friday 4:30 AM–11:30 PM, Saturday 5 AM–11:30 PM,
Sunday 6 AM–11:30 PM

☛ *A gorgeous landmark with diner food and a devoted following*

The lure of the snappy blinking red neon sign, hypnotizing everyone driving past at dusk, may have something to do with this Moody's enduring and flourishing business.

The meat loaf, turkey roasted upside-down, and cream pies at this 1930s diner have pleased so many customers that by now over a million have eaten here. In 2002, at the 75th-anniversary celebration, 31 members of the extended Moody family were involved with running this place.

The food on Moody's long menu is basic, mostly homemade plain fare, modest sandwiches, and traditional dishes. That explains the reasonable prices, perhaps the main reason local patrons fill this place for early suppers. A souvenir store for T-shirts and cabin rentals have succeeded here too.

Morse's Sauerkraut
(207) 832-5569
3856 Washington Road (Route 220)
www.morsessauerkraut.com
Hospitality—Overwhelmed sometimes (don't go on Saturday), otherwise fine
Restaurant open for breakfast 8–10:30, lunch 10:30–4, Thursday through
Sunday; Monday and Tuesday 9–4; closed Wednesday
Store hours 9–6, closed Wednesday.
Entrées $7 to $9

☛ *Too small for the extent of its business, but offering good German food and great kraut*

In fall, when the newly harvested cabbages had completed their fermentation and were transformed into fresh sauerkraut, the former owner of this Germanic outpost would put an ad in the paper: "Kraut's ready." Everyone who cared knew what that meant.

Today Morse's still makes sauerkraut all year long, and still sells the most in fall, made with the new cabbage crop. Some customers wait until November to get the kraut made with cabbage that's been sweetened by the frost. But whatever they prefer, there is always kraut here, made fresh with all its beneficial bacteria, now understood to be a crucial part of a healthy human being. Articles about that are on the walls.

David Swetnam and Jacquelyn Sawyer have expanded the shop, a store and delicatessen crammed with German breads, chocolate *babka* from Brooklyn, and Schaller & Weber sausages. You can eat sauerkraut served up to you in the four-booth restaurant, another addition, or buy it to take home.

Farm Stands and Bakery

Beau Chemin Farm Stand (207-832-5789), 1749 Finntown Road.
A right turn north of Moody's Diner, 3½ miles down the road after the turn. This organic farm raises endangered heritage breeds of livestock like Buff Orpington chickens and Suffolk Punch draft horses. Wool is sheared from Leicester Longwool sheep and other breeds, dyed, and spun. You can pick your own raspberries and flowers, and buy produce. Weekends in summer may be a good time for a visit to see the farm, if you call ahead.

Borealis Breads (207-832-0655), Route 1 (across from Moody's Diner).
Open Monday through Saturday 8:30–5:30, Sunday 9–5. Moist, chewy, and crusty is how the company describes its own breads, and we know that is the exact truth. The *ciabatta* is tender as well, an object of worship fresh from the oven. We love the rye and the multigrain. The slow-rising technique Borealis employs gives the bread its distinctive flavor.

Spear's Farm Stand (207-832-0483), 1526 Atlantic Highway (Route 1).
Open 9–6 daily in-season. Squash and pumpkins and corn overflow the shelves in the harvest weeks of fall. **(Also at 14 Center Street in Nobleboro just off Route 1.** Open Monday through Saturday 9–5).

Maine produce gets spicy hot at Beth's Farm Stand in Warren.

Warren

Beth's Farm Stand (207-273-3695), 1986 Western Road.

With signs guiding you here both from Route 1 and from Route 90, this short drive brings you to such an abundance of fine produce you won't want to miss it. Piles of tomatoes, corn, onions, and pints of blueberries are for sale, along with many other kinds of produce at this landmark farm stand.

CHAPTER 6

The Blue Hill Peninsula and Deer Isle

I T SEEMS AS IF THE PEOPLE WHO LIVE on this strangely beautiful stretch of the coast have a special intensity about their food—more of them are starting food businesses, growing produce, or baking bread with more skill and more attention than on other parts of the coast.

The good fortune lies on both sides. The bakers can make a living, because the customers are there to buy what they make. The farmers can sustain their farms, because the people around them want to eat what's growing on their neighbor's land.

The Deer Isle farmer's market is jammed, with people lined up and waiting to make their purchases, the kind of line you might see at a vendor's truck in New York City's Union Square. It was a sight to give you hope, to make you wonder if we could, someday, share a culture that loved good, fresh, flavorful food—one that could leave behind a sorry indulgence in junk food that has no taste worth talking about, and no nutritional value beyond sheer calories.

If you're going to indulge, after all, why not indulge in something delicious? Why not trade in the can of soda for a piece of pie, at the very least? There are several women on Deer Isle who can make you a pie worth eating.

Blue Hill

Arborvine Restaurant and The Vinery
(207) 374-2119
Main Street, Tenney Hill
www.arborvine.com
Open for dinner Tuesday through Sunday 5:30–9, July through Labor Day;
Wednesday through Sunday until New Year's Day; Friday through Sunday until
May; Wednesday through Sunday in May and June. The Vinery has the same
summer hours; closed after Labor Day until Memorial Day weekend.
Entrées $22 to $29

☛ *A very popular fine-dining place with consistent, quality food and
lovely grounds and rooms*

The handsome old, beamed dining rooms here were filled up every night of
our visits, the parking lot was overflowing, and we never managed to snag a
table. We'll try again next year and meanwhile regale you with the menu, confident from all the praise we heard bestowed on this restaurant's hospitality
that you will enjoy a meal here.

Roast rack of lamb with a basil pine-nut crust ($29) and pork tenderloin
with green apples ($23) give a glimpse of the direction of the meat entrées. I
would probably start with the Damariscotta River oysters ($12), but then I'd
do that anywhere that serves them. Unique to Arborvine would be the smoked
scallops and trout with horseradish cream ($10).

A chocolate gateau with raspberry puree and a pear crisp with whipped
cream are on the dessert menu.

The Vinery, open only in summer, can take care of some of the overflow at
the Arborvine, although you may have to wait a while for a table. With white
walls and a bar, this place is more casual. Friends of ours did not like having to
pay for bread. Wines start kindly down at $14, and the list is long enough for
some intriguing bottles between the high-priced greats and those economical
good-enoughs.

The Wescott Forge
(207) 374-9909
66 Main Street
www.thewescottforge.com

The upstairs lounge of Blue Hill's Wescott Forge includes a handsome bar.

Hospitality—The service here is utterly accommodating.
Open for lunch 11–2:30, dinner 5:30–10 Monday through Saturday; Columbus
Day through Memorial Day open Wednesday through Saturday
Entrées $18 to $31
Handicapped accessible on the main floor, reservations recommended

☛ *Sophisticated, but not overcomplicated, the dinners here are studies in careful contrasts and freshness.*

The tables set along the glass windows on the river are the first to be reserved, so ask for one yourself. Watching the flow of that water to the sea is a pleasant way to interrupt your reverie about the very fresh mussels, or an excellent shrimp spring roll with a fine crunch to it.

David Sweimler is the chef, and past work in New York City's bistro Quatorze, Café Luxemburg, and Lespinasse. His partner in this business, Anneliese Riggall, runs the business with years of experience as well. The old wood floors, the front patio in summer, and fireplace in winter create a comfortable atmosphere, only troubled by a high noise level when crowded.

Try something from the fine wine list while you contemplate the menu, like an Easton Amador Zinfandel ($8), but rely on the salad, like one with greens, pear, and candied pecans ($6), with a tart vinaigrette neither too light nor too heavy. Cheese plates and smoked seafood plates are another good way to get things started.

Seared scallops in ginger-miso broth ($24) with coconut sticky rice (the rice is a house specialty) were perfect. Chicken stuffed with sausage and served with scalloped potatoes was the rich dish of the evening, an exact fit to one appetite. One small issue with a steak cooked beyond my preference was quickly made right with another plate of sliced, rare meat, and its sautéed greens were exquisite.

Peach and rhubarb crisp ($7) was another example of the way it all comes together here, crisp and buttery on top, tender and tart-sweet inside. The chocolate soufflé was just as dark and intense as anyone could wish for.

Lunch, Pizza, Takeout, Wine, and Bakeries

Blue Hill Food Co-op Café (207-374-2165), Main Street (Route 172), P.O. Box 71.

Open year-round Monday through Friday 8–2, soup and sandwiches available until 7, Saturday 8–6, and Sunday 9–1. Some people say this is the best place in town for lunch. Considering the taste of the delicious golden seafood stew, with crabmeat and lemongrass, that seems about right. Robin Byrne learned about cooking at the Natural Gourmet Cookery School in Manhattan, and her partner in the business, Joe Porada, grew up in a restaurant in Binghamton, New York. Between them the café is turning out high-quality soups, baked goods, and three standard salads, as well as daily specials. Many dishes are vegan; all use organic ingredients. Sesame noodles, red curry chicken salad, and fine hummus are a few of the choices, and dessert could be a strawberry bar.

The Blue Hill Wine Shop (207-374-2161), Main Street, P.O. Box 71.

In addition to a large selection of wine from around the world, this 27-year-old shop sells a full range of teas and coffee, cigars and tobacco. The 90 varieties of wine are sold in an old stock barn—penciled descriptions of the cattle once sold there are on the wall. Port and sherries are available too.

The Fishnet (207-374-5240), Main Street, P.O. Box 720.

Open in summer Sunday through Thursday 11–8, Friday and Saturday 11–9; in fall and spring daily 8–4; closed Columbus Day through March. This is the drive-in and take-out place the locals recommend for fried seafood, with hamburgers and hot dogs for the kids. It has been in the same family for years and is known for good fish-and-chips. For $16.95 in 2006 you could enjoy a 1½-pound lobster with corn on the cob and chips, or a lobster roll for $10.99. Steamers, side orders of fried fish, and ice cream and homemade desserts. A tiny dining room with five gold-wood booths is to the left of the order counter.

Pain de Famille (207-374-2565; www.paindefamile.com), Main Street, P.O. Box 1437.

Open in summer 8–5 Monday through Friday, 8–4 Saturday, closed Sunday, off-season open at 7 AM. The plain room of this bustling bakery, now owned by Beth and Michael Gallo, is filled with goodness; a counter and baskets are filled with the creations of the women working across the room. Focaccia rounds ($3.50); francese, a white country loaf ($2.95); and field wheat loaves (all $3.50) are a few you can find here. *Pane al ciocolatto,* chocolate bread ($3.95), smells fabulous coming out of the oven. Maine Grains Bread flies out of the bakery. The Nutty Bird Bar ($2.50) resembles something from the bird feeder, but it was fabulous, with pumpkin seeds, walnuts, pecans, almonds, sunflower seeds, flax seeds, tahini, and honey—and I wish I had one right now. Sandwiches and wraps are stocked in the cooler, and pizza is in a rack. All natural, organic, and vegetarian options abound.

Pain de Famille co-owner Beth Gallo measures out dough for baking.

The Pantry (207-374-2229), Water Street.

Open for breakfast and lunch 7–2 Monday through Friday. This tiny place has staying power, making eggs and omelets, bagels with cream cheese, and Belgian waffles for breakfast, and more for lunch, since 1988. The Melina-PMS Crab sandwich intrigued me, but the Reuben, the turkey sandwich with Swiss cheese, and the good chowders might have more mass appeal. Crabmeat and lobster rolls too. There's outdoor seating, and all orders can be wrapped to go. Blueberry shortcake for dessert, and self-serve coffee at the counter.

The Blue Hill Farmer's Market is held Saturday 9–11:30 late May through Labor Day weekend at the Blue Hill fairgrounds, and then at the Congregational Church parking lot, in downtown Blue Hill. Lore Lipkvich, of Garden Lore, sells a goat's-milk cheese here that got raves at a College of the Atlantic tasting; her 15 goats live in Mariaville, and she makes ricotta, feta, and flavored chèvres from their milk. She also sells cage-free eggs, and goat's-milk soap, which would make a fine souvenir.

Brooklin

The Brooklin Inn
(207) 359-2777
Route 175, P.O. Box 25
www.brooklininn.com
Hospitality—Obliging and charming on our visit
Open for dinner daily in summer, in winter closed Monday and Tuesday
Entrées $18 to $34

☛ *An inn with a welcoming, casual atmosphere and well-made dinners*

The old rooms here have seen years of hospitality, something host and innkeeper Chip Angell, who led us to our seats, excelled at himself. He made us all comfortable with a little banter, returning to open the bottle of good wine we'd ordered at his recommendation.

Since the menu mentioned the possibility of children's portions, or a special dish, we asked; and the chef offered to make tricollatura pasta with butter and Parmesan, to our young guest's delight. The adults were off and running with appetizers. Peekytoe crabcakes ($10) with chive-cilantro mayonnaise and pineapple salsa were packed with crab, crusty, and well-flavored. A large, poached pear sat on spinach leaves with slices of Manchego, sweet pecans, and maple vinaigrette ($8), a perfect combination. Paul Brayton's mussels, a full pound with Dijon sauce, kept one of us busy for a long time as she savored the mustard's sharpness against the plump, fresh Blue Hill mussels' salty sweetness.

There were ships all around us—ships' flags, and photographs, and models. The sea was nearby, certainly, in the bouillabaisse put in front of me, with halibut, haddock, clams, scallops, and mussels in a clear broth with tomatoes, and wonderful grilled lengths of crusty bread, well-buttered.

Wild salmon ($23) slightly too cooked for my taste, came with forbidden rice, a black, chewy grain that made a good contrast with the sweet flesh of the fish that also gained with a horseradish sauce. A special shiitake mushroom risotto pleased with its melting texture.

For dessert, the Chocolate Seduction Cake seduced. "It's like eating fudge," one of my companions said, so be forewarned.

The menu credits the suppliers of most of the meals' ingredients, letting you know that Johnny White caught the lobster yesterday. I credit the inn with doing right by them, and chef Kyla Randell for making that night out a pleasure for us all.

Brooksville

Oakland House Seaside Resort
(207) 359-8521, 1-800-359-7352
435 Herrick Road, Herricks Landing
www.oaklandhouse.com
Hospitality—Outgoing and warm
Open daily from the end of June through September for dinner
Entrées around $20

☛ *Fine food and wine served in a lovely old inn*

This wonderful place, a family resort with elegant old cabins set along the sea, serves dinner to its own guests and to the public during the summer months. With a dining room reserved for families and another for people without children, you can find the right spot for yourself.

When I had the pleasure of spending a night here as a guest of friends, we dined together in a small room, just the five of us. The youngest guest was

The Oakland House Seaside Resort, with a separate dining room for diners without children, serves fine dinners and is open to the public in-season.

hard put to eat her small pizza, and some pieces of cut-up fruit, before she raced out to the lawn to play with other guests' children.

But the rest of us were preoccupied by the Crab Tower, crab and fresh greens sandwiched in crisp wontons, and the smoked salmon rosette with a touch of vanilla sour cream, and then the soup of creamed spinach, broccoli, and leeks from the garden.

A salad of tender romaine, fennel, and Brie was generous with the mild cheese, and dressed lightly.

A bottle of Echeverria Reserva Cabernet Sauvignon ($27), a 2003 from Chile, from the good wine list went nicely with the sirloin with mushroom and port sauce, the lamb chops with mustard-honey sauce, and the seared tuna with Japanese ponzo sauce. Executive chef Woody Clark puts these dishes together with a light hand, letting the meat and fish dominate the flavors, while touches of ginger and wasabi, for instance, spiced the mild, sweet tuna.

Pecan griddle cakes with poached pears and a light caramel sauce was one of the buttery desserts, light, and not too large—just right when the evening is getting dark, and the children's laughter out in the gloaming comes softer as they tire. It's time to walk back to the cabin.

Bagaduce Lunch (207-326-4729), 19 Bridge Road (Route 176).

Open daily 11–7 from May to the second week of September. This take-out place is set beside the Bagaduce Falls, where a reversing tide rips up and down its narrow channel at the ebb and flood. The area is famous for its horseshoe crabs and haunted by beautiful birds—eagles, ospreys, and herons among them—looking out for their own lunch.

I enjoyed a crabmeat salad made with local greens and tomatoes. The crabmeat, mixed with mayonnaise, was delectable. The onion rings were a different matter, not elegant, but delicious all the same, thin, crisp, hot, and oily. An overflowing paper dish of fried scallops ($10), with perhaps 16 big scallops and good tartar sauce, were succulent and tender; and the clean picnic tables scattered along the waterside make for lovely alfresco meals. Ice cream and sundaes, too.

Buck's Harbor

Rendezvous
(207) 326-8531
Route 176
Open daily for dinner in summer 4–9:30 (bar until 11:30); off-season open Thursday through Sunday 5–9:30 (bar open to 11)
Hospitality—With a crowd there was a short delay, but end of summer staff shortages can't be helped
Entrées $15 to $24
Reservations advised on weekends

☛ *A Greek influence adds interest to this good menu of Maine fish and meat.*

Located behind the Buck's Harbor Market, this space has been a restaurant for years; in its latest (2006) incarnation a few Greek specialties jazz up the menu, from a Greek salad ($8.50, or $12 with grilled organic chicken)—perfect hot-weather food with romaine, cucumbers, tomatoes, feta, and kalamata olives— to spanikopita. Crabcakes, mussels, and lobster risotto are on the list too.

Oven-roasted baby artichokes ($10) proved tender and good with a little green chili, garlic, and Manchego. The Mediterranean meze had a really wonderful *tzatziki*, as well as *melitzanosalata,* with creamy roasted eggplant, and garlic feta with walnut pesto, all great on the grilled sourdough ($10).

Seared scallops ($24) came on roasted-garlic spinach cream with mashed mascarpone Yukon gold potatoes, rich as sin. The spanikopita from a family recipe ($15), with salty light spinach filling and a flaky crust, made our vegetarian friend's evening a pleasure—and the top sirloin ($24) made mine, again with those rich potatoes.

Rigatoni crab pasta and handmade ravioli filled with artichokes, asparagus, ricotta, and buffalo mozzarella, in tomato cream sauce, was another rich dish worth tasting.

On Thursday, Friday, and Saturday nights here three simple pizzas are on the menu: a Margherita ($10) with its classic mozzarella and tomato topping, one that adds hot Italian pepperoncini, and the Quattro Stagioni ($12.50), with ham, mushrooms, and artichokes.

The wine here is good and the atmosphere friendly and low-key—and next time I won't miss the fried zucchini blossoms ($9).

Buck's Harbor Market (207-326-8683), Route 176.

This general store has a bakery that's got the best pizza, on Friday and Saturday, on the peninsula, according to one food lover in Blue Hill. Fresh bread, a selection of cheeses, fine wines, and beer. Cookies and muffins too, and fresh produce from Barbara Damrosch and Eliot Coleman's Four Season Farm in Brooksville, and Blue Sky Farm in Monson.

Castine

The Castine Inn
(207) 326-4365
Main Street
www.castineinn.com
Open for dinner May through Columbus Day; tasting menus on demand off-season, on Wednesday, Saturday, and Sunday in summer; pub menu Wednesday through Sunday in summer, through Saturday off-season. Closed after Columbus Day through April.
Five-course tasting menu $85; with paired wine, add $40. Pub menu $6 to $10.

☛ *The chef, Tom Gutow, runs a kitchen that leaps with creativity.*

The Castine Inn is a destination for a certain kind of Maine tourist, the one with the nose for fantastic menus. Tom Gutow, whose Castine Inn dining room was ranked in the country's top 50 hotel restaurants in 2002 by *Food & Wine* magazine, is a master of elegant meals that move quietly from one brilliant flavor to another, the tempo building, the intensity deepening. He calls his six-course tasting dinners "going to the theater."

His menus, and his business, are always changing—he may introduce an à la carte menu in the future. His dishes span the range of the seasons, emphasizing Maine, and have featured grilled foie gras with Lambert cherries, buttery lobster with liquid corn tortellini and basil, slow-roasted salmon with green apple, chicken with a chicken liver brochette, a rhubarb float with Socrates Cucumber Sorbet, an apple tart with cardamom, and a chicory chocolate cappuccino to end.

In the pub you might find chicken soup with house-made broad noodles in the fall, in summer Mediterranean seafood soup with mussels and rouille, or a Seal Cove Farm feta and black olive salad ($7). More possibilities include an avocado martini—the Castine Inn version of guacamole—crispy risotto cakes ($6), and signature Castine and Penobscot Bay crabcakes ($10) that were featured in *Gourmet* magazine. The secret? They're made mostly with crabmeat, with a very little bit of egg, milk, and cracker crumbs.

Dennett's Wharf Restaurant and Oyster Bar

(207) 326-9045
Sea Street
www.dennettswharf.com
Open spring through fall daily for lunch and dinner
Entrées $9 to $17

☛ *An old sail and rigging loft now brews beer and serves lunch on the waterfront.*

The bar is made with Georgian lumber shipped here for a bowling lane, rediscovered under the linoleum during a renovation, and transformed into the world's longest oyster bar—now the site of Maine's oyster-eating contest. Oysters are shucked to order; you might as well get in some practice.

Steamers, lobster cakes, and fried clams also are on the appetizer list. Seafood lasagna, with scallops, shrimp, and cheeses in a white sauce, sounds rich. You can get a steamed lobster, or barbecued ribs and steaks, or roast chicken. Burritos, BLTs, lobster rolls, and a crabmeat melt for lunch.

Pentagöet Inn

(207) 326-8616, 1-800-845-1701
Main Street, P.O. Box 4
www.pentagoet.com

Hospitality—Well-trained staff do a great job serving dinners.
Open daily for dinner at 5:30 May through October
Entrées $18 to $24

☛ *One of the best meals on the coast of Maine, for ambience, service, and great food*

Everything seemed to come together at the Pentagöet Inn. The glass of wine I drank on the porch at the end of a long day of traveling put me in the right mood, and there was the wonder at the folded terry-cloth towels in the bathroom, in a stack waiting for use, with a basket to drop them in. How could they keep up? But on my previous two visits the room was impeccable.

Castine's famous elms still tower over Main Street, and you can admire them from the porch. Inside, yellow chintz wrapped around cream poles at the windows, and red walls negated the feminine assault of the china knickknacks.

A puree of artichoke hearts, garlic, and oil came with warm focaccia to get us in the mood to eat. The salad with Gorgonzola toasts, port-pickled grapes, and olive oil ($7.50) had a fascination; the grapes were a cross between a raisin and a fresh grape, tasting more of fruit than wine, but delicious and a lovely contrast with the Gorgonzola. A glass of Spy Valley Sauvignon Blanc, from New Zealand, fruity and intense, kept pace with the strong flavors.

A lobster tail and claw meat, mussels, and scallops, all tender, lay bathing in a dark rosy broth in the bouillabaisse ($28) I ordered, a special; flakes of luscious cod lapped in the peppery, fennel soup and filled my mouth with its perfection, and a long piece of crouton with lobster butter kept up the pleasure.

My friend's enormous plate of *gemelli* pasta with pulled Smithfield ham, peas, and shallots in black truffle cream could not be devoured so thoroughly, but she loved it just the same and put down her fork with regret.

For dessert, a blueberry tart triumphed with a preponderance of berries over lemon curd, and the pecan pie's light filling stood well with the sweeter maple ice cream.

Bakery and Lunch

Bah's Bakehouse (207-326-9510), Water Street.

Open Monday through Saturday 7–5, Sunday 8–5 in-season. Delicious danishes and raspberry scones are made here, where a customer can put together a meal to carry out in a wicker basket to a table with an umbrella in the yard on a fine day. Soups and sandwiches and creative salads. Hot coffee.

Castine Variety Store (207-326-8625), 1 Main Street.

Open 5 AM–9 PM in summer, 5 AM–8 PM in winter. Inexpensive crabmeat or lobster rolls in summer, pizza, and a big collection of videos for rent. The old counter from a long time back in this old-fashioned store makes a good setting for a milk shake.

Deer Isle

Whale's Rib Tavern
(207) 348-6615, 1-888-778-7505
20 Main Street, P.O. Box 69
www.pilgrimsinn.com
Open daily for dinner May through November
Entrées $7 to $25

☞ *Popular, well-made standards fill the menu.*

Steaks, fish, and specials are made here. The roast duck with pomegranate and raspberry, and other more formal meals familiar from when the dining room went by the name of the Pilgrim's Inn are gone; but the dining room is crowded with folks who don't miss them, though an occasional longtime guest still does. They can dine on the steamed lobster, which never leaves the menu.

More ownership changes came a year after the dining room became known at the Whale's Rib; the owners as of our publication date are Tina Oddleifson and Tony Lawless.

A grilled rib eye ($18.95 for a "queen," or $22.95 for a "king") and broiled haddock ($14.95) are popular.

Ice Cream and Pies

Harbor Ice Cream (207-348-9360), 11 Main Street.
Open Monday through Saturday 11–8, Sunday 12–8, May through the end of September. This place sells Gifford's ice cream in cones, sundaes, and frappes. The food otherwise isn't anything to write home about, or hear about either.

Susie Q's (207-348-6013), 17 Sunset Cross Road.
Open Monday through Saturday 9–3 in summer; call for hours after Labor Day. Fresh-baked pies from Susan Scott, one of the owners of the Fisherman's Friend

Restaurant (see page 233). Blueberry, raspberry, and strawberry-rhubarb pies, muffins, cakes for parties, and blueberry and raspberry crisp also are available. Crab quiche.

Isle au Haut

The Keeper's House
(207) 460-0257
www.keepershouse.com
Open late May through late October
Entrées are included in the price of a night's stay.

☞ *A trip to a beautiful island where the innkeepers' dinners have been delighting visitors for years*

Jeff and Judi Burke, the hosts at this restored lighthouse station, feed their guests wonderful meals. The adventure of making your way out here and staying in the living museum of the lighthouse station no doubt sharpens the appetite, but all our friends who have had the pleasure of enjoying their meals praise them. You might start with a hot lobster dip, or six-onion soup, and a garden salad, then enjoy grilled salmon with herb butter and roasted red potatoes along with fresh-baked bread. End with fresh peach pie and coffee or tea, and then it's time to listen to the surf outside your inn window.

Little Deer Isle

Eaton's Lobster Pool
(207) 348-2383
Blastow Cove Road
www.eatonslobsterpool.com
Hospitality—Helpful and experienced at this traditional lobster place with salads
Open for dinner 4:30–9 mid-June through Labor Day, weekends from Mother's Day and until Columbus Day
Entrées $8 to $39 (baked stuffed lobster)

☞ *The view off the porch of a nearby island and distant hills makes all the fresh seafood delicious.*

There is full service here nowadays, with starters like lobster stew ($14 a bowl), steamed clams ($12), and a garden salad ($5). You also can enjoy lobster salad ($17) served with lettuce, tomatoes, and cucumbers, or a lobster roll ($12) served with french fries.

The peaceful setting at the end of winding Blastow Cove Road, with a chorus of crickets in late summer and stretches of water leading to the area's thematic softwood-covered hills, makes this spot one of the best settings in Maine. I guess that's why the prices are a little higher than elsewhere. Twin lobsters, served with salad and french fries, or a baked or mashed potato ($34), would be worthy of this landscape.

Fried fish and shellfish dinners would be too ($16 for either clams or scallops, with a salad and choice of potato). Broiled scallops or haddock are offered, as are strip steaks, grilled chicken breast, and crabcakes.

Crabmeat

Crabmeat pickers sell fresh crabmeat from their shops or homes here, including two on Route 15. Cheryl Robinson sells Maine peekytoe crab harvested by her husband, Dick, from her shop, **The Krusty Krab (207-348-2285).** According to a Salt Institute article by Molly May, Cheryl has been picking crab, a niggling, difficult job, for "as long as she can remember." A second sign on Route 15 before the causeway is at **Angela Murphy's house (207-348-6495),** where you can also purchase freshly picked crabmeat. Just down the road **Sonia Bunt (207-348-9958),** on Blastow Cove Road, has 20 years of experience and can come up with a spare container if the harvest has been good.

North Brooklin

The Lookout
(207) 359-2188
Flye Point Road (2 miles down)
www.thelookout.biz
Open for dinner 5:30–8:30 Tuesday through Sunday, June through Labor Day; Wednesday through Sunday until mid-October
Entrées $18 to $32
Reservations recommended

☛ *The buzz says this place makes the best meals in the area.*

This beautiful setting—an old white farmhouse above a long stretch of rolling grass and lines of Queen Anne's lace that trail to the blue water, with a large white tent glimmering down there—may present one of the most picturesque views around.

Jonathan Chase, well-known here for past work at the Pilgrim's Inn and earlier at his own place in Blue Hill, is the chef. He started one August menu with Cuban black bean soup with crème fraîche ($7), and crostini with fig, olive, and white anchovy tapenade ($8).

Mushroom, asparagus, and ricotta strudel with roasted shallot, red pepper, and garlic coulis ($17) would impress most vegetarians.

But a meat-eating customer like me might be more engaged by the Alsatian choucroute with kielbasa, chicken-shiitake sausage, knockwurst, and red potatoes ($17). Ale-braised lamb shank with maple barbecue sauce ($20) and grilled sliced flatiron steak with Roquefort walnut butter ($19) are two more beacons on the list.

Fruit crisp and a flourless chocolate cake are usually on the dessert menu.

Stonington

The Cockatoo
(207) 367-0900
24 Carter Lane
Hospitality—Whatever you want, someone here will help out, including other customers.
Open 12–8 for takeout in summer
Entrées $11 to $22
BYOB

☛ *On a warm night, the outside patio is a kind of heaven overlooking Webb Cove, while the spicy seafood heats up your mouth.*

Suzen Carter was Suzen Diniz before she married a fisherman and moved to Stonington eight years ago. She's Portuguese, from New Bedford, Massachusetts, with ancestors from the Azores, and she loves to cook. She loves to cook so much that when she first moved here she would bring her food to the bank and to the gas station, just to share it and because she didn't know anyone on the island. "Why don't you open a restaurant?" people asked. Her husband said the same thing, and he had expanded his fish store just down the hill from their house. She started out small one summer and by the end of the season was amazed.

"It was all word of mouth," she said. Remembering the previous Saturday night when the tables in the outside patio were full, and a line of 14 people waited for takeout, she felt confident that she would be mixing up more of her shrimp Mozambique ($16.95), a garlicky, pungent dish, and her Portuguese sole ($15.95), full of saffron and rice, for seasons to come.

"We don't have anything frozen," she said. Her husband's three fishing boats bring in supplies for the little fish store, and a day-old harpooned swordfish sat in the cooler. Clams are dug, shucked, and fried within a day.

"You don't even need any seasonings," she said, even though she'd shown off the bag of Portuguese salt, Peniche, a moment before—it adds "fresh out of the water flavor," she said.

The clams ($16.95) are part of the word going from resident to visitor and back as people turn in on the dirt driveway off Oceanville Road to Carter's Seafood and the Cockatoo, and they proved to be the best we had tried that summer. The only seating is at the outside tables, where you carry your order from the take-out window. Bring your own bottle of wine to this party. But if you arrive at an off hour, expect to set up your own spot to lunch—and the back patio can be too hot in the heat of the afternoon. One customer helped us plug in a fan.

The aging dancing cockatoo, Peaches, favors a Latin beat and sings to the music, crowing with her gray tongue and bobbing with evident delight, ruffling her white feathers and the few orange ones, and then studying you intently with her round black eyes.

This customer enjoyed doing a little gardening before lunch at the Cockatoo.

The Fisherman's Friend has moved down in view of the sea.

The Fisherman's Friend
(207) 367-2442
5 Atlantic Avenue
Open for lunch and dinner in summer, closing earlier in winter; closed on Monday
Entrées $7 to $18

☛ *A local favorite for fried fish and Maine lobsters*

The lobster stew and chowders are always ready here in this Maine seafood restaurant. Crabcakes, lobster rolls, and other things to eat in-between, like hamburgers and grilled cheese fill the categories for every kind of diner. Tony and Lauren Bray run the restaurant (also co-owned by Tony's mother, Susan Scott, and her husband, Jack Scott) in its new location along the water, with 140 seats downstairs. An outside deck seats 40 when the sun is shining. The pies, more than 20 listed on occasion, can really get your heart beating, though one visitor found them disappointing. Give them another chance and let me know what you think. Blueberry, raspberry, and strawberry-rhubarb pies are just a few you're likely to run into here.

The Harbor Café

(207) 367-5099
Main Street
Open for lunch and dinner year-round, closing early on Sunday in winter
Entrées $9 to $19

☞ *An informal restaurant with friendly service and simple meals*

The Harbor Café sits up over Main Street in a clean, light-filled room, with a view of the water, pine booths, and white walls stenciled with ivy. Specials, like scallop chowder, were up on the board, and the day's vegetables included pickled beets, corn, stewed tomatoes, and coleslaw. Standard sandwiches and seafood rolls, with hamburgers and salad plates, provide lunch. Dinners are a variety of fried fish and shellfish, and a ham steak or sirloin.

Homemade desserts included apple-raisin, Toll House, blueberry, and raspberry pies, and Key lime cheesecake.

Lily's Café

(207) 367-5936
Route 15, P.O. Box 653
Hospitality—Quick and cheerful service
Open in summer for breakfast and lunch Monday, Tuesday, and Friday 7–4, and Wednesday and Thursday until 8 for dinner; in winter Monday, Tuesday, and Friday 7–3, and Wednesday and Thursday until 7 for dinner
Entrées $7 to $13

☞ *A charming, casual spot for good food; organic ingredients in the recipes*

Smells of baking fill this old gray-clapboard house on the corner of Route 15 and the airport road. The tendency is toward organic, with a produce stand open in summer for vegetables from places like Brooklin's Carding Brook Farm. A lot of their produce is used in the soups and other dishes in the restaurant.

Breakfast starts with eggs, moves on to a big assortment of pancakes, and includes bagels, homemade granola with Greek yogurt, and hot organic oatmeal with raisins and maple cream. Island Acre Farm breakfast sausage is $2 a link, and organic coffee is $1.50, with free refills.

Lunch could be Ethel's barbecued pork sandwich, boneless pork simmered in a raspberry barbecue sauce on French bread, or crabcakes made with island crabmeat and served with salad, bread, and curry-mayo dipping sauce. There's

The Harbor Café has an eat-all-you-want fish fry on Friday in winter.

a vegetarian burger made from scratch with nuts, cheese, and brown rice; lentil salad; Chinese noodles; and a baked fish sandwich on rye. Apple pie, chocolate cake, and blueberry muffins are all made here.

Maritime Café
(207) 367-2600
27 Main Street
www.maritimecafe.com
Hospitality—Local talent makes for quick, intelligent service.
Open daily in-season 11:30–2:30 for lunch, 5:30–8:30 for dinner
Entrées $6 to $20

☛ *A stylish café with upscale prices and a great deck*

The deck over the water, with tables under umbrellas, is the favorite spot here; but the inside dining room looks sleek, with taupe-and-black-striped upholstered wall benches, dark wood tables, white walls, and rope-encrusted sconces.

Dinner specials, like grilled salmon, add a few more choices to the short menu, with crabcakes, barbecued ribs, baked haddock, and lobsters for dinner.

Lunch is pretty much the same, with a lobster roll ($13), a crab roll ($11),

Lunch is refreshing above Stonington Harbor on the Maritime Café's outdoor deck.

a very ordinary hamburger with flavorless meat, chips, lettuce, and tomato ($7), and haddock, turkey, and veggie sandwiches.

My lobster salad ($20) satisfied with a generous amount of lobster mixed with mayonnaise, but there wasn't much to like about the greens, a grocery tomato, and cucumbers too familiar with a refrigerator. A side dish of roasted creamed corn held some interest, with the toasted corn kernels in creamy sauce. The glasses of ginger lemonade ($2) were full of fresh lemon and the astringent sharpness of macerated ginger.

We went a little crazy about the blackberry pie; sweet and dark, with a crisp and chewy topping, it was served hot with ice cream and whipped cream and woke us up from our lunchtime ennui.

Smoked Seafood, Lobsters, Coffee, Takeout, Wine, and Ice Cream

Carter's Seafood (207-367-0900), 24 Carter Lane.

This is the source of the great fresh fish and shellfish at the Cockatoo (see page 231). All types of fresh fish, clams, mussels, lobsters, and shrimp are sold here.

The Clown (207-367-6348), Main Street.

Open mid-May through mid-October. A branch of the Portland wine store, you can buy wine here, along with some items of European kitchenware. Wine tastings held the second Friday of every month.

The Espresso Bar at the Inn on the Harbor (207-367-2420), Main Street, P.O. Box 69.

Open 11–4:30 Memorial Day through Columbus Day. You can get an espresso made with Lavazza coffee and sip it on the back deck over the water. Accompany it with fresh carrot cake ($3.95), a blueberry scone ($1.50), or Chastity's superb peanut-butter balls (60¢ each).

Island Cow Ice Cream, Main Street.

This little seasonal ice-cream store sells Smiling Hill Farm Ice Cream.

Stonington Lobster Cooperative (207-367-5564), Indian Point Road; Sunshine Seafood (207-367-2955), Old Quarry Road; Fifield Lobster (207-367-2313), Fifield Point Road; and Greenhead Lobster (207-367-0950), Ocean Road—all sell lobsters.

Stonington Sea Products (1-888-402-2729; www.stoningtonseafood.com), Route 15.

Open Monday through Friday 10–4 and Saturday 10–2 in summer, Monday through Friday 10–4 in winter. Fresh fish is sold here—tuna, swordfish, and lobster—as well as an array of smoked seafood, from salmon to mussels to fish and other products, including smoked fish pâtés, flying fish roe, and seaweed salad. I adore the smoked mackerel. It's low on the food chain, low in mercury, and high in omega-3s.

Island Cow Ice Cream in Stonington sells Smiling Hill Farm Ice Cream from Maine.

The Take Out (207-367-6363), Atlantic Avenue.

Open in-season Sunday through Thursday 10:30–8, Friday and Saturday until 9. This place has the best crab rolls around.

Stonington Farmer's Market is held from the end of May to the end of September on Friday, 10–noon, at the Stonington Community Center, also known as the old school. Many farmers contribute to this busy event. Bob Bowen of Sunset Acres Farm (go to www.sunsetacresfarm.com to see "The Girls") brings his and his wife Anne Bossie's fabulous goat cheese, like the Baga-duce Button, a bloomy rind cheese with a creamy inside, as well as eggs, meat, and chicken. He can get you a 200-pound pig if you need one for a pig roast, as he did for the Isle au Haut centennial celebration in 2006. It was so heavy, they had to winch the pig up off the boat into a pickup on the dock, but it tasted delicious after hours of slow, careful roasting.

Sunset

Goose Cove Lodge
(207) 348-2508, 1-800-728-1963
300 Goose Cove Road
www.goosecovelodge.com
Hospitality—Local college students can be a little overwhelmed, but they are kindness personified.
Open for dinner Tuesday through Sunday from late May to early October
Entrées $16 to $20

☛ *A perch over a classic view of islands of pointed firs, with high-quality meals*

The end of the season is always a roller coaster for the inns and restaurants on the Maine coast that depend on students for staff. It happened that our dinner at Goose Cove coincided with the Sunday-night closing of a nearby inn, and the restaurant was packed.

But although our young waiter was stretched, he'd learned his trade over the summer and could be snagged on the fly to fulfill requests quickly.

Peekytoe crabcakes, and seasonal grilled vegetables, like asparagus and pep-pers, are brilliant beginnings on the list, along with mussels and fried calamari.

This restaurant features salads with pleasant touches, like BLT salad with sautéed shrimp and Gorgonzola with greens, tomato, and bacon, or sautéed scallops on arugula with feta.

The dining room, paneled in knotty pine and set on two levels, takes advantage of the wonderful view out over the almost mythic islands around Deer Isle, covered by the pointed firs that spread their mats of roots over the red granite bedrock and hang on for dear life. As the fog crept up over the water, the customers in the crowded dining room reveled over their good bottles of wine—chosen from a list that features Portuguese reds and other finds, modest and expensive—and dug into plates of slow-cooked ribs, or veal and pork lasagna from a family recipe.

There is always a fresh fish special, and something for vegetarians, both lacto-ovo and vegan.

Desserts the night of our visit were Chocolate Trinity Parfait, too creamy for a chocolate lover, and a cranberry-blueberry crisp that needed more sugar.

Spencer Pies (207-348-9346), 151 Sunset Road (Route 15A), P.O. Box 64.

Irene Spencer sells pies she bakes fresh in her modest home alongside Sunset Road; a hand-lettered sign announces PIES when she's in the little gift shop beside her home. The blueberry pies were going for $15, and she had made cherry and lemon meringue earlier in the summer. She hopes to stay open until September and reopen for summer in May but would be happy to make pies to order any time of the year.

CHAPTER 7

Ellsworth to Hancock & Mount Desert Island

THE TRADITION OF SUMMER VACATIONS HERE, the heavy traffic, and the relentless crowds make this area the site of fierce restaurant competition. Many fail, some within a single summer.

Chefs seem to move around these businesses pretty regularly, too.

The hopping nighttime sidewalks of Bar Harbor are thronged with hungry people who will make someone's fortune. We can only hope the customers seek out the good things, the places like Café This Way and the Bagel Factory, and other businesses that bake and cook with integrity.

Acadia National Park

Jordan Pond House
(207) 276-3316
Near the Bubbles
www.jordanpond.com
Hospitality—College students make this place hum, with quick and intelligent service.
Open for lunch and tea 11:30–6 and dinner 6–9 late June through Labor Day, until 5:30 through Columbus Day, until 4 through late October (no dinner after Columbus Day)
Entrées $11 to $20

☛ *The quintessence of refreshment in a national park*

Tea and popovers with strawberry jam and butter are welcome pleasures when the hikes are over and the sun has decided to shine over Jordan Pond, or you can get a table inside this often crowded building and evade the cold mist of fall.

We made a reservation an hour distant at the reservation window outside the restaurant door and walked down the trail that skirts Jordan Pond. Then we doubled back. With the low overcast that troubled our visit, the hot tea and hot popovers were especially tasty.

You can eat a regular lunch in the dining room or on the lawn, with lobster rolls, curried chicken salad, chowders, and salads to choose. Dinners of crabcakes ($19.50), penne pasta, baked scallops, or a steamed lobster are served after 6.

Bar Harbor

Café This Way
(207) 288-4483
14¹/₂ Mt. Desert Street
www.cafethisway.com
Hospitality—Professional and friendly
Open for breakfast Monday through Saturday 7–11, Sunday 8–1; for dinner 5:30–9, mid-April through October
Entrées $17 to $23

☛ *Sophisticated and casual, with an emphasis on pronounced flavors*

Fruit or spice or cheese or garlic often tie into the main dishes to make their tastes loud and clear. The pork chops with dark cherry-Dijon glaze ($16) is fragrant with roasted garlic and sage, and the Thai grilled salmon ($17) gets revved up with sweet chili lime sauce.

Dinners here are extolled, and because this is one of the town's longer lived spots the recipes are creating loyalists. If you must indulge in lobster in cream, this looks like the place to do it, with lobster sautéed in heavy cream and Absolut citron, served over linguine with spinach and roasted red peppers ($23).

If you can keep going for another course, there's chocolate-raspberry truffle cake, or a blueberry pie from Morning Glory Bakery (see page 251).

Breakfast can be simpler. The granola ($5.75), with honey and cinnamon yogurt and blueberries and bananas, makes a delicious start. Bagels with cream cheese, red onion, tomato, and either smoked salmon or smoked trout are another admirable classic.

But the list of omelets would satisfy the sharpest morning hunger and sustain the steepest climb on a ladder trail in Acadia.

Eden Vegetarian Cafe
(207) 288-4422
78 West Street
www.barharborvegetarian.com
Hospitality—Effortless and accommodating
Open 5–9 daily mid-May through Mid-October
Entrées $13.50 to $16.50

☛ *Beloved by vegetarians and anyone who enjoys good meals with vibrant ingredients*

Yes, there is no meat, but that is not the reason you need to call for a reservation for dinner at this popular place. The food is outstanding.

One appetizer, fried peach oyster mushrooms from Mineral Springs Farm ($7) with a fennel salad and lemon aioli, is a menu mainstay that delights. Summer tomato bisque ($6) with croutons can't be beat, when the summer tomatoes come into their glory.

A salad of local greens, and a *panzanella* salad of marinated cherry tomatoes, cucumbers, crusty bread with basil and sherry vinaigrette, are both $6.50; and for another $2 you can add grilled, marinated tofu.

For a late-summer meal, the changing menu offered Rosa Bianca eggplant stuffed with vegetables and butter bean *tangine,* on Moroccan couscous, with spicy harissa ($16). A feast here enjoys an entirely guiltless quality, allowing a diner to consume the recommended daily vegetable servings all at once, gloriously. Pesto *orecchiette,* the little ear-shaped pasta, is served with arugula, basil, and pine nut pesto; and green beans, tomatoes, and roasted cremini mushrooms. Indonesian coconut, green chili, and peanut braised tempeh come on a mung bean noodle and vegetable salad with citrus and tamarind dressing.

Bog Juice, from swamp-grown local cranberries ($3), is sweetened with maple syrup, organic like almost everything here. Most of the wine list is organic, and bottles are priced from $20 and up; Richmond Plains Sauvignon Blanc ($28), from New Zealand, is light and herbal, with a taste of grapefruit.

Havana
(207) 288-2822
318 Main Street
www.havanamaine.com
Hospitality—Awfully good-looking servers, swift and competent
Open for dinner daily 5–9 in summer
Entrées $16 to $33

☛ *A fun restaurant with Latin style, serving Cuban-inspired food*

The shadows of the big dark black-eyed Susans crept up the teal and adobe red walls as the waiters swerved back and forth in their indigo cotton shirts and black pants. The hair on both the men and women servers, uniformly dark on our visit, was swept back into sleek buns.

A place with Latin style is a rarity in Maine, and Havana may owe some of its reputation as "the best restaurant in Bar Harbor" to its atmosphere of away. It's cool and fussy. The little piece of toast with shrimp pâté and four capers, "compliments of the chef," was pleasant. Was that peach-vanilla butter with the poppy seed–orange corn bread? The bread was almost sticky and gooey, cakelike, and not engaging. The glass of simple *vino verde* washed away the taste, and the server came by with the crumb scraper to keep us spiffy.

The halibut was fine with its dry rub and toasted *pepitas* crust, a mango *mojo* alongside a sweet pairing. The rice was a bore, but the fresh vegetables, vinegar-tinged green and red peppers, and red onion along with a roasted banana delivered some excitement.

The medium-rare pork chop with another dab of roasted banana and maple chipotle barbecue sauce was also fine. We liked the mashed potatoes enriched with olive oil.

Desserts include guava mousse in a chocolate-dipped waffle cone and Nicaraguan *tres leches.*

Mache Bistro
(207) 288-0447
135 Cottage Street
www.machebistro.com
Open for dinner daily from 5 Memorial Day through Labor Day, fewer nights off-season
Entrée $13 to $25

☛ *Praised as one of the best restaurants in Bar Harbor*

Mache opened in 2000 and got a new owner in 2004: Rachel Swords. Her manner is low-key and relaxed, and the ever-changing chalkboard menu is focused on making things as good to eat as possible, with minimal fuss. Seven to eight entrées and seven appetizers are seasonal.

A warm chèvre salad ($6), or *gemelli* pasta with porcini marinara and shaved Manchego ($7), might be an appetizer.

Duck breast has a reduction of blueberries with thyme, shallots, and ginger thrown in ($23), served with mashed potatoes with lots of butter and milk.

Seafood stew, skate wing, cod with kohlrabi greens, red chilies, and pearl couscous with local vegetables, were passing through the fall menu. Chicken coq au vin, Swords said, is a popular dish—an organic chicken leg cooked with pancetta, white wine, and vermouth, and "falling off the bone delicious," with bacon and parsnips.

Swords bakes the bread, often focaccia with a topping like Asiago with roasted red peppers. She is also in charge of all the desserts. Chocolate bread pudding is one; another is chocolate chip meringue and raspberry Pavlova with fresh whipped cream. That best seller, crème brûlée ($7), is served spiced in fall, in summer with orange blossom and ginger. Mt. Desert Island Ice Cream Company makes a great blackberry cabernet sorbet, and during blueberry season Swords added to her blueberry cobbler their cinnamon-cardamom ice cream.

Maggie's Restaurant
(207) 288-9007
6 Summer Street
www.maggiesbarharbor.com

Hospitality—Accommodating and friendly service
Open for dinner 5–9:30 Monday through Saturday, June through late October
Entrées $16 to $24

☛ *With an emphasis on fresh, local seafood and produce, this place delivers delicious meals.*

The owner of this enduring establishment, its long presence in tumultuous Bar Harbor a clue to its quality, started out with a fish market, filleting fish she bought from local fishermen. The restaurant benefits from her sharp eye for freshness, and the local creatures are still the ones that are served here.

Starters feature produce from the owners' own garden in an organic greens salad with cherry tomatoes and Sunset Acres Farm goat cheese, a delightful cheese made in Brooksville. Smoked salmon with caper-mustard sauce comes from nearby, and so do the mussels steamed with herbs and wine. Pizzas are offered for children who can't face the seafood.

Maine shrimp, cherrystone clams, mussels, potatoes, and chorizo in saffron-tomato sauce is a good Maine version of spicy fish stew beloved around the Mediterranean. Scallops with bacon, fresh corn, and roasted red peppers take that classic pairing of pork and shellfish in another direction.

Everyone lauds the lobster crêpes, always on a menu that otherwise changes.

The pale green tablecloths with flowered underclothes, and the porch room with lace swags in the windows and little white lights, show the comfortable house, a few steps off Cottage Road, at its pristine best. With Spanish guitar music on the stereo and a dish of the zesty lemon cake ($5.50) filled with lemon curd and strewn with long strands of lemon zest, there is nothing to detract from a summer evening.

Except, perhaps, your yearning for your companion's blueberry sundae with lemon ice cream and whipped cream. But she'll let you taste the dark sauce, like a liquid pie filling, and make the night sweet.

McKay's Public House
(207) 288-2002
231 Main Street
www.mckayspublichouse.com
Open daily for dinner at 4:30 year-round
Entrées $17-$20

☛ *A casual restaurant that's a fine choice for quality food in a range of entrées*

"We like to get as many fresh ingredients as we can, all over the menu," said Sue Ericson, manager of McKay's. The restaurant uses local produce from several organic farms and serves beer from each of the local breweries.

Renovations on the second floor have installed a granite wine bar, with seats for six, and a couple of tables, where you can choose from the full menu. Live jazz and other music is played upstairs periodically, mostly weekends. Shepherd's pie with lamb and, in winter, pub specials like bangers and mash or chicken potpie are typical.

Grilled filet mignon with lobster mushroom confit, slow cooked with olive oil, was a fall special. Seafood risotto with scallops and shrimp is so popular that the place can't take it off the menu. Another favorite is the fish-and-chips. During the winter the specials will be on the Web site.

There are about 10 stools at the bar, and food is served there too. Because McKay's is open year-round, it feeds a lot of locals. In summer an outside garden is filled with tables with umbrellas and lanterns hang from plant stands, doubling the seating for the crowds that migrate here in good weather.

Michelle's Fine Dining
(207) 288-2138
194 Main Street
www.michellesfinedining.com
Hospitality—A waitstaff trained to take special care of the customers
Open for dinner and breakfast May through October
Entrées $26 to $34

☛ *Formal and traditional elegance, and meals for a special occasion*

The rooms are filled with antiques, and a piano bar is open Thursday and Sunday night; appetizers are served, and cigars are available.

For one local businessman who dines at Michelle's as often as once a week, the filet mignon is the draw. Topped with a medallion of Roquefort, and served with a zinfandel demi-glace, the meat is aged to perfection and cooked "blue," just the way he likes it.

For dessert you can have zabaglione with berries, a crème brûlée ($10), or a dessert soufflé; there are five soufflés, from Grand Marnier to Maine raspberry ($14).

At the breakfast buffet ($12.95 per person) you can help yourself to hot smoked salmon, mini bagels—unfortunately somewhat stale and hailing from the supermarket—and herbed cream cheese in a room with pink-lilac walls. The granola full of macadamia nuts and dried cranberries was great and looked splendid in its small, gold-rimmed bowl. Nut-crusted bacon, with a bit of sugar thrown in, was somewhere over the top for my taste; but the hot home fries actually benefited from the chafing dish.

Ornately framed, lighted artwork and bud vases with single red roses on the tables, each covered by two tablecloths, made the atmosphere tranquil. Dinner must always be a special occasion here; the setting exactly right for a big romance or a weekly escape.

2 Cats

(207) 288-2808, 1-800-355-2808
130 Cottage Street
www.2catsbarharbor.com
Hospitality—Raucous and energetic, this place is hopping, but the food can be slow in coming.
Open daily for breakfast 7–1 in summer; call for winter hours
Breakfast $7 to $15 (dinner may be offered in the summer)

☛ *As long as the staff issues are ironed out, this is a fun place to eat breakfast.*

On an overcast morning the lawn at 2 Cats is swarming with customers awaiting the signal to pounce—their names will be called by the boisterous maitre d'. Meanwhile, we are all drinking coffee we poured for ourselves inside and fabulous fruit smoothies made up at the counter.

"Hairy kitty!" the man yells, and everyone laughs.

"It's frenetic," I say to the man at the counter, "Is it always like this?"

"Always," he confirms.

A bottle of champagne pops at a table on the porch. It's someone's birthday, and the servers deluge her with attention.

When we are led to a table on the terrace, the momentum is still with us. More coffee is poured, and a hot chocolate is sped along to take off the chill.

But, as it turned out, the chef had gone missing, the kitchen was understaffed, and everyone's breakfast was seriously delayed. The couple next to us got theirs half-price, because their wait exceeded an hour. Our French toast and eggs Benedict arrived in 45 minutes. The poached eggs were fabulous, the French toast was dry, but we had to get going to catch the *Island Explorer* to Northeast Harbor.

We will return to try the famed omelets with smoked salmon or smoked trout, the muffins that ran out that blue morning, and the granola sold by the pound to its dedicated customers.

Maybe we'll order champagne.

Breakfast, Lunch, Casual Dinners, Takeout, Coffee, and Candy

The Bagel Factory (207-288-3903), located on Cadillac Avenue in a cul-de-sac off Cottage Street.

Open 7 AM–2 PM Tuesday through Sunday year-round. Agnes Smit, 68, makes bagels the old-fashioned way, first boiled and then baked. "It's what makes the difference in a bagel," she said. She sup-plies dozens each week to the Blue Hill Co-op Café and Bar Harbor restaurants.

"People buy my bagels and bring them back to New York," she said, laughing because it seemed a little crazy.

In the late 1970s and '80s she ran the Sunflower Bakery, which delivered whole-grain bread to lots of Maine co-ops, and then ran the Geronimo Café. She's had her hands in a lot of dough, and knows how to make the best, always a pleasure to encounter if the Maine coast has deprived you of good bread, as it can.

Her healthiest bagel might be the one made with spelt flour; the rest are sour-dough. She also makes bialies on Friday and pretzels, filled with mustard and cheese, on Thursday. She makes vegetar-

Agnes Smit's fresh bagels, made in her Bagel Factory in Bar Harbor, are beloved.

ian chili every day and other soups with whatever's in-season. She's only allowed six chairs because her place is a takeout, but the size works for her. In nice weather you can sit in the sun outside and devour your toasted bagel in peace.

Ben and Bill's Chocolate Emporium (207-288-3281; www.benand bills.com), 66 Main Street.

Truffles, fudge, and many, many other sweets, along with a fine selection of ice cream and gelati ($4.25 for gelato in flavors like toasted almond, pistachio, peach, wild strawberry, blueberry, and sour apple).

J.H. Butterfield and Co. (207-288-3386), 152 Main Street, P.O. Box 181.

Sandwiches include chicken salad ($3.95), cream cheese and olive ($3.75), and egg salad ($2.95). Wine, beer, cookies, and much else.

The Morning Glory Bakery (207-288-3041), 39 Rodick Street.

Open Monday through Friday 7–4, Saturday 8–2, from spring until Thanksgiving. Fresh bread is baked here, from a nutty and delicious whole wheat to honey oatmeal, sourdough, and baguettes. Sticky buns, scones, cookies, and pies like blueberry, apple, pecan, and strawberry-rhubarb are all excellent. Sandwiches, including a BLT with avocado and herb mayo ($5), soups, quiche, and salad of the day are sold for lunch.

The Opera House Internet Café (207-288-3509), 27 Cottage Street.

Ben and Bill's Chocolate Emporium sells gigantic ice cream cones and fine gelati.

Check your e-mail and enjoy a cup of coffee and a Ghirardelli chocolate brownie, bagels, and other good things on the honor system—you tell the cashier what you ate. An art gallery features paintings by the owner—local landscapes, animals, and portraits.

Rupunini (207-288-2886; www.rupunini.com), 119 Main Street.

Open 11 AM–midnight daily in summer. Pasta, steak, burgers, good microbrews, and indoor and outdoor seating are all at this very popular restaurant in the middle of the Bar Harbor scene. Maine's Spinney Creek oysters are sold from the raw bar, along with other specials. Shane's Ice Cream from Maine could go on the apple crumble pie for dessert.

The Bar Harbor Farmer's Market is held Sunday 9–noon in the YMCA parking lot on Main Street, Mother's Day through October. One particularly

good find here is the goat's-milk yogurt from Painted Pepper Farm. Organic goat's milk from this Steuben farm comes from Nigerian does and is packaged in 6- and 16-ounce glass jars in plain, or flavors like maple cream and honey-ginger. This thick and creamy treat can be mail ordered when it's not summer-time (207-546-9777; www.paintedpepperfarm.com). They also make balsam fir wreaths.

Bernard

Thurston's Lobster Pound
(207) 244-7600
Steamboat Wharf Road
Open 11–8:30 Memorial Day through Columbus Day; closed Labor Day
Entrées $8 to market price for lobster

☛ *The insiders' favorite lobster pound, for lobster rolls, chowder, and great lobsters*

With plastic sides available to wrap around the outside porch, this place carries on into the cooler weather and is sitting pretty on the warm days when the breeze lifts up from the waves and floats past your table. The working harbor here is a charming prospect, and the pound hasn't become overwhelmed by success. Fresh lobster, corn, and alternatives. Salads were added to the menu under new owners when this well-loved spot was sold in 2006.

Bucksport

Farm stand with the pies, 227 Route 1, 1 mile north of the Bucksport Bridge and just south of the junction of Route 1 and Route 46.
The pies here are sold by the lady of the house, who sits under a green awning. She might not tell you her name, but she'll tell you she bakes 21 pies at a time, and got up at six to do it. She's been here for more than 50 years. Her daughter makes jam. From June 1 to September 21 you are likely to find her near the yellow pie sign, selling strawberry, blueberry, strawberry-pineapple-rhubarb, and strawberry-rhubarb pies.

Ellsworth

Cleonice

(207) 664-7554
112 Main Street
www.cleonice.com
Hospitality—Intelligent and friendly
Open daily for lunch 11:30–2:30, tapas and desserts 2:30–5, dinner every
night from 5
Entrées $19 to $24; tapas $2.50 to $7.50
Reservations recommended, especially on
weekends

☛ *Real Mediterranean flair with seafood
and meat dishes makes the food sing.*

In a long room lined by a dark wooden bar
and booths, with five ceiling fans slowly
revolving, you can't help but feel ready for
some noir event, some romantic entangle-
ment, some Peter Lorre–like stranger sidling
up to seek your help. The cool glass of Man-
zanilla, a dry sherry perfect with the tapas,
assists the illusion. Downtown Ellsworth was
never so exciting.

When the fellow tourists come into focus it
won't matter, because you have already got
your tapas, your order quickly filled from the
food kept behind the bar. The little bowl of
scungilli salad, made with Maine's own ubiq-
uitous periwinkles (the temptation to scare the
children with them is great), gives your mouth
something to learn, the black-striped snails
chewy and resilient and their salad of green

*The tapas are put together at the
bar in Cleonice, where small
dishes and the fine dinner
entrées are fresh and wonderful.*

olives, fennel, red onion, and peppers a bright complement. Grilled sardines,
flown in from Greece, were drizzled with balsamico, while the calamari salad
was all tender small squid in lemon and olive oil, with a few salty black olives for

contrast. The rich spanikopita was deeply flavored with lots of creamy feta; baba ghanoush sizzled in the mouth with garlic flavor.

Htipiti, whipped, spiced feta, served with crunchy pita bread, is a fiery tapas worth tasting; and so are the splendid *boquerones,* marinated silken-skinned white anchovies, off a list of specials. The lemon-leaf-wrapped veal Italian meatballs, mild and pale in color, held a succulent lemony juice. And how I regret not being able to try chef-owner Rich Hanson's smoked shad roe spread ($7) or oysters Rockefeller ($8).

But though the temptation is to eat from all the little plates, the dinners here are possibly better, with a bigger range for meat and seafood.

Trenton Bay clams in garlicky white or spicy red sauce ($19.50) on linguine is the "same recipe that had lines around the block in Boston's North End," according to the menu. Risotto ($21.50) is concocted with produce from the restaurant farm in Bucksport: chanterelles, *chicoria,* radicchio di *Treviso,* fresh herbs, and *farro.*

Lamb chops marinated with *charmoula,* a Moroccan spice paste of cilantro, parsley, lemon, olive oil, garlic, cumin, and paprika, and Merquez sausages ($22.50), come with grilled eggplant, preserved lemon, pepper sauce, and pine nuts. Grilled Maine sirloin with pesto Genovese and roasted heirloom tomatoes ($25.50) take the sweetest advantage of the harvest season on this astoundingly appetizing menu.

Jasper's Restaurant and Motel
(207) 667-5318
200 High Street (across from the Ellsworth Shopping Center)
Hospitality—Grown-up female servers take good care of all their customers.
Open for lunch and dinner daily 11–9, June through mid-October, 11–8 the rest of the year
Entrées $7 to $26

☛ *Down-home meals made with Downeast harvests*

This restaurant has been around forever, serving mostly seafood, some steak, and Sunday specials like roast pork and baked stuffed chicken. George Henry, the chef, has been cooking here since 1969, feeding locals through the winter and taking care of summer visitors and their hunger for lobster.

Henry bakes a boneless breast of chicken with a cornbread stuffing and serves it with either gravy with cranberry sauce or a cranberry cream sauce. Sunday lunches in winter bring a large church crowd and feature that chicken dish, along with another Sunday special, roast pork loin with pork gravy, served with applesauce and a choice of potato, vegetable, and salad. On the day we called, Henry was fixing baked acorn squash with brown sugar and butter and steamed Swiss chard from Crossroad Farm, an organic farm in Jonesport. Sometimes he adds a little malt vinegar to the chard. Mashed turnip sometimes makes the list as another fresh vegetable.

"I have been here for so long that I'm getting gray," Henry said. "I hear, 'Boys, you still do things the way you always did,' so I guess that must mean something." Henry certified that he uses real food, and although he does sometimes use frozen items, most of the meals come from fresh ingredients like those vegetables. It's on the strength of those vegetables that I include him here.

Four dining rooms, including one with a bar, seat about 50 per room.

Union River Lobster Pot
(207) 667-5077
8 South Street (right turn off Route 1, just before the Main Street bridge)
www.lobsterpot.com
Hospitality—Well-trained, efficient, and helpful
Open daily for dinner 5–8:30 mid-June through mid-September, for lunch until Labor Day
Entrées $14 to $25

☛ *Well-known for good food, from great lobster to sophisticated fish*

With outdoor cookers set up cheek by jowl to the live lobster tanks, you could count this place as one ready to appeal to tourists interested in one thing only.

But Union River pushes that envelope and offers fresh fish served in ingenious ways. The teriyaki style makes a fine swordfish dinner, and a cilantro cream works deliciously with halibut. Other fish could be given a Cajun rub and then served with a salsa full of mango, papaya, honeydew, and jalapeños. Chef-owner Brian Langley recommends the maple-mustard glaze for salmon fillets. Fish served in the St. German style gets a crown of buttered crumbs.

"We walk a fine line between casual and out of the ordinary," Langley said. Visitors often crave a lobster dinner, but locals come here for the fresh fish that Langley gets daily from Maine Shellfish, a big local distributor.

Steamers ($8.95 for 1 pound, 2 pounds for $15.95) were tender and fresh from a generous serving. A shore dinner with a 1½-pound lobster ($27.60 in 2006) was the choice of our youngest dinner companion, a boy who delights in lobster and has for years.

Steamed outside in large cauldrons, the lobsters at the Union River Lobster Pot are as fresh as this morning.

Just six wines are available by the glass, and they are modest drinks, with all the emphasis here going to the fish. Fresh-picked lobster meat fills the lobster rolls and salad plates ($18.95).

The 72-year-old baker, who has worked for Langley for 20 years, knows exactly how to make pie; and strawberry, blueberry, raspberry, and pecan are often on the list.

The location makes the meal special. The grassy banks of Union River are now healthy and clean—and the haunt of a graceful eagle. Bring a glass of wine outside to wait for a table, and sit along the river to watch the bird survey the water.

Food Markets, Bakeries, Coffeehouses, and Ice Cream

John Edward's Market (207-667-9377; www.johnedwardsmarket.com), 158 Main Street.

Crossroad Farm and other organic produce, organic local eggs, Equal Exchange coffee, and a large selection of wine are all sold here.

Maine Grind (207-667-0011), 192 Main Street.

Open Monday through Thursday 7–5:30, Friday and Saturday 7–7, and Sunday 8–3. Opened in 2006, this clean, fresh space is on the first floor of an old downtown building. It is a wonderful place to gear up with good coffee and perhaps bagels and lox, a croissant, or a slice of carrot cake while you enjoy the wireless Internet connection or browse a favorite newspaper.

Morton's Ice Cream (207-667-1146), 9 School Street.

Open year-round Tuesday through Saturday 12–8. This ice cream store is located at the first right south of the traffic light at the intersection of routes 1 and 3, adjacent to The Maine Grind. With a bigger space and more seating, this shop will be offering homemade soups during lunch, as well as ice cream, Italian gelato, and sorbet—like peach-mango, or blood orange and grapefruit— that are all homemade. Ten different kinds of gelati include cappuccino, and one ice cream flavor with a following is Key lime with pineapple. Chocolate-wasabi gelato attracts the risk takers. The ginger ice cream uses fresh and crystallized ginger and has a nice bite.

The Riverside Café (207-667-7220; www.theriversidecafe.com), 151 Main Street.

Open for breakfast and lunch weekdays 6–3, Saturday 7–3, and Sunday 7–2. This bright space with big windows bustles in the morning. Egg sandwiches, pancakes, French toast made with homemade bread, and lots of muffins make breakfast selection difficult. For lunch you can choose from the substantial sandwiches and soups, salads, vegetarian selections, and homemade pies.

Rooster Brothers (207-667-8675), 29 Main Street (Route 1).

This business roasts its own coffee beans, imbuing the atmosphere with a lovely smell. Brewed coffee can be bought in take-out cups; you also can buy freshly roasted beans, whole or ground. Upstairs is a store full of kitchen equipment.

The Ellsworth Farmer's Market is held Monday 2–5:30, Thursday 2–5:30,

and Saturday 9:30–noon, June through October in the parking lot of the Maine Community Foundation at 245 Main Street.

Le Domaine
(207) 422-3395, 1-800-554-8498
Route 1
www.ledomaine.com
Hospitality—Highly trained, polished service
Open for dinner Tuesday through Sunday 6–9 early June through mid-October
Six-course prix fixe $35 special, or à la carte

☛ *A fabulous French wine cellar matched with exquisite French cuisine*

You can travel far in this dining room. Although Nicole Purslow has sold her restaurant, her training and know-how carry on in the kitchen under another chef. Its menu remains the epitome of Provençale cooking.

In the bright dining room, copper pots gleam around the mantel of the big fireplace; the tablecloths glow with green and yellow; and the careful, attentive service raises your awareness that things here are a little more serious than they might be elsewhere.

Vilma Cruz Miguel is the chef at the Mexican Restaurant in Hancock.

There's the *pâté de foie maison,* a pâté that Purslow's words still describe as impossible for her to improve. You get the sense that she's tried, but can't best, perhaps with some exasperation, her mother's original creation.

Entrées included braised lamb with grilled eggplant, and *escalope de veau* ($29.50), thin slices of veal served with a wild mushroom cream. And there was a filet mignon bordelaise ($31.50), garnished with Roquefort butter.

The *tarte au framboise,* a pastry shell filled with custard and raspberries, would make a fine end, as would the bread pudding with rum-soaked currants and cream.

The Mexican Restaurant
(207) 598-7297
Route 1
Hospitality—Friendly and full of assistance
Open daily 11–8
Entrées $5 to $13

☛ *Authentic Mexican meals and a fun atmosphere*

The pretty dining room in this branch of the first Mexican Restaurant, in Harrington, is a perfect place for a break from Route 1. Settle into a booth and order an *horchata* ($2.99), a Latin American drink made with milk, cashews, and spices like cinnamon and sugar. While you eat the fried tortilla chips and spicy salsa, you might be able to listen to the Spanish rap music. I tried the *machaca* ($10.99), a dish of shredded beef with eggs and green peppers, which was rich and savory. *Camarones al mojo de ajo* ($10.99), shrimp sautéed in garlic with rice and beans; tacos suaves ($2.99), soft tacos stuffed with roast pork and guacamole with chorizo; or the chicken burrito ($6.99) are also good meals here, where the refried beans are almost soupy, the cheese is creamy, and the yellow rice is full of flavor.

Tidal Falls Lobster Restaurant
(207) 422-6457
Tidal Falls Road (look for the sign 8 miles north of Ellsworth on Route 1)
Hospitality—Come to the window and order, and the food is delivered to your table.
Open last week in June through Labor Day
Entrées $2.25 to $19
BYOB

☛ *The most fabulous view in Maine, with high-quality lobster to go along with it*

For the most part, this restaurant serves steamed mussels with garlic butter and steamed lobster. A New York strip sirloin steak, lobster salad, hamburgers, and hot dogs also are available. The side of garlic bread is unique to lobster places.

Fresh-squeezed lemon juice mixed in a ratio of 3 cups of juice per gallon of sweetened water make the good lemonade, served with lemon zest and mint.

"We make our own coleslaw, potato salad. We have a baked crab dip, made with cream cheese, bubbly and browned on top and baked in a 4-ounce cruet," said Karin Wilkes, the restaurant manager. Tidal Falls is now owned and operated by the Frenchman's Bay Conservancy, which protects area lands. "It's made the place more widely known, for one thing," Wilkes said.

An indoor pavilion holds 40 people, but outside is a grassy picnic area with 10 to 12 picnic tables.

"People have told me that we have the best lobster around, but we don't know why," said Wilkes.

It could be because the water off Schoodic Point, where they get their lobsters, is so cold, or because the water in their holding tank is pumped from the ocean, or because the beasties don't hang out in the tank for more than four days.

But the setting and its incredible view are what distinguish this place from all others. "The tide comes into a narrow rocky inlet. When the tide reverses and the bay empties, it's just like somebody poured a pitcher of water over the rocks," Wilkes said. It's noisy, and most people sit on one side of the tables to watch. Eagles, cormorants, ospreys, and blue herons visit at low tide. Seals are more frequent at high water.

You can bring your own wine or beer. The restaurant will provide complimentary wine glasses, a little elegant touch in the casual environment. A private dining area on a deck, seating four, overlooks the falls. It could be yours for a $25 reservation fee. All the profits go to the conservancy.

Food Markets and Takeout

Mano's Market (207-422-6500), 1519 Route 1.
Open 7–6 Tuesday through Saturday, year-round. Deidre Dority and Adam Bishop now own this store, and keep it open through the winter with a line of 15 sandwiches, twice-baked potatoes, macaroni and cheese, meatloaf, and chicken potpie. There is indoor seating. Wines are from $8 to $15, with more

expensive choices stocked in summer. Local farms provide rotisserie chicken, cooked in a French outdoor cooker, and produce comes from Jonesport's Crossroad Farm and Gouldsboro's Mandala Farm. Fresh berries come from a place just down the street, along with morning harvests of greens that are fresher than fresh. Rock City Coffee Roasters coffee comes from Rockland.

Sullivan Harbor Farm Smokehouse (207-422-3735; www.sullivan harborfarm.com), 1545 Route 1, Hancock Village.

Open Monday through Saturday 9–5:30 in summer, Monday through Friday 9–5 in winter. The large new building on Route 1 is a handsome showcase for delicious smoked salmon. The salmon is served from Boston to Florida at Legal Sea Foods restaurants, in Connecticut at the Mohegan Sun casino, and at the Simon Pierce Restaurant in Quechee, Vermont.

In the Maine retail store, thousands of pounds of salmon fillets, farm-raised two hours away in New Brunswick, Canada, are delivered each month. After lying embedded in coarse salt, draining water, and achieving a firmer texture, the salmon is cold-smoked, packed, and ready to eat ($24 a pound).

Sullivan Harbor Farm also sells smoked scallops ($15 for a half pound), pastrami salmon ($12 for a half pound), and roasted and smoked rainbow trout. All prices listed above are at the store; mail-order pricing is different.

Hancock Point

Crocker House Country Inn
(207) 422-6806
Point Road
www.crockerhouse.com
Open daily for dinner from May 1 to October 31; weekends only in late March, and November and December
Entrées $22 to $30

☛ *High-quality dinners in a comfortable, friendly inn*

Chef-owner Rich Malaby and his wife have been here since 1980, polishing and polishing some more. The dining rooms are charming, comfortable, and elegant.

The meals start with thoughtful appetizers, such as oysters on the half shell ($9.95) and oysters Rockefeller ($10.95). The warm artichoke and lobster dip is one classic, and the pâté mousse is another.

Classic entrées are presented as well, with filet mignon au poivre ($27.95) and rack of lamb ($27.95). Roast duckling with a Grand Marnier–ginger sauce tweaks the classic enough to bring it up-to-date. In the Crocker House Scallops ($25.95), mushrooms, scallions, garlic, and tomatoes lend their goodness to sautéed scallops, served with rice pilaf, and bring some Mediterranean flavor to the meal.

With a loyal, repeat clientele with its own favorites, some things on the menu are there to please them; other items change.

Wine and beer are served here, where the sound of a bell buoy floats into the windows from the restless sea.

Islesford

The Islesford Dock
(207) 244-7494
Little Cranberry Island, or Islesford
www.islesford.com, click on "Islesford Dock Restaurant"
Hospitality—Good in extremity, and graceful under pressure
Open daily for lunch and dinner mid-June through Labor Day, Sunday brunch
Entrées $8 to $23
Beal and Bunker (207-244-3575) runs a ferry service to Islesford from Northeast Harbor

☛ *Great meals on an island that is easily accessible*

Maybe Little Cranberry is too accessible? Perhaps that was going through the mind of one of the Islesford Dock's owners, Dan Lief, as a lunch traffic jam ensued when the second delivery of hungry tour-boat visitors appeared at his door. Customers clamored to eat, and their boat was due back soon. He assured them there was plenty of time.

We agreed to eat at the bar and got to sit quickly. Watching the action, rather more interesting than the lovely view, at least for a while, we enjoyed a meze plate ($13)—tiny smoked mussels and garlicky, lemony hummus on baked pita wedges accompanied by a relish made with chopped onion, carrot, cucumber, red pepper, and feta, with some fresh fruit and olives on the side. That simple plate, always on the menu and always changing, is one reason we were all here, glad to enjoy the fresh tastes the kitchen assembles.

But Islesford Dock wouldn't be so impolitic as to neglect the typical seaside dishes. Clam chowder, steamed clams, and crabcakes are on the list, next to tuna tartar, grilled calamari, Szechuan eggplant, and grilled asparagus. There's a de rigueur steamed lobster right up alongside the Caribbean seafood stew, a cinnamon and chili flavored stew of shrimp, halibut, and mussels. Pasta Rustica mixes *orecchiette* with Parmesan, white beans, and summer vegetables. Those dishes are available if you take a dinner cruise out here, or happen to live on the island.

The hamburgers ($9), served with fresh-cut fries, are juicy and full of flavor, and made an 11-year-old, a 15-year-old, and a 50-year-old content at the bar. The question of whether to order strawberry or blueberry crisp threw us for a moment, until we each ordered one and shared. Both were scrumptious with ice cream, and a quiet walk around the island afterward was all we needed to make the pleasure of our visit complete.

A huge garden is the source of much of the greens. In 2007 Cynthia and Dan Lief will celebrate their 15th year as restaurant owners here; they started coming in 1972, and rented for 15 years on vacations from New York City as a school teacher and a banker, respectively.

Manset

XYZ Restaurant
(207) 244-5221
Bennet Lane at 80 Seawall Road (Route 102a)
Open for dinner at 5:30 on weekends Memorial Day through June, daily in summer through Labor Day, then weekends until Halloween
All entrées $22

☛ *The real thing in regional Mexican cuisine, with flavors from the far south*

Robert Hoyt and Janet Strong started this restaurant elsewhere in 1994 and made slow progress for a while. But the word about the food got out, reached the city newspapers, and began drawing crowds. "X" stands for Xalapa, capital city of the state of Veracruz, "Y" for Yucatán, and "Z" for Zacatecas, a central state in the north of Mexico—all places Hoyt and Strong have traveled. They recreate the meals they enjoyed in this charming space, built in 2004, with a bright red-and-white interior and vivid flower-printed tablecloths.

Everyone starts with the XYZ Margarita ($6.50), made with fresh-squeezed

COURTESY OF XYZ

XYZ serves brilliantly seasoned and subtle Mexican dishes and killer margaritas.

lime juice—one reason the restaurant used up 1,800 pounds of limes one summer. Limeaid is another.

A signature dish is the chiles rellenos made with rehydrated dried ancho chilies that are stuffed with cheese and corn, or with *picadillo*—a savory sweet mix of fruit, pork, and beef—and then roasted.

The rich flesh of the dark red anchos held a slightly piquant flavor, luxuriously rich, and a wonderful complement to the creamy corn and mild cheese.

Queso fundido, a cheese appetizer with XYZ pork chorizo ($8), was out when I sat down for a late reservation; and so were *chiles verdes* ($8), fresh roasted green chilies with *cotija* cheese. But a sweet, smooth avocado soup with a whiff of tequila was a fine beginning, and the *lengua en escabeche,* ($8) beef tongue in vinaigrette, was a lovely salad of mild meat and tart sauce.

For dinner there were tastes of chicken in a dark sauce of *pasilla* chilies, with tender meat and intense chili flavor. *Pollo con naranja* was made with chicken, oranges, ancho chilies, and hot *de arbol* chilies, with a spicier, sweet flavor. Tender pork with tomatillos, poblanos, and chile California was mixed with ground almonds, creating a fine blend of sharp, tangy, and savory.

For dessert it's easy to enjoy the frozen lime pie and a perfect, simple flan.

A helpful children's meal is suggested—a quesadilla made with cheese, or cheese and beans ($6).

Mount Desert

Beech Hill Farm (207-244-5204), 171 Beech Hill Road.

The farm stand here is open Tuesday, Thursday, and Saturday from late June to October. This organic farm grows wonderful greens and lettuces, strawberries, raspberries, and apples, and lots of flowers.

Northeast Harbor

Breakfast, Lunch, and Takeout

The Colonel's Restaurant (207-276-5147), Main Street.

Open April through October for breakfast, lunch, and dinner. A full bakery means there's an array of breakfast baked goods from which to choose. Breakfast is served in the space behind the storefront, with some tables outside, but service can be haphazard. Pizzas, fried seafood, and burgers are available for lunch and dinner.

The Docksider (207-276-3965), 14 Sea Street.

Fried seafood (using partially hydrogenated vegetable oil), chowder, and boiled lobsters. This place began as the Docksider in 1979, and it was Flick's Place before that—in the 1950s or '60s. With seats for 50 and a take-out window, it's a busy place. The lobster rolls ($15.95), with 4 ounces of lobster picked in this kitchen (as long as they can keep up; some meat is bought during the summer rush), are made with mayonnaise; special order with butter, or nothing, on a toasted hot dog bun. Crabcakes from a special recipe have been made since 1981. Gifford's Ice Cream.

The Full Belly Deli (207-276-4299), 5 Sea Street.

With a few tables and a big selection of sandwiches, this is a good spot to gather supplies for a picnic lunch, maybe a south of the border sandwich with turkey, cheddar cheese, guacamole, tomato, lettuce, and sprouts. All the classic favorites are on the menu too, from egg salad to roast beef. Baked goods for morning coffee, and desserts like brownies and cookies.

Redbird Provisions (207-276-3006), 11 Sea Street.

Open for lunch and early dinner June through September. An upscale place to stock up, with pan-fried codfish cakes, crabcakes, and salmon cakes all made here for the main course. Not your standard fried food and not much lobster, but carrot-ginger and truffled porcini mushroom soups make different meals for anyone tired of fried clams. No pies, but they bake berry tarts and cakes with fresh Maine blueberries. Everything is geared to go, but dining in is getting more emphasis. Beer and wine served.

Northeast Harbor Farmer's Market is held Thursday 9–noon on Huntington Road across from the Kimball Terrace Inn, from the end of June through August. Smith's Smokehouse in Monroe makes smoked meats and smoked cheeses; their blackstrap jerky is particularly fine, as is the Canadian bacon and smoked chicken breast.

Otter Creek

The Burning Tree
(207) 288-9331
71 Otter Creek Drive (Route 3)
Hospitality—A busy place with experienced service
Open for dinner June through Columbus Day, closed Tuesday in summer, closed Monday and Tuesday after Labor Day
Entrées $19 to $25

☛ *A premier fish and vegetarian restaurant that grows many of its ingredients*

The Burning Tree works at making vegetarian dishes really succeed, like a mint-flavored edamame wonton soup with miso broth, shiitake mushrooms, summer squash, and spicy tofu; and a watercress cheese tart with shredded beet and dill pasta.

But it does very well by all its meat and fish, too. Appetizers have included a squid salad with shiitake mushrooms, bamboo, ginger, and sesame seeds, and a curried crab salad with mango and crispy *pappadum*. A country pâté served with pickled grapes and toasted sourdough bread could nicely precede the prosciutto-wrapped scallops, glazed with orange-rosemary and served with arugula and Parmesan on linguine.

Red meat is not served here. Instead there is a great array of finely designed fish and chicken dishes. Crabcakes and bouillabaisse with saffron aioli are old favorites, and the broiled halibut with Pernod and green peppercorn sauce could easily become a new one. Grown organically, the greens in the salad and much else come from gardens outside the door of the restaurant.

Southwest Harbor

The Claremont Hotel
(207) 244-5036
Clark Point Road
www.theclaremonthotel.com
Open daily for dinner 5–9 mid-June through the third week of September; lunch 12–2 and cocktails 5:30–9 in The Boathouse, by the water
Entrées $20 to $25

☞ *Elegant, old-world surroundings, with good food*

Even though this hotel no longer requires its male dinner guests to wear a jacket and tie, and has done away with the jacket collection kept handy for that purpose, you can still dress up for a dinner out here. Why not? No jeans or shorts are allowed.

The dining room is as good looking as they come, with eloquent views of Somes Sound. An adjoining bar is open the same hours and season as the dining room, or you can enjoy a cocktail or lunch in July and August at **The Boathouse,** with its fabulous views from an open porch.

Start with seared rare tuna ($8) with Roquefort blue cheese sour cream, or grilled shrimp cocktail ($9) with homemade tomato and chili sauce. Malpeque oysters ($11), the Europeans in Maine's waters, are served on the half shell, and Prince Edward Island mussels ($8) come roasted with butter, garlic, shallots, and white wine.

For a main course the flatiron steak ($24) is accompanied by goat cheese and scallion mashed potato, and the roast chicken ($20) has a rich side of mascarpone and Parmesan polenta. Paella Claremont Hotel-Style ($25) has all the right ingredients for Spain, with shrimp, chicken, lobster, littleneck clams, and chorizo in saffron rice.

Fiddler's Green
(207) 244-9416
411 Main Street
www.fiddlersgreenrestaurant.com
Open for dinner from 5:30 to close except Monday
Entrées $16 to $26

☛ *With a wide range and a big menu, there is a dish here for everyone*

Mesquite-smoked duck with pomegranate-apple chutney ($12) and crabcakes with a three chili and mango sauce ($11) are two possible appetizers.

Dinners on the changing menu range from sirloin steak with walnut truffle butter and fries ($19) to scallops with asparagus, spinach, tomato, pancetta, and Parmesan ($23) to my old favorite, a Livornese sauce with capers, olives, garlic, and olive oil, this time on trout ($18). Smoked fish, ravioli, bread, and pastries are all made here.

Head of the Harbor
(207) 244-3508
Main Street
Open daily for lunch and dinner 11:30–8:30 in-season
Entrées $9 to $18

☛ *Seafood with a view, and gingerbread for dessert*

This long dining room sits on the top of a rise and overlooks the water. Inside it's hung with lobster traps and buoys, and the kitchen serves up the standard fried seafood with a few special touches, like the fried Maine shrimp, tiny and delicate creatures that require a deft touch with the heat.

Fish chowder ($5.99) is not thickened, and the tartar sauce is made here. The onion rings are freshly made, too, thin and crisp. Fried pollock and french fries ($8.99 small, $9.99 large) come with salad, coleslaw, and the vegetable of the day. Some people in your group might be grateful for the chicken Parmesan or the seafood salad plates. Desserts are plain, simple, and appealing, like the gingerbread with whipped cream ($3.50) and the root beer float. The very limited wine and ale list has drinkable Blackstone Merlot and a couple of Casco Bay microbrews.

Red Sky

(207) 244-0476
14 Clark Point Road
www.redskyrestaurant.com
Open daily for dinner 5:30–9 from mid-June to September, closing more frequently off-season and for January and part of February
Entrées $17 to $29

☛ *The latest up-to-date addition in the upscale food world of Mount Desert Island*

Patrons of this cool bistro praise the leek and tomato tart and the lobster risotto with porcini. Owners Elizabeth and James Lindquist seek out the best local produce suppliers to make it all happen. An aged New York strip sirloin is always on the menu, along with varying homemade pastas. Elizabeth sometimes offers her favorite duck dish, a roast breast in a plum wine demi-glace ($24) with fresh plum salsa.

The wine list carries as many as 100 bottles, averaging $30, and 10 wines are available by the glass. House-made crusty bread rounds out the meals, along with organic greens from several local farms. Maine shrimp dumplings ($7) or fried oysters ($10) make fine beginnings.

Maple-glazed baby back ribs ($21), grilled scallops with chile-molasses glaze ($24), and halibut with a *panko* crust, sesame soba noodles, and a cucumber salad ($25) show influences from the American South and Asia.

Desserts are made here and range from a bittersweet Belgian chocolate pudding ($7) to gingerbread with fresh ginger juice, caramel sauce, and cream cheese whipped cream to a peach tart, "when there're peaches around." A cheese course is another spectacular way to end a meal.

Lunch, Breakfast, Takeout, Wine and Cheese, and Ice Cream

Eat-A-Pita (207-244-4344), 326 Main Street.

Open daily for breakfast 8–12, and lunch 8–4 in-season. Call in an order for one of the salads or a stuffed pita sandwich, like curry chicken with carrots, celery, and onion ($6.95), or a Greek salad, olives, and feta stuffed pita ($5.95 for a small). A crabcake sandwich on a bulky roll ($8.95) is a respectable version of the sought-after dish, and the sandwiches are generously portioned. Dinner is served in **Café 2,** all in the same colorful space with old wood tables. Seafood, meat, and vegetarian entrées are served Tuesday through Sunday from 5 to 9.

Little Notch Bread and Café (207-244-3357), 340 Main Street.

Open Monday through Saturday 7:30–8, closed Sunday in summer; Monday through Saturday 8:30–6 or earlier off-season; call for hours. The local source for good bread, with loaves of sourdough, French baguettes, whole-grain breads, focaccia, and more. Sandwiches, simple pasta dishes, and pizzas. Also cookies, brownies, scones, and sticky buns. An apple galette and many pastries.

The Quiet Side Café and Ice Cream Shop (207-244-9444), 360 Main Street.

Open in-season for lunch and dinner. Fish and clam chowder, sandwiches, and salads, along with fried fish and hot subs, are all on the menu. Ice cream is available in 20 flavors; surely one will go with homemade blueberry pie.

Sawyer's Market (207-244-3315), 344 Main Street.

The smell of ham floats across the worn wood floors of this grocery store and across Main Street.

Sawyer's Sips (207-244-4550), 4 Clark Point Road.

Open 6:30 AM–10 PM in summer. A wine bar that is owned by the same owners of Sawyer's Specialties (see next page), serving cheese and olives, bruschetta, desserts—and much more—for breakfast, lunch, and dinner.

Opening up for the sandwiches at Southwest Harbor's Eat-A-Pita.

Sawyer's Specialties (207-244-3317), 353 Main Street.

Carries an excellent wine selection—more than 1,000 varieties—and has a cheese case with finds. Both can supply you with whatever provisions you need.

Southwest Harbor Farmer's Market.

Held Friday 9–1 in the St. John the Divine church parking lot, on Main Street, across from the Bar Harbor Bank. Back Bay Farm brings organic vegetables, Schartner Farm supplies fruits, Udder View Farm makes goat cheese, Bread Box Bakery in Orland offers bread. Far Pointe Fibre in Steuben sells hand-spun wool and wool products.

Town Hill

Breakfast, Lunch, Beer and Ale, and Barbecue

Atlantic Brewing Company (207-288-2337, 1-800-475-5417; www.atlanticbrewing.com), 15 Knox Road.

Tours of the brewery are given, for free, at 2, 3, and 4 Memorial Day through Columbus Day. Free tastings of all the beers, and of Old Soaker Root Beer, are offered in the gift shop, another prime location for a good souvenir. With malts and hops imported from England, and Bar Harbor water, Atlantic Brewing makes a caramel-brown ale called Bar Harbor Real Ale that tastes great. I like all of the ales, and the Coal Porter is my favorite porter.

Bar Harbor Summer Ale, a seasonal, is always new when summer comes. Blueberry Soda, new in 2006, really tastes like blueberries.

Take a tour of the brewing facility and then enjoy fine barbecue next door at **The Knox Road Grille,** open 11:30–8 daily in summer, to really taste how the ales and beers work with a meal. On Saturday an all-you-can-eat barbecue ($15 per person) is a real festival, and outdoor seating makes a summer day as good as it gets.

Mother's Kitchen (207-288-4403), Route 102 (next to Salsbury Hardware, a fun stop itself).

Open Monday through Friday 8–2. Here are the sandwiches that you would make at home, but might not be able to organize. The Summer Kitchen ($6.25) has smoked turkey, avocado, bacon, lettuce, tomato, and creamy dill sauce on sourdough bread. The servings are very large here, so try splitting one—if you can agree to one—and enjoying it at a picnic table outside, where the staff bring your order out to you. Grandpa Jack ($5.75), with meatloaf, was out by the time we arrived—it often runs out early—but Rocco's Art ($6.50), with roasted

The locals flock to Mother's Kitchen for lunch and enjoy their choices outside.

eggplant, local feta, artichoke, and olive relish on onion-walnut dill bread was delicious. Desserts like blueberry crumb cake, cut in massive hunks, are enough for the whole family. Salads, pies, muffins, scones, coffee, and breakfast sandwiches, too. If you call early you can preorder that Grandpa Jack.

Trenton

Trenton Bridge Lobster Pound
(207) 667-2977
1237 Bar Harbor Road (Route 3)
www.trentonbridgelobster.com
Hospitality—You pick the lobster and hand it off to be cooked.
Open for lunch and dinner Monday through Saturday, Memorial Day through Columbus Day
Entrées vary with the market price for lobster.

☛ *A classic place to rip open a crustacean and enjoy*

For more than 50 summers, the wood fires under the big cookers have sent up their steam and pulled over passing cars. Boiling seawater cooks the lobsters with the touch of salt that makes the flavor laugh out loud. The menu sticks to what is good with lobster—steamed clams, coleslaw, potato salad, and butter. You can also order a few other lobster or shellfish dishes, including a lobster roll, lobster stew, clam chowder, and a lobster or crab cocktail. But mostly you are here for the essence of Vacationland—the salty, buttery, tender, sweet meat of lobster.

Maine's Own Treats (207-667-8888), 68 Bar Harbor Road.
Open Monday through Friday 8–6, Saturday 9–5, Sunday 10–5, closing two days before Christmas and opening up again in May.

Every treat—from chocolate to jam, maple syrup to mustard, apple butter to lobster stew—is stocked on the crowded shelves here. There's plenty to take home as a gift or as a present to yourself. You can open them one day in February and recall the summer in Maine.

8

CHAPTER 8

Schoodic and North

THIS FAR EAST END OF MAINE, and of the United States, always has been renowned for its dramatic landscape, fringed with boreal forests and combed by winds rushing off the sea. Here you can stand on promontories overlooking the Atlantic and ride out over the water to an island to approach the puffins, with both the birds and their admirers enjoying a lonely emptiness found nowhere else on the coastline of the Lower 48. You can hike down a half mile of bog bridge on the Bold Coast Trail, or around a boardwalk on a bog in Lubec, and encounter ravens and eagles.

You can see and smell and breathe a vigorous world kept, for the most part, clear of people.

For the same reason, unfortunately, it hasn't been all that easy to find a great meal here.

The places people have liked and crowded, like Helen's Restaurant in Machias, might just never have been as good as people claim. And right now some of them aren't good at all. Some feed people with processed and frozen foods that may keep prices low and require less work in the kitchen, but the meals leave customers hungry, however high the plate is filled. Their stomachs might feel full, but their souls are starved.

You can always ask for what is fresh. I've tried, and if people are being straight, the places listed here use as much fresh fish as they can. I've listed those that use fresh food, including fresh fish and fresh vegetables, when they can get them.

But sometimes red tide arrives on the Maine coast in summer and shuts down all the clam flats, keeping the local clammers from making any money and forcing the local fried-fish places to use frozen or canned clams for their clamoring customers.

That might be a great time to choose a different kind of shellfish.

Lobsters, thank goodness, are always fresh in Maine, however much companies finagle with freezing methods designed to get them to Japan. But a clam shack could use frozen lobster meat for its lobster rolls. They might save money that way, or time, but it won't taste as good. Ask if the lobster rolls are made with fresh-cooked lobster that's been shelled by the restaurant.

Scallops are in-season between September and mid-April. Picked by divers starting in December, scallops are a good choice if your visit comes later in the off-season.

Rising to the challenge of finding great ingredients, more and more people in Downeast Maine are finding ways to make a living making dinner. The owners of the Artist's Café in Machias blazed a path eight years ago, and more entrepreneurs since have followed suit, giving more choices to diners eager to find good cooking.

Farther Downeast in East Machias and Lubec, newcomers are at work building up business for fine provisions like pastured, organic, heirloom pork. Their livelihoods may be supported by folks down south, but the locals can buy from farmers like those at Old Sow Farm if they seek them out.

In Calais, and elsewhere, keeping things the same has proven exactly the best approach. The same bread pudding that might have pleased your grandparents on their visit is ready for your own meal, when you want to order it, at the Chandler House.

A few other places sustain the oldest, simplest traditions, like using fresh berries for pie. If the newest places think they are starting that practice, let them.

Birch Harbor

Bunkers Wharf
(207) 963-2244
260 East Schoodic Drive
Hospitality—Fabulous. This place is run with an emphasis on welcoming people and taking care of them.
Open for lunch and dinner from before noon–10 PM May through October
Entrées $18 to $29
Reservations appreciated

☛ *A fun, friendly, and sophisticated place with delicious seafood and meat*

The big dining room with a tall ceiling and knotty pine paneling overlooks Bunkers Harbor, a tranquil working cove full of lobster boats at their moorings. A tall stone chimney holds a fireplace to warm up the early spring and late fall nights, and an outdoor patio welcomes customers in the warm weather. For dinner the tables are covered with white tablecloths, and customers in summer fill the space with happy conversation. Bunkers Wharf is immediately recognizable as a neighborhood restaurant, frequented by people who know where to go for good food.

Dinners off a sample menu include steamed lobster, plain and simple, but augmented with roasted corn bread pudding ($25.95). Roast duck ($22.95) with maple Dijon glaze is served with mashed potato and wilted spinach.

Chicken and sausage farfalle with a Parmesan cream sauce ($17.95) was the goal of one of us from the moment her eyes lighted on it on the menu. Rich and strongly flavored, it made a pleasurable meal, though the portion was enough for an Olympic athlete.

We chose a simple maple crème caramel for dessert, and the tender custard set on rays of chocolate sauce was a good finish to the intense flavors of the main course. The evening's four desserts were presented on a silver tray festooned with scrolls and spirals of various colored sauces. Along with the custard that night, you could have chosen a brownie with mocha-rum sauce, a flourless chocolate cake, or a piece of cheesecake.

The lunch menu lists hamburgers, a haddock sandwich, a lobster roll, and fish-and-chips, as well as a couple of salads. And appetizers looked tempting, with Gorgonzola, chèvre, and mozzarella pizza and lobster stew.

This is the place to go when you're exploring Acadia National Park's Schoodic Peninsula, which is as lovely as its more famous setting on Mount Desert Island.

Calais

The Chandler House
(207) 454-7922
20 Chandler Street
Hospitality—An experienced staff takes good care of the customers
Open for lunch 11–2, for dinner 3:30–9 daily Memorial Day through Labor Day; closed Monday off-season
Entrées $13 to $29

☛ *An old-fashioned restaurant that serves inexpensive, good food*

The average dinner usually runs $20 here, including drinks—lunch amounts to $10.

For 25 years the Chandler House has been serving good meals at modest prices, and William Condon, who has been there 15 years, just wants to "keep doing what we've been doing." His father started the business that seats 40 and still has tables covered with tablecloths in the nicely decorated rooms.

"Everything is like you would make at home," Condon told me. All the soups are homemade, the chicken dishes are fresh. The chicken salad is made from poached chicken that is pulled apart in the kitchen, not with canned or frozen chicken.

Fresh seafood comes locally from Canada, and a local clammer, William Mitchell, brings fresh clams once a week. Chandler House chefs shuck them to make chowders and fried clams.

The restaurant's signature dish, prime rib roasted on the bone, is served every night with Yorkshire pudding ($16.95, $18.95 for extra large). The dinner rolls, crusty and tender, are made in the kitchen too.

Desserts are homemade. Blueberry pie is $3 with ice cream, or you could try strawberry shortcake, walnut cake, or a hot fudge sundae. Condon's grandmother devised the recipe for the bread pudding ($3 with whipped cream), made with milk, bread, coconut, raisins, cinnamon, eggs, and sugar.

Chandler House is located behind McDonald's, and slightly out of the way. But, "When people find us, they usually come back," Condon said.

Columbia

Anthony's Farm (207-483-2260), Main Street (just off Route 1).
Open May through October. This farm stand sells strawberries, blueberries, and vegetables in-season.

Blue Barrens Farm (207-483-4196), 88 Pea Ridge Road.
Hours depend on the harvest; call ahead, June through October. Preserves are available over the phone, and you can pick your own crops at the farm or buy them picked for you at the farm stand. Strawberries, raspberries, and blueberries.

Columbia Falls

County Road Cranberry Bog (207-483-4055), 1256 Route 1, 1 mile past Route 187 toward Machias.
This shop is open in October and November; products are available for shipping year-round. Judy Farnsworth makes cranberry vinegar, cranberry jam, blueberry syrup, cranberry syrup, cranberry-pineapple and cranberry-orange jams, and hot pepper jelly. Fresh cranberries are sold when they're ripe, usually the first week of October. Frozen berries are available in winter. The bog is visible from Route 1, and visitors love to go check it out.

Molly's Orchard (207-483-4178), Point Street, which runs out from the village, a turnoff from Route 1.

Open in early summer for pick-your-own strawberries and in the fall for pick-your-own apples, this farm is run by Rick and Jolene Farnsworth.

Wild Blueberry Land (207-483-2583; www.wildblueberryland.com), Route 1.

You cannot fail to see this great big blue geodesic dome on the ocean side of Route 1 when you drive this way. There are blueberries inside, pies are being baked, and jars of blueberry jam, syrup, and dried blueberries are for sale. The store will overnight ship frozen blueberries anywhere you like. A 10-pound box costs $24 (plus shipping).

East Machias

The Riverside Inn
(207) 255-4134
Route 1
www.riversideinn-maine.com
Hospitality—Two summer servers, working weekends off-season, care for up to 20 guests.
Open for dinner 5–8 Tuesday through Sunday late May through mid-September, Thursday through Sunday the rest of the year; open for Sunday brunch year-round, except closed in January
Entrées $18 to $23

☛ *An ambitious restaurant that has grown its business mostly by word of mouth*

The Culinary Institute in Albuquerque, New Mexico, gave Rocky Rakoczy, 56, a degree in advanced culinary studies in April 2003, at the same time that he and his wife, Ellen McLaughlin, 50, bought the Riverside Inn.

"We were planning on having an inn with a small restaurant in a small dining room," he said. They found this one along the tidal Machias River.

With a nearby university, a hospital, and Washington Academy, a prep school started in 1865 that brings people to the area from all over the world, Rocky and Ellen decided East Machias was the place for them. It didn't hurt that there wasn't a lot of competition.

Retired from American Airlines after 35 years as an operations crew chief, Rocky is enjoying his new life as a restaurant chef.

Dinner meetings for the hospital doctors, guest speakers at the university, and staff parties for nearby schools fill tables on off-season nights, and regular summer visitors return with high expectations.

"We serve a variety of menus, different kinds of lamb, a London broil, pork medallions, Jamaican baby back ribs, butterflied pork chops," Rocky began. He listed weekly specials and five different kinds of fish, including a lobster dish served over pasta with capers and cream. The inn's broiled salmon strips, stuffed with crab, scallions, shallots, and mushrooms combined with paprika, lemon pepper, and mayonnaise, and served with a turmeric-dill sauce, is the most popular dish. Rocky calls it "the pride of the Riverside."

Coming in second is Lambs Shezaseis, a boneless leg of lamb butterflied and stuffed with red pepper, feta, and spinach laced with garlic. Rolled and seared, then baked to order in individual servings, this is usually served with asparagus or a sautéed vegetable and sweet potatoes a l'orange, made with sweet potatoes, Yukon Gold potatoes, carrots, parsnips, pineapple, and pearl onions, all baked in orange juice with nutmeg and ginger.

Thirty wines, with 7 available by glass, 23 beers, and a basic full bar satisfy the customers, who like to make reservations for the holiday menus that are served on Valentine's Day, Christmas Eve, and New Year's Eve.

Eastport

Raye's Mustard Mill (207-853-4451, 1-800-853-1903; www.rayes mustard.com), Route 190. P.O. Box 2.

The center of all things mustard. Tours of the mill, which has been making mustard since 1903, and its old stone grindstones are given at 10 and 3 weekdays and some Saturdays, if mill operations allow it. The retail store sells good mustard varieties along with other things from

Raye's Mustard Mill in Eastport grinds mustard seeds on its original grindstones.

this region at the farthest eastern tip of the United States, including Mainely Smoked Seafood.

Gouldsboro

Winery and Farm Stand

Bartlett Maine Estate Winery (207-546-2408; www.bartlettwinery .com), P.O. Box 275 (a half mile south of Route 1, 23 miles east of Ellsworth; watch for signs).
Open May to October; call or stop for hours. One of the most pleasant hours you can spend lies at the end of a short wooded path in the tasting room of the Bartlett Maine Estate Winery. Your well-spoken host will pour tastes of about eight different wines made here, describing each one with well-wrought phrases. There is no obligation to buy, and the tasting is free.

I went home with a bottle of Winemaker's Reserve 1999 Pear Wine, aged in French oak barrels for at least 12 months. The bottle was signed by vintner Robert Bartlett. At $25 it was one of the winery's more expensive bottles. I drank it with a venison tenderloin and thoroughly enjoyed its clear, dry flavor.

Bartlett wines are growing in fame, winning awards and diverting grape wine lovers to an occasional glass of fruit wine, a far different creature from the horrible apple wine you might be ashamed to have loved when you were underage. These wines, from the modestly priced Coastal Red, made with blueberries and apples, and Coastal White, pear and apple, to the pricier bottles of reserve and dessert wine are sophisticated, delicate, and good with a wide variety of meals. We drank the Coastal Red at a Maine bar to accompany Thai mussels. The glass of wine, with a fruitiness that worked well with Thai curry sauce, was great.

The winery buys its fruit and blends it to achieve its different wines. Mead, made with Maine wild blossom honey and spring water, is a strange creature, but it made sense in those woods, as it does in the Tolkien woods, and perhaps I should make a better acquaintance. That was the driest at my tasting. The sweetest was a blackberry wine it would be possible to drink with dessert, but that really explains the existence of thimble-size cordial glasses. I still don't know if I would recommend the semi-dry blueberry wine to go with smoked seafood, as the wine host did, but I'm a convert to these wines with spicy meals and roasted meat, and grateful for these new pleasures.

Darthia Farm (207-963-2770, 1-800-285-6234; www.darthiafarm.com), 51 Darthia Farm Road.

Open Monday through Saturday 8–5, May through October. Run by Bill and Cynthia Thayer, this organic farm made a covenant with the future to remain intact and organic. The Thayers plow and haul wood out of the forest with the strength of three purebred Haflinger draft horses—Gus, Teddy, and Stefan. Cynthia writes novels that paint her land and fictional neighbors in lucid, fascinating colors, and spins and knits sweaters and other garments with the wool of her farm's sheep. You can buy both the novels, published by St. Martin's Press, and the handmade garments in the farm store. You could also buy raspberries, raspberry jam, winter squash, tender lettuce, or whatever is in-season. The blueberry-rhubarb jam tastes great on toast.

Harrington

The Mexican Restaurant
(207) 483-2002, (207) 598-7297
Timkin Pike Plaza
Hospitality—A little Spanish helps, but you'll be well taken care of without any at all.
Open daily
Entrées $5 to $9

☛ *Run by Central American immigrants who make delicious, authentic Mexican, Guatemalan, and El Salvadoran food, served in plain quarters*

The restaurant shares space with a store that sells foodstuffs to the area's growing Latino population; restaurant and retail are divided only by a line of bead curtains. Clear plastic sheets cover the plastic laminate tables, and the brown-plastic bench seats are attached to the table. That utter informality makes it comfortable to browse around the store shelves while you wait for your order, examining the matte-brown seed pods of tamarind, for example, in a crate on the floor.

The shop and restaurant owner's mother, Rubenia Ayala, took good care of us without speaking a lot of English. We worked it out with our own rudiments of Spanish, confined to words like *enchilada verde* and *burrito*. I ordered the *tamarindo* to drink, and was served a tall cup of icy, very sweet tamarind-flavored water that slowly turned delicious as I drank it and grew accustomed to the new flavor.

The menu provides the plain English for all items. A tostado, for instance, is one crisp corn tortilla topped with, among several choices, a ceviche made with cooked shrimp marinated in lime juice with tomatoes, onions, cilantro, and fresh avocado ($2.99). The quesadilla was a 13-inch flour tortilla folded and grilled, with sour cream, cheese, *carne asada,* and guacamole ($7.99). We could have tried a burrito with beef tongue, mole, onions, cilantro, and green sauce ($7.99), or with fried catfish, tartar sauce, and chopped tomato salsa ($7.99).

But the chicken, cheese, and avocado burrito ($6.99) was perfect for a young friend. It was stuffed and very fresh, the flavors were pleasant, and the meat was tender as butter.

Another selection, two enchiladas verdes stuffed with chicken and topped with green sauce, Monterey Jack cheese, and sour cream, proved extraordinary after a long fishy haul up the Maine coast. The soft, fresh tortillas were lit up by that hot green sauce, which set the stewed, melting chicken on fire. The sprinkle of Jack cheese proved mild and sweet, a small quantity of fresh cheese curds, not a molten lead blanket you might have assumed was standard south of the border.

You wouldn't necessarily know any better, if you ate most of what passes for Mexican in Maine (but see XYZ in Manset, page 263, for another exception).

Inside the kitchen Tereza Fidelina, from El Salvador, was stirring a huge pot of pork ribs in a spicy red sauce. Anyone who lives nearby has a God-given opportunity to eat the wonderful food she devises and the hotter Mexican dishes that Juan Perez, the owner's husband, grew up eating when his family moved from Guatemala to Mexico, before they found their way to Downeast Maine.

Latino immigrants pick Maine's blueberries and apples and pack Maine's sardines, and some of them have started to settle here. About 100 live in nearby Milbridge, and people from all over Central and South America depend on Doris Ayala's place to find the supplies for their meals, or to eat them already prepared. Doris, who is from Honduras, started the store in 2001, the restaurant in 2002, and added a Hancock branch in 2004. She serves Venezuelans, Cubans, and Puerto Ricans, to mention just a few, along with the Mainers and visitors who make their way here. I heard of a couple from Oklahoma who were grateful to get here now and then and eat real Mexican food, instead of the bastardized versions served elsewhere, where the flavors are toned down to a faint echo, or a defeated whimper, and the plates are paved with cheese.

Dallas' Lobstah (207-483-2227), Route 1.

Open Tuesday through Sunday 11–8 in summer, Thursday through Sunday 12–7 in early fall. This new spot has an outdoor lobster cooker for lobster lovers, and uses local clams for its fried dishes. A few tables outside make a nice spot for the classic Maine summer meal. Clean and simple.

Jonesboro

Chandler River Lodge
(207) 434-2540
654 Route 1
Open for dinner Tuesday through Saturday from 5; summer hours may change
Entrées $29 to $35

☛ *A new entrant to the far Downeast fine-dining list, from an experienced local*

Two of the three dining rooms overlook the Chandler River at this old inn where upscale meals are now served. Chandler Scallops, stuffed with crabmeat and beurre blanc ($30) and pecan-crusted pork medallions with cranberry port sauce ($29) were two entrées described by new owner Beth Foss. Shrimp and lobster scampi is served on whole wheat linguine ($35).

Foss, who is one of the chefs here, bought this inn in fall 2006. She is also the owner of the Bluebird Ranch Restaurant in Machias. She said, "It's the type of cooking I've always wanted to do."

Salads are served with a blueberry vinaigrette made in the area from Foss's recipe. You can buy a bottle of it for $6.50.

Different flavors of crème brûlée, raspberry and Kahlúa, and a chocolate torte (all desserts $7) are sweet endings.

Jonesport

Tall Barney's Restaurant
(207) 497-2403
Main Street
www.tallbarneys.com
Hospitality—Intense ribbing from the fishermen if you are a "flatlander" translates as endearment (really)—but ignore them and enjoy the quick assistance of the servers.
Open daily year-round for breakfast, lunch and dinner; Mondays and Tuesdays closes at 2
Entrées $7 to $23

☛ *Pleasant, renovated rooms full of conversation among the tables, and great, simple food*

A newcomer might want to be warned about the Liars' Table, a long table angled down the dining room, aslant just like the claims made by its occupants, fishermen and locals who find anyone amusing, especially each other, and still would be likely to try to save their life in a crisis. They are irritating men you wouldn't want to miss meeting, or live without.

When John Lapinski heard a description of this place and that table on NPR in 2002, he called up the restaurant and asked if it was for sale. In three weeks he bought it. He sold his insurance business in New Jersey, and then he moved to Jonesport with his wife, Linda, to join the Liars' Table, or at least listen to it.

Linda makes fabulous pies and tarts, like one we enjoyed made with blueberries from Sanford Kelly's fields overlooking the bay, and another, a tart with tender cake-like crust beneath the berries. Her lemon meringue ($3.25) features a high meringue and sweet lemon filling. You also might find blueberry pound cake or apple crisp on the dessert table.

The chocolate mousse cake at Tall Barney's Restaurant in Jonesport gets all the love.

But the owner doesn't fancy sweets. Lapinski said he came here to change his life—and did. He lost 90 pounds and stopped needing medication for his type 2 diabetes. How? He became more active, he said, spending three days a week as a sternman on a lobster boat in the summer and fall. But mostly he slowed down when he ate.

"I don't sit down and wolf a meal any more," he said, "I sit down and enjoy it." That means he pushes a plate of food away when he's finished—he doesn't let it finish him.

He also managed to renovate the restaurant, installing a new kitchen and fixing up the dining room, while never closing for the first year and a half he owned it. In 2007 he plans to open a retail counter in the back dining room, for fresh fish and Linda's great baked stuff.

The standard Maine fare of chowders, fried seafood, and meat is what the menu is all about. Lapinski has hiked up the quality, getting scallops from a local boat when it's scallop season. The clams are also local. Biscuits with sausage gravy, a classic Downeast meal, are $4.29.

Crabcakes ($7.79) are big, thick and packed with crab meat. A lobster cake burger ($11.99) is made the same way, both held together with a little white sauce, which doesn't interfere with the flavor of the shellfish. You can also find grilled wild Sockeye salmon ($13.99) on the changing menu.

Sometimes Lapinski barbecues beef on a grill outside, cooking steaks and chops. His customers enjoy that, and so does he.

Farms and Bakeries

Crossroad Farm (207-497-2641), 314 Crossroad.

Dinah Bracha and Avraham Pearlman run a huge organic farm here, growing 30 varieties of lettuce alone. You can get produce by calling ahead, asking for it, and arranging a time to pick it up. Crossroad Farm supplies produce to many of the best area restaurants, stocks John Edwards, a store in Ellsworth, and makes regular trips south with the harvests. On our visit we met up with Linda Lapinski, who was picking up some broccoli for Tall Barney's, the restaurant she runs with her husband (see page 286). That was lucky, because otherwise we might not have met the farmers—they were out in the fields, hard at work.

The Mason Bay Berry and Egg Farm, home of the Farm Bakery, with a produce stand (207-497-5949), 1561 Mason Bay Road (3 miles from Route 1 on Route 187).

Open 10–6 Monday through Saturday in July and August, closed Thursday, Saturday, and Sunday in September. Special orders taken all year. Lois Hubbard is known for her gingersnaps, as well as blueberry and raspberry pies. Honey whole wheat and cinnamon-raisin bread are favorites. Fudge is another big seller; flavors include peanut butter and chocolate raspberry.

Vegetables and fruits—among them tomatoes, cucumbers, squash, pumpkins, and Pontiac Red, Russet, Yukon Gold, and Kennebec potatoes—are for sale at the farm stand here. It's open the same hours, or as long as vegetables last.

Lubec

Bacon and Sausage

Olde Sow Farm (207-733-2569; www.oldesowfarm.com), 1050 County Road.

Jessica Zanoni and her husband are raising Tamworth pigs, a heritage breed, on 150 acres here, and the bacon, sausage and pork that results is extraordinary. The pigs are outside in the summer, feeding on grass and bugs, raising the Omega 3s in the meat. As this farm grows you'll be sure to find its products on menus and in stores. They sell fine leaf lard and a wide variety of cuts, from chops to hams.

Chocolate and Ice Cream

Monica's Chocolates (1-866-952-4500; www.monicaschocolates .com), 56 Pleasant Street.
Open daily 8 AM to 8 PM, year-round. Monica Elliot, who grew up in Peru, brought her first chocolate recipe here from a childhood shared with family chefs. With the years she has added fillings and presentations to her chocolate line, like a pistachio cream made with organic pistachios from Sicily. I tried her Maine-inspired sea urchins and fell in love. The smooth, light caramel, toffee, and Peruvian filling comes wrapped in a crisscrossed dark chocolate shell, perfectly delectable. Fortunately there is no need to get to Lubec to taste them, because you can order what she and her family make online. But if you are in town, her shop is the best spot to come for a treat and to shop for gifts to bring home with you. Her molded chocolate scallop shells are lovely.

A favorite of the candies made at Monica's Chocolates in Lubec are the sea urchins, which begin as these caramels.

Phil's Not-So-Famous Homemade Ice Cream. Open 1 PM to 9 PM, closed Tuesday, in season. With vanilla fudge chocolate chunk, caramel cashew, and black raspberry on offer in this pretty little house by the entrance to the bridge to Campobello, it's probably going to be famous soon.

Machias

The Artist's Café
(207) 255-8900
3 Hill Street
Hospitality—Completely attentive
Open for lunch Monday through Friday 11–2, dinner Monday through Saturday
5–8 early spring through mid-October
Entrées $20 to $30

☞ *Unpretentious but full of goodness, this place feeds the heart and soul.*

Susan Ferro, an artist, has cooked for 10 years in the restaurant she started in the midst of a culinary wilderness. Her customers will be grateful when the doors reopen in the spring.

"I thought I was going to shape the food I served," she said with a laugh. "My customers have shaped my business." She serves up some entrées, for instance, with a cream sauce people dote on.

Her paintings are part of the décor in the pretty, small rooms of her building on a hill on the way into Machias, and the artfully arranged meals could put you in mind of their colors and design. But if that doesn't, the lunchtime sandwich menu will, with its choice of the Impressionist (sliced chicken with pesto mayonnaise on a baguette, $6.50) or the Surrealist (grilled and undoubtedly dripping Swiss cheese, with fresh garlic and dill butter on two slices of the anadama).

You could order a lemon square ($1.50) or an oatmeal chocolate-chip cookie for dessert, likely portraits of what the regular lunch crowd rightfully admires from the kitchen.

Ferro gets her bread shipped up from Boston but makes a few special loaves herself. The likely problem of her baker's business being bought and the bread losing its quality troubles her as she strives to serve the best quality food she can both afford and find. She gets her haddock from Campobello, serving it one week sautéed with bread crumbs and a mix of summer squashes, red peppers,

The owner of Machias's Artist's Café, Susan Ferro, is also the painter of the art on the walls.

and shallots, along with a tomato salad and homemade tartar sauce.

Her roast turkey dinner comes with a piece of homemade sausage made by Joe Parisi (see below), one of the many people she has found to work with, a local version of the slow food movement that's improving the dining Downeast. Farms provide some vegetables, like those in the caponata, made with eggplant, tomato, onions, and olives, that accompanies her thin breaded veal chop

($24), a perfect version as tender as you can wish for. Kris Pinot Grigio ($5 a glass, $15.99 a bottle) make a perfect drink with it.

She and her customers have long agreed about the gingerbread ($6), with its sliding topping of really fresh whipped cream. The tiramisu, chocolate gâteau, and cheesecake (all $6) are sometimes part of the dessert menu. And the coffee is just as strong as she likes it, even if that's something to which some customers might object.

The Inn at Schoppee Farm
(207) 255-4648
Route 1
www.schoppeefarm.com
Open Thursday, Friday and Saturday by reservation
Entrées $36 to $44
BYOB

☛ *A small dining room with a focus on individual attention*

David and Julie Barker, originally from Machias, opened this inn in November 2004. They run their restaurant in a handsome room in the old house. Entrées of seafood and beef, and occasionally lamb and bison, from local sources are among the meals. Rooms also are rented here, and goats whose milk makes goat cheese and yogurt are raised.

Markets and Festivals

Joe's Sausages (207-255-0054), 14 West Street.
Open Monday through Friday and most Saturdays 8–5, call for winter hours, closed in February. Joe Parisi, whose parents immigrated to the United States from Sicily, makes sausage and grows a huge vegetable and fruit garden. His peers in the food business extol his sausage, made fresh with no preservatives from pork deliveries that come twice a week. One neighbor called him, "An Italian sweetheart from the old country." The usual hot-spicy and mild-sweet varieties are embellished with the addition of wine, or Romano cheese, garlic, and parsley. Call ahead to place an order for seasoned pork roasts, or to check on weekend hours. Starting in mid-May, his 4,000 asparagus plants start their two months of production. By July 1 the strawberries are ripe for about three weeks, and you can pick your own. In late summer the eggplant and peppers, along with essential flat-leafed parsley, are among the produce he sells. He also main-

tains the farthest Downeast outpost of Micucci's, a Portland wholesale business, with Asiago, Fontina, fresh mozzarella, and Parmigiano-Reggiano available for purchase. He sells Cinqueterre Farm bread (see page 295). He also goes to New Jersey to get Cento and pepper cheese from Locatelli.

There's a picture of a pig on his lawn, which is on the first street south of the post office.

The Machias Farmer's Market starts in early May and goes through October, located on Route 1 across from Helen's Restaurant, Saturday 8–noon. There often are farmers selling produce in this location other days of the week as well.

The Machias Maine Wild Blueberry Festival (Machias Chamber of Commerce, 207-255-4402; www.machiasblueberry.com) rolls around

the third weekend of August, and has been celebrated for more than 30 years. The blueberry is central, and stars in the blueberry pancake breakfast early on Saturday in Machias's Centre Street Congregational Church. Blueberries blaze out in all kinds of desserts in the church vestry all day long. You are sure to find pie and muffins and much else.

But in between meals with blueberries, the festival presents a Friday night fish-fry, and on Saturday volunteers serve lunches that feature chowder and lobster, crabmeat, and chicken rolls.

The wild blueberry pie–eating contest might be doable next year, if you practice hard enough.

Milbridge

44 Degrees North
(207) 546-4440
17 Main Street
www.44-degrees-north.com
Open daily 11–9 in summer, Sunday closing at 8, winter same but closing at 8 every night. The pub closes at last call.
Entrées $8 to $26

☛ *A friendly place with popular dishes*

Starting in 2004, this restaurant has thrived. Jan Rossi, manager for her family's restaurant, keeps things running smoothly with professional courtesy.

A best-selling appetizer is scallops wrapped in bacon, grilled on skewer, brushed with mango chipotle sauce if you like ($7.50). Another is steamed mussels, the best ever with no grit, with fresh garlic and white wine ($5.75).

Seafood lasagna ($14.95), with haddock, scallops, shrimp, and crab sautéed in garlic wine sauce, is layered with lasagna noodles, ricotta, and mozzarella. Columbia Crest Chardonnay ($5) or the Kris Pinot Grigio might taste good with that. Grilled Atlantic salmon—plain, with avocado butter, or with sesame-ginger sauce—appeals to many who dine here.

But on Friday and Saturday night the number one seller is the slow-roasted prime rib ($14.95).

Some of the desserts made here are seasonal. In the summer you will be likely to find blueberry crisp, in the fall, apple crisp. Wintertime brings out the bread pudding, and in spring, fresh fruit pie reappears, like the flowers and the leaves outside.

Takeout and Fish Market

Joshy's Place (207-546-2265), High Street.

Open Monday through Saturday 11–9 in summer. We're sure the woman in the counter window here isn't always so surly, but maybe you should try to catch her earlier in the day, or earlier in the summer.

She wasn't keeping folks away, however, from this crowded Route 1 pit stop with an inexpensive lobster roll and haddock burger. Ice cream comes in four sizes, a really nice feature for the littlest customers and people who opted for that double-bacon cheeseburger. You also can go for soft serve ice cream, hard ice cream, a milk shake, or a banana split.

Tibbets Seafood Market (207-546-3435), 13 Main Street.

Open 9–5:30, daily in summer, Tuesday through Saturday in winter. Haddock, hake, tuna, sole, swordfish, lobsters, crab—the full array of fish, with local clams and everything from Maine unless it's not in-season or doesn't swim by.

The Milbridge Farmer's Market runs from the end of May through October, Saturday 9–noon, at Main Street KELCO Employee parking lot (the wreath factory). Back Bay Farm, owned by Matt Herbruck and Kelly Mason, grows organic vegetables, eight varieties of potatoes, lettuce, heirloom tomatoes, snap peas, and shell peas. Kelly makes homemade Castile soap made with olive oil and scented with herbs and essential oils in eight varieties, as well as skin care products like a lemon verbena body lotion ($9.50 for 8 ounces; look for it at www.reallygreatskin.com).

Pembroke

Cinqueterre Farm and Bakery (207-726-4766), Ox Cove Road.

Open Memorial Day through Labor Day, but call first, as this small operation could be on the verge of retirement. This farm down a road off Route 1 does a big business in the summer selling fresh baked goods. Baguettes, raisin bread, multigrain bread with ground flaxseed, and French country bread are among the loaves baked here. With so few good bakeries in the area, some residents invest in a freezer's worth from Cinqueterre to get through the winter. Pies can be ordered or bought if you're lucky, and jams are made throughout the summer. The bread is for sale in Machias at Joe's Sausages (see page 292).

Yellow Birch Farm (207-726-5807), 272 Young's Cove Road.

Call for hours. Organic vegetables and chicken, pork, and lamb, along with balsam Christmas wreathes available by mail.

Perry

The Friendly Restaurant
(207) 853-6610
1014 Route 1 (just north of Route 190)
Hospitality—Straightforward and fast
Open for lunch and dinner 11–8 in summer, closes earlier off-season
Entrées $6 to $12
Reservations recommended on weekends

☛ *Good cheap food and drink*

This popular local restaurant was owned by Sheldon and Priscilla Patterson, who bought it 17 years ago. After Sheldon died and Priscilla retired, their son Robert and his wife, Jennifer, took over. Jennifer has been working here since 1990, after she married into the family.

Lobster rolls and seafood are the main draws; the lobster overflows its bun.

Asked what she thinks makes the place special, Jennifer said, "I think our portions. We give a good portion."

Daily specials are offered all day, from corn chowder with grilled cheese ($4.79) to a Reuben sandwich ($4.09) to Caesar salad with chicken ($5.79). Jennifer makes lemon meringue pies and blueberry pies when the blueberries are in-season. She also makes a chocolate raspberry pie—a layer of raspberry, a layer of cream cheese, and whipped cream covered by a layer of melted semi-sweet chocolate—a brilliant concoction for which we can vouch.

Weekend nights are really busy, with Friday-night reservations a must. Three or four tables are filled with patrons who come every Friday and keep a standing Friday night reservation.

Cheap wine, either Almaden Chablis or Mountain Burgundy ($1.50 a glass), beer, and mixed drinks make the dinners taste even better.

"Everybody knows everybody around here.... Usually you'll see people hopping from table to table," Jennifer said. With her kids in a school of only 118 students, Jennifer is glad to stay right where she is, where the traffic doesn't amount to much and the person in the passing car is very likely to wave hello.

Smoked Salmon

Mainely Smoked Salmon (207-853-4794; www.mainelysmoked salmon.com), 555 South Meadow Road.

Open when they're home, often at 4 in afternoon on weekdays and all day on weekends.

John Constant, who has worked in the salmon business for 15 years, sells hot- and cold-smoked salmon. It can be ordered through the Web site and shipped overnight.

At $15 a pound for cold-smoked salmon, he also is selling it inexpensively.

Constant won't use wild fish, because, he said, they can be caught at the wrong time in their life-cycle and make a poor-quality smoked fish. The fish Constant buys are prepared for harvest with special diets and precise culture.

He builds houses for a living. "I pound nails when I'm not doing this," he said. Look for him and wife Karen at local fairs and the Bangor Folk Festival.

Prospect Harbor

West Bay Lobsters in the Rough
(207) 963-7021
Route 186, (3 miles from Route 1)
Hospitality—Simple, friendly assistance in a plain setting
Open for dinner 5–8, May through October

☛ *A place to concentrate on eating lobster, with great fixings and no distractions*

With four picnic tables and two linoleum tables set in a plain interior, this place is exactly what's in its name: rough. Since that is also exactly how lobsters are best enjoyed, many of us interested in a lobster dinner will opt to come here. The plastic tablecloth with the big bowl set in the middle are familiar from family clambakes, where informality is the rule and the pleasures of the table reside in the taste of the food. You can choose your own lobsters out of the tank and wait for them to be cooked on the outdoor stove.

A menu on a board lists the simple offerings, starting with hard-shell and shedder lobsters—people often prefer the hard-shell because their meat fills the shell. However, while a shedder will drain a lot of water, its soft shell is awfully easy to get inside. The lobsters that have most recently shed can be torn apart with your hands. Some of the older hard-shells can require a hammer blow, or a rock, to smash through that dark red carapace, convenient when you are right on Maine's rocky shore but perhaps less fun elsewhere.

If you bought a big old hard-shell, take a break from the labor with an ear of corn ($1), coleslaw ($1.75), or a dish of baked beans that are cooked daily from either soldier beans, the northerners' preference, or pea beans, favored by Bostonians. According to Gina Clark's research, northerners acquired their preference for soldier beans when they found that those beans stayed soft after being frozen and reheated, as when they were hauled from lumberjacks' camps to the day's work in winter woods in a lunch pail. Pea beans became hard.

When the time comes for dessert, there is pie and ice cream.

Takeout and Fish Markets

Down East Deli (207-963-2700), junction of Routes 186 and 195, P.O. Box 230.

Open daily 11–8 in summer, 11–7 in the off-season.

Using bread shipped from Boston bakeries, this deli's Philly cheesesteak sandwiches contain sliced Delmonico steak, cheese, mushrooms, green peppers, and onions. Leon Harrington, the owner, said he's had customers from Philadelphia who tell him his Philly cheesesteak is as good if not better than ones at home. The Italian hoagie includes Italian capicola (a spicy ham), salami, pepperoni, and Virginia ham, with a choice of vegetables and a homemade Italian dressing made of oil and vinegar with herbs.

A lot of people in Maine call an Italian anything on a hoagie roll, Harrington said, but an Italian made south of Maine always contains that variety of meats, and other people expect them when they ask for an Italian.

The previous owner had an excellent menu, Harrington said, that he has not changed so much as built on since he reopened the business in October 2003, after it was shut for a year and a half.

Pizza ranges through 30 or more toppings, made with hand-stretched New York dough. Harrington said owners of competing pizza places come to his place to eat pizza, a claim I cannot prove.

Prospect Harbor Trading Company (207-963-7956), 178 Main Street (Route 186).

Come between 11 and 3; closed Sunday in June, July, and August. Lobsters are available here throughout the year, though they're scarcer in the winter. By 3 PM lobster boats are arriving and it's impossible to serve retail customers. As many as 20 lobster boats deliver to this company, which ships out most of the shellfish to Inland Seafood the same day.

When she was going to bed one night in October 2003, manager Sylvia Smith saw two Gouldsboro residents in a boat, towing the company's full lobster crates away from the dock. She trained a light on them and called 911, telling the operator not to put the alert on the scanner. "Otherwise you'd get everyone showing up down here," she said. She told the 911 operator to call an officer on the patrol-car phone. The thieves were caught at a different dock. "Good thing I didn't go to bed 15 minutes earlier," she said.

Stinson Seafood Company (207-963-7331), Prospect Harbor.

This is a subsidiary of Bumblebee Tuna, and the phone number given takes consumers to operators in San Diego. Beech Cliff Sardines, the kind packed at this plant, cannot be bought at the plant, but they are for sale at Hannaford and Shaw's supermarkets and local stores. On a coast that once had many fish packing plants, only this sardine plant and one in Bath remain. Some of this area's growing Latino population—which supports the wonderful Mexican Restaurant in Harrington (see page 283)—work at the Prospect Harbor plant.

Robbinston

Katies on the Cove (207-454-3297; www.katiesonthecove.com), 9 Katie Lane.

Open June 15 through September 15, 10–5:30 Tuesday, Thursday, and Friday; 10–5 Wednesday; 10–3 Saturday. This little store sells handmade chocolates that are easy to love. Between the end of October and March, they can ship the candies, but have stopped shipping during warm weather.

Maine potato candies, otherwise known as Needhams, chocolate-covered coconut creams, are made here, along with old-fashioned mint patties and chocolate-covered dried blueberries and cranberries. The Web site is a lot easier to get to than the store, if you aren't driving north from Eastport to Calais. But if you are, look for the yellow house covered with flowers, and consider buying the coffee creams. You can buy the candies farther south at Maine's Own Treats, on Route 3 in Trenton on the way to Mount Desert, or at Raye's Mustard Mill in Eastport (see page 281).

Steuben

Bushey Enterprises (207-546-2804), Route 1.

Open 8–4 Monday through Saturday; December 1 through April 15 for fresh scallops; live lobsters available year-round. Maine shrimp (fresh in January and February) can be bought frozen, whole, or peeled, and frozen haddock, flounder, and scallops are available year-round. Ask to be called when fresh fish is delivered; it goes into the freezer after one day.

Sullivan

Chester Pike's Galley
(207) 422-8200
2336 Route 1

Open daily 6–2, except Sunday 7–2; Friday night fish-fry; call for winter hours
Lunch $5 to $5.50

☛ *Plain food made with care, from real cream to homemade bread*

Opened June 18, 2004, the first summer was busy from the get-go. Breakfast and lunch feature home cooking, with homemade breads and hamburger and hot dog buns, and homemade blueberry jam.

"The Chester fries are getting pretty popular," part-owner and baker Amy McGarr said, who listed the ingredients as home fries with green pepper, onions, ham, and cheddar cheese. Blueberry pancakes ($5), with homemade blueberry topping and fresh whipped cream, not out of a can, McGarr insisted, and with fresh-picked blueberries during the blueberry season, are another favorite.

Apple pancake and Belgian waffle sales don't keep up with sausage gravy over a biscuit ($3). It sounds bad, McGarr admitted, but people like it.

Lunches include club sandwiches on homemade bread—a turkey club is $5.25 and so is a Reuben. The Downeaster haddock sandwich goes for $5.25.

Jane Fogg, McGarr's business partner, makes a great seafood chowder, McGarr said, and it's not too thick.

McGarr and her partner worked years ago at the Everglades Club in Palm Beach, Florida, but both are originally from Bar Harbor. McGarr returned in 1994. Fogg came back more recently, decided to buy a restaurant, and enlisted McGarr's help.

The place seats 50, with a separate barroom, but though they do serve wine and beer there is not a big bar scene, because it wasn't something McGarr and Fogg wanted.

A Sorrento women's group comes in every Tuesday morning, putting two tables together. It's the perfect kind of breakfast scene for them.

Tracey's Seafood
(207) 422-9072
Route 1 (next to the Grange Hall)
Hospitality—Helpful and friendly
Open for lunch and dinner 11–7 daily in summer, closed Monday through Wednesday off-season; closed early October through February
Entrées $9 to $16

☛ *A family business with counter service and an indoor area to eat boiled lobsters*

This place has a wood-fired lobster and clam cooker outside, just like its more famous southern competitor by the Trenton Bridge. The Friday night fish-fry, serving up fried haddock with salad or coleslaw and french fries or onion rings, keeps business busy until 8 that weekend night. Polly Tracey and her husband, Levon, a lobsterman, make sure their supplies are the freshest. The clams come straight from a nearby processing plant where they are dipped in hot then cold water, shucked, and then "capped"—cut away from the siphon. They are delivered every morning to Tracey's to be fried. A clam dinner tastes good with a large order of onion rings. For dessert, there's a three-scoop cone of hard ice cream. Fried foods are served through the ordering window, as are ice cream cones and sundaes.

Farm Stand

Amber's Best, Route 1.
Open July through October. Amber, the farmer's daughter, died of cancer in 2004; this farm stand sells her favorite vegetables and fruits.

Zucchini fills the bin at Amber's Best Route 1 farm stand in Sullivan.

Whiting

Look's Gourmet Food Company (207-259-3341; www.looksgourmet food.com), 1112 Cutler Road.
If you can't find someone right away in the little retail shop of this food processor, you might, like me, speak to a man taking a delivery of fresh cream. The good stuff seems to go into the cans of lobster and clam chowder made here, so when you can't enjoy it fresh, open a can from Look's and remember Maine.

The retail store at Look's Gourmet Food Company in Whiting stocks all kinds of chowders.

Whitneyville

First Frost Farm (207-255-4773), 172 South Main Street.

Jon Robichard sells produce at the Machias Farmer's Market, delivers to seniors in the senior farm share program, and sells vegetables from the farm itself. He grows 60 varieties of vegetables and herbs, along with some blueberries and melons. Potatoes, like the Russian Banana, French fingerling, and All Blue, and lots of basil, from Sweet Genevieve to Purple, are some of the many fruits of his labors.

Winter Harbor

Chase's Restaurant
(207) 963-7171
193 Main Street
Hospitality—Helpful and fast
Open 7 AM–9 PM in summer, 7 AM–8 PM or earlier off-season, closes at 2 Sunday
Entrées under $10

☛ *A plain restaurant with inexpensive food and friendly manners*

This country restaurant feeds its local customers simple, popular favorites like a fried haddock sandwich or fish-and-chips ($8.95 for a small). The breakfast mainstay is the small special—two eggs as you like them with a choice of sausage, bacon, or ham and toast and coffee ($3.95). The pies are reliable. We asked the friendly waitress, Beth Gilman, what was homemade and she brought out a slice of coconut cream pie. Under clouds of stiff whipped cream the coconut filling was sweet as sin, just the right consolation for pulling into town when Gerrish's, the ice cream and sandwich place, had closed at 3, and dinner places were not yet open.

Chase's has been around forever. When we visited years earlier, it was filled with tobacco smoke. The atmosphere is clear now, obedient to the state law banning cigarette smoking in restaurants.

"Most people are glad there's no smoke," Beth said.

Fisherman's Inn Restaurant
(207) 963-5585
7 Newman Street (at the flagpole)
Hospitality—They go out of their way to make sure you get what you'd like.
Open for lunch 11:30–3, dinner 4:30–9 mid-May through mid-October or later depending on business
Entrées $14 to $23

☛ *The motto is "Real food, done well," and the casual atmosphere, home baking, and personal attention make it a standout for Maine seafood.*

The owner of this restaurant, Karl Johnson, also owns the Grindstone Neck of Maine smokehouse just up Route 186 (see page 305), so working with seafood, finding great sources, and knowing his suppliers is an old habit. That makes the Grindstone Neck appetizer a good choice. For $8.95 you can taste smoked salmon, mussels, scallops, and shrimp, with a relish of capers.

The restaurant's clam chowder has won in local competitions. The lobster bisque ($5.95 a cup, $10.95 for a bowl) is made with homemade stock and a little sherry, and is well-provided with lobster meat.

More than a hundred pounds of lobsters are cooked here every day, for bisque, lobster pie, and lobster salad, among other delicious things.

Knocking out a wall has created a water view, giving the dining room a panorama of Winter Harbor.

Mussels from Hancock, caught or grown within a 15-miles radius like most of the Fisherman's Inn seafood, can be ordered either steamed with white wine or cooked in a spicy Thai sauce. Johnson and his son go to Thailand every year for formal training in Thai cooking, and that has also resulted in the menu's crispy Thai-style salmon, made with fresh lemongrass, *galangal* and other Thai ingredients, like Kaffir lime leaves. A dozen plants provide the last for Johnson, but he has to import the rest.

The short wine list, with most wines available by the glass, include Pepperwood Grove Pinot Noir from California ($6.95 a glass, $28 a bottle), Dr. Weins-Prum Riesling from Germany ($6.50 a glass, $26 a bottle), and Las Brisas Sauvignon Blanc from Spain ($4.95 a glass, $20 a bottle). "We serve underexploited, reasonably priced wines," Johnson said.

The most popular item, the seafood mixed grill, includes steamed lobster tail, broiled fresh haddock, and scallops wrapped in bacon, all served with a pot of native shrimp and crabmeat in drawn butter.

There is always a strangely colored lobster in a tank at the Fisherman's Inn in Winter Harbor.

Pat Weaver, in his 50s, has been baking delicious pies and making all the desserts since 2000. Blueberry pie is very good, and the most popular, but it would be hard to forgo the chocolate espresso tart or fresh strawberry shortcake (in-season).

And you will want to make the acquaintance of whatever odd-colored lobster is hanging out in the tank by the front door. Lobstermen keep the tank supplied, and some of them have been taking the strange-colored ones and throwing them back in one place along the coast, a waitress told us, so the next one here could be white, yellow, or plaid.

Casual Eating, Takeout, and Food Markets

The Barnacle (207-963-7733), 159 Main Street.

Seasonal takeout owned by Gail Nelson, who works at the Winter Harbor Post Office.

J.M. Gerrish Provisions (207-963-2727), 352 Main Street.

Open 8–3 Tuesday through Saturday, closed Sunday and Monday. Roxanne Quimby bought this old-fashioned soda fountain and took it upscale with espresso and machiato. The old stools, with brass footrests shaped like a flat stirrup, are gone from the checkerboard tile floor next to the counter, where you can order ice cream ($2 for a small cone) in flavors from vanilla to peanut butter. Or you could opt for a fruit smoothie ($4.25). Sandwiches, salads, and soups can be enjoyed here or to go. The blueberry crumb cake is perfect with coffee.

Grindstone Neck of Maine (207-963-7347, 1-866-831-8734; www.grindstoneneck.com), 311 Newman Street (Route 186).

Open daily 9–5 in summer, after Labor Day Monday to Friday 9–5. On the day we dropped in, some other visitors from away instigated a tasting, and we had a chance to compare the farm-raised Atlantic salmon ($6.50 for 4 ounces), the organic, farm-raised Scottish salmon ($8.95 for 4 ounces), and the wild salmon ($9.50 for 4 ounces), all cold-smoked on the premises. The high fat content of the Scottish fish made it more "buttery," and that and the Atlantic were both delicious; but the taste of the wild salmon, with its intense, near-scarlet deep orange, rang like a bell in our mouths. It has a lower fat content and a more intense clean flavor. It's also more expensive. Grindstone Neck buys truckloads of it from Alaska to smoke and pack during its three-week season, but it travels far to get to our wild-salmon-less East Coast.

Grindstone Neck also makes smoke-roasted salmon, maple-cured trout, and smoked haddock, scallops, and mussels.

The Winter Harbor Farmer's Market is held in the parking lot of Mama's Boy Bistro 9–noon Tuesday and goes from June to September. Mandala Farms, one of several present, sells their organic produce, from arugula to melons to sweet corn. They also raise cashmere goats, so you might be able to buy some of the nicest yarn around.

Index